'This book is an essential read for anyone interested in sustainability, tourism and event management. It brings together a strong collection of contributors to offer a comprehensive guide to green events and green tourism with case studies from around the world.'

Dr Paul Spencer, Projects and Operations Manager at Winchester Business Improvement District, Chair of Festivals in Winchester and Visiting Early Career Researcher Fellow at the University of Winchester, UK

'The UN Sustainable Development Goals (SDGs) call for action by all actors from every sector across the globe and this includes event and tourism management worldwide. This book provides a comprehensive guide to making sustainability a reality within the industry and an excellent key text for all event and tourism management courses and programmes. The inclusion of international case studies enables the guidance and information provided, to be brought to life in an accessible way.'

Professor Carole Parkes, Professor of Responsible Management, University of Winchester Business School, UK. Special Advisor to the UN PRME (Principles for Responsible Management) initiative

Green Events and Green Tourism

As the appetite for leisure travel and events continues to grow at an exponential rate, the impact on the environment and local communities is becoming an increasing concern, not least by the users of the services. Green approaches to tourism and events are growing in popularity and present an opportunity to identify both solutions to significant environmental and societal problems and new approaches to business.

Green Events and Green Tourism looks at key frameworks, guidelines, principles and benchmarks that support the application of sustainability in practice. The five sections of the book cover themes of governance, accreditation, certification, innovation, priorities, trends, ambitions and consumer behaviour, and the chapters include examples of best practice in the organisation of music and arts festivals, special interest tourism, the green management of outdoor sites and the management of sports events. Readers will benefit from insightful case studies from around the globe.

Hugues Séraphin is a Senior Lecturer in Event and Tourism Management Studies at the University of Winchester, UK.

Emma Nolan has 25 years' experience as an event management practitioner and academic, is a Senior Fellow of the HEA and is working towards her PhD at the University of Chichester, UK.

Green Events and Green Tourism

An International Guide to Good Practice

Edited by Hugues Séraphin and Emma Nolan

Taylor & Francis Group

LONDON AND NEW YORK

First published 2019
by Routledge
2 Park Square, Milton Park, Abingdon, Oxon OX14 4RN
and by Routledge
605 Third Avenue, New York, NY 10017

First issued in paperback 2020

Routledge is an imprint of the Taylor & Francis Group, an informa business

British Library Cataloguing-in-Publication Data
A catalogue record for this book is available from the British Library

Library of Congress Cataloging-in-Publication Data
A catalog record has been requested for this book

ISBN 13: 978-0-367-73369-8 (pbk)
ISBN 13: 978-1-138-33475-5 (hbk)

Typeset in Times New Roman
by Wearset Ltd, Boldon, Tyne and Wear

Contents

Figures

Tables

Contributors

Editors

Emma Nolan has 25 years' experience as an event management practitioner and an academic. This includes working in visitor attractions, theatres and local authorities and delivering events for a variety of clients including political parties, the TUC and the NHS. She moved into academia in 2008 and worked as a Senior Lecturer in Project and Event Management at the University of Winchester for several years. She is a Senior Fellow of the HEA, has an MA in Education and is currently working towards her PhD at the University of Chichester. Emma recently published her first book, *Working with Venues for Events* (Routledge, 2018), and her current research interests are centred on the MICE sector. She is specifically interested in exploring the site selection process in the organisation of association conferences.

Hugues Séraphin is a Senior Lecturer in Event and Tourism Management Studies. He has also been the Programme Leader for the Event Management programme at the University of Winchester for three academic years (2015–2018). He has expertise and interests in tourism development and management in post-colonial, post-conflict and post-disaster destinations. He has recently published in *International Journal of Culture, Tourism, and Hospitality Research*, *Current Issues in Tourism*, *Journal of Policy Research in Tourism, Leisure and Events*, *Journal of Business Research*, *Worldwide Hospitality and Tourism Themes*, *Journal of Destination Marketing and Management*, and *International Journal of Business and Emerging Markets*.

Contributors

Jane Ali-Knight is a Professor in Festival and Event Management at Edinburgh Napier University and a Visiting Research Fellow at Curtin University, in Western Australia. A recognised academic, she has presented at major international and national conferences and has published widely in the areas of wine tourism, tourism, festival and event marketing and management. She has also edited seminal textbooks in the area of Festival and Event Management.

Her current research interests include the career destination of festival and event graduates; the use of social media in festivals and events; and the growth and development of festivals and events in emerging tourism destinations. She has extensive experience in designing and delivering undergraduate, postgraduate and professional courses in tourism and festival and event management, both in the UK and overseas.

Ericka Amorim is a native of Brazil who currently resides in Portugal. She is an expert in marketing and international business, with a heavy emphasis on tourism marketing. As such she understands the need for tourism security as a marketing tool in a highly unstable world. She is currently studying for her PhD at the Universidade Nova in Lisbon, Portugal.

Olga Andrianova is a Project Manager and co-founder of Volga Trader, an international business consulting company located in Russia/Saratov (www.volga trader.com). Volga Trader undertakes projects to help UK businesses to achieve results in export sales, setting up operations and trading activities in Russia. As a business journalist, she worked in the Russian Far East, including Kamchatka where she joined the team of volunteers to prevent nature pollution and after the years in the Far East she joined Green Agency (www.green-agency.ru) in Moscow and now helps to develop eco park projects and open air festivals for youth, using her experience in international cooperation and her capacity as a journalist. She arranged the trip to Lake Baikal for a group of tourists to experience the wildlife, to learn about the local people and nature, and the material collected allowed her to write a book about this trip to increase public interest in unique places on the planet that need people's attention and care.

Graham Berridge is a National Teaching Fellow (2010) and Deputy Head of the Department of Tourism & Events at the University of Surrey. He has an international publication record and is the author of *Event Design and Experience*. In 2008, he was Visiting Academic for Events Management at the University of Queensland in Brisbane, Australia. He is a founder member of the Association of Events Management Education and served as a Committee member until 2008. His interest specifically lies in the study of event design and creating experiences. In particular, he is keen to develop our understanding of how individuals experience planned events and to develop a richer insight into these through, amongst others, 'experiential ethnography' research. He has undertaken consultancy work to study people's experiences of both commercial and public sector environments.

Marisa P. de Brito is Lecturer and senior researcher on sustainability and the circular economy at the research group 'Events & Placemaking' of the NHTV Academy for Leisure, Breda University of Applied Sciences, Netherlands. She does research in the area of Events and Placemaking, mostly related with sustainability, entrepreneurship and performance. Her recent projects include Sustainable Strategies for Events, Places and Destinations. She has also worked on sustainability projects of fashion, and oil and gas supply chains, besides having additional work on closed-loop supply chains, circularity, and on the management of humanitarian organisations, using qualitative or quantitative techniques. Her research interests and research drive is on conducting research for the improvement of processes, organisations and places.

María M. Carballo has a PhD from the University of Las Palmas de Gran Canaria. She is currently a part-time Professor at the University of Las Palmas de Gran Canaria and a researcher at the University Institute of Tourism and Sustainable Economic Development (TiDES) and UNESCO Chair of Tourism Planning and Sustainable Development. She specialises in economic welfare theory and the analysis of tourist preferences.

Rita R. Carballo has a PhD from the University of Las Palmas de Gran Canaria. She is currently a part-time Professor at the University of Las Palmas de Gran Canaria and a researcher at the University Institute of Tourism and Sustainable Economic Development (TiDES) and UNESCO Chair of Tourism Planning and Sustainable Development. She specialises in cultural, experience and security issues in tourism and their marketing implications.

Elena Cavagnaro is head of the Research Group 'Sustainability in Hospitality and Tourism', on drivers of pro-social and pro-environmental behaviour at Stenden University of Applied Sciences. She studied classical philosophy in Rome and Naples, and later at the VU University in Amsterdam. There, she got her doctoral degree in 1996. Her philosophical background turned out to be a good basis for her career at Stenden University. In 1997, she started there as a teacher of (business) ethics at the Retail Business School. During this time, she started her research into sustainable entrepreneurship in the service industries. From 1999 to 2008, she worked on developing the Master of Arts in International Retail Management. In 2004, she was appointed lecturer in Service Studies. In addition, she teaches sustainable development and leadership at Stenden. Together with George Curiel, Cavagnaro authored the book 'The Three Levels of Sustainability'. It was published in 2012 and became a bestseller. The vision of sustainability described by the authors in this work is at the basis of the lectureship's research.

Monica M. Coroş is a Lecturer in Travel Agency Management, International Tourism Operations, Cultural Tourism, Entrepreneurship and Purchasing Management in the Department of Hospitality Services, Faculty of Business, Babeş-Bolyai University of Cluj-Napoca, Romania, where she completed her Doctoral Degree in Management with a thesis on Tourism Demand and Supply Management. Her research covers topics related to destination management organisations, sustainable tourism, rural tourism, entrepreneurship and SMEs.

Rachel Dodds is a Professor at the Ted Rogers School of Hospitality and Tourism Management at Ryerson University in Toronto, Canada. Her research focuses on sustainable tourism, CSR, sustainable livelihoods and greening festivals. She has also developed a number of sustainability guides for industry, including a greening festival guide.

Frédéric Dosquet is Professor of Marketing at ESC Pau with a doctorate in management science and a Master's degree in marketing and communication from ESCP-Europe. He has written 15 books and more than 20 book chapters in the fields of marketing, tourism and events management. In recent years, his research has focused on the Camino de Santiago, most notably its political, managerial and environmental dimensions. He has presented his work at numerous international conferences and published his findings in academic journals. He is a member of the association El Centro de Documentación e Investigación del Camino de Santiago.

Maribel Osorio García currently works at the Centro de Investigación y Estudios Turísticos (CIETUR), Universidad Autónoma del Estado de México (UAEM). She does research in Social Theory, Urban/Rural Sociology and Qualitative Social Research.

Anu Treesa George is a PhD candidate at the Tourism and Events Research Group in the College of Business at Victoria University, Australia. Her research interest is in responsible tourism, hospitality and events industries, green growth strategies and community well-being. Her research focuses on mitigating sustainability challenges by developing a practical framework that combines the green growth concepts with responsible tourism to enhance the sustainable practices in tourism industry.

Oana A. Gică is an Associate Professor in the Department of Hospitality Services, Faculty of Business at Babeș-Bolyai University of Cluj-Napoca, Romania. She holds a Doctoral Degree in Management. Her main research topics are entrepreneurship and SME management, strategic planning, sustainable tourism and rural tourism.

Tatiana Gladkikh is a Senior Lecturer in Business Management at University of Winchester, UK. She joined academia after 11 years of management, academic and consultancy roles at the Ministry of International Relations of the Saratov Region Government and Volga Region Academy for Civil Service in Russia, and is an independent business communication consultant in the UK. Her research interests are focused on globalisation and the emergence of global identity in the context of international business. Her book *The International Business Environment and National Identity* was recently published by Routledge (2017). She holds a PhD in Russian and East European Studies from The University of Birmingham. She is a member of the Chartered Institute of Linguists and a transnational education consultant for the Global MBA programme at the Edinburgh Business School. An enthusiastic advocate of ecotourism, she has climbed 82 Munros (mountains higher than 3000 feet) in the Scottish Highlands, including the Inaccessible Pinnacle on the Isle of Skye and the Fisherfields, a range of six Munros in the Heart of the Fisherfield Forest, one of the wildest places in Scotland.

Min Jiang is a Senior Research Fellow at the College of Business, Victoria University, Australia. As an environmental lawyer by training, she has led and coordinated a number of policy-oriented, interdisciplinary research projects in adaptation to climate change, sustainable tourism, green growth, and water governance. She has published internationally in academic books and top-tier academic journals including *Journal of Cleaner Production, Journal of Sustainable Tourism, Annals of Tourism Research, Current Issues in Tourism*, and China's top tourism journal *Tourism Tribune*. She is the author of *Towards Tradable Water Rights: Water Law and Policy Reform in China* (Springer, 2017). Her previous work has focused on Australia, China and the South Pacific.

Maximiliano Korstanje currently works at Universidad de Palermo. He does research in Epistemology, Applied Philosophy and Aesthetics. His current project is 'Thana Capitalism and the rise of death seekers'. He is the Book Series editor of *Advances in Hospitality, Tourism and Services Industry*, and senior advisory board member of Cambridge Scholar Publishing UK. He was visiting Professor at University of Leeds, UK, University of La Habana Cuba, TIDES University of Las Palmas de Gran Canaria (Spain) among others. He is Emeritus Editor of *International Journal of Cyber-Warfare and Terrorism* and co-editor for *International Journal of Risk & Contingency Management* and Scientific Editor of *Estudios and Perspectivas en Turismo*.

Carmelo J. León has a PhD from the University of Las Palmas de Gran Canaria and an MSc in Economics from the University of Manchester, UK. He is the Director of the Management Board of the University Institute of Tourism and Sustainable Economic Development (TiDES) at the University of Las Palmas and holds the UNESCO Chair of Tourism Planning and Sustainable Development. He specialises in environmental and socio-economic aspects of tourism and the environment, and in developing the marketing implications of analysing tourist preferences.

Erick Leroux is an Associate Professor of Marketing at University of Paris XIII. Head of International Sustainable Tourism Management Association, he has also written several books in the fields of sales force management, commercial negotiation and tourism. In recent years, his research has focused on marketing and sustainable tourism.

Thierry Lorey is Professor of Marketing at ESC Pau and an assistant researcher at the University of Bordeaux. After obtaining his doctorate from the University of Toulouse 1 Capitole (2012), he created the Department of Agro-food Studies at ESC Pau, becoming one of its co-directors. In addition to his research into the marketing of wine, culture and spirituality, which has been published in many leading French and international journals, he has studied various aspects of the Camino de Santiago, most notably with respect to tourism and territorial and public management issues. Much of this work has been carried out in collaboration with Spanish universities. He is also a member of the association El Centro de Documentación e Investigación del Camino de Santiago.

Judith Mair lectures in Event Management in the Tourism Cluster of the UQ Business School, University of Queensland, Australia. Her research interests include events and sustainability, in particular greening of events and festivals, and the impacts of events on community and society. Her recent projects have focused on researching the links between events and social capital; examining the potential for events to act as spaces for pro-environmental behaviour change; and assessing the potential impacts of climate change on the tourism and events sector.

Thomas Majd holds a doctorate in management science and is an Associate Professor in Marketing. As well as running his own company, he is the director of the Bachelor in Business and Management programme at Groupe ESC Troyes (South Champagne Business School) in France where he teaches marketing, distribution and commercial negotiation. In recent years, his research has focused on marketing intelligence, tourism marketing and commercial negotiation.

Ovidiu I. Moisescu is an Associate Professor in Branding, Public Relations, Marketing Places and Tourism Economics at the Babeş-Bolyai University of Cluj-Napoca, Romania. He completed his PhD in Marketing at the West University of Timişoara (Romania), and a postdoctoral research post at the Babeş-Bolyai University of Cluj-Napoca (Romania) and the Corvinus University of Budapest (Hungary). His research focuses on brand equity, CSR, tourism marketing and place branding.

Teresa Moore is a Director at A Greener Festival and co-founder of the annual Green Events and Innovations (GEI) Conference in London and the European Sustainability think tank GO Europe. Formerly Head of Department of Music and Event Management at Bucks New University, Teresa has undertaken research into sustainability, live music and events. Most recently she published the findings of a Live Music Census of Bristol, UK (March 2016) with UK Music highlighting the economic and social contribution of grass-roots music venues to the local economy. She has carried out a series of festival surveys focusing on audience attitudes to environmental issues at music events (2008, 2012 and 2013) and worked with Julie's Bicycle researching 'Audience Travel to One off Music Events' (2009). She is Editor and contributor to the new *Purple Guide for Event Organisers* (2014) and is currently undertaking a PhD in sustainability and event management, focusing on pro-environmental behaviour change.

Jess Ponting is an Associate Professor at San Diego State University where he founded the Center for Surf Research in 2011. He has lived and worked in surfing research in five countries and advised governments in Portugal, Papua

New Guinea, Fiji, the Maldives and Indonesia on the management of surfing tourism and surfing events. He also co-founded the International Association of Surfing Academics and has published extensively in the areas of surfing and sustainability. He co-founded the Surf Park Summit series of conferences and has produced some of the first published research concerning sustainability, surfing and the emerging surf park industry.

Sandra Sun-Ah Ponting is a Lecturer at the L. Robert Payne School of Hospitality and Tourism Management, San Diego State University. She has a research background in the professionalisation of tourism and events workers and an interest in the sustainability of events, corporate identities and their processes of change.

Deborah Popely is an Associate Professor at Kendall College (Chicago, USA), where she teaches sustainable management of hospitality and tourism. Her interests include green meetings and events, standards and certifications, and sustainable supply chain management. She consults with destinations and venues on planning and certification related to energy efficiency, water conservation, waste management and local procurement. She is currently conducting research on the impact of water scarcity on hotels in arid tourism destinations.

Sarah Schiffling has always maintained an extensive volunteering commitment while working in the logistics and aerospace industries. Combining her expertise with her engagement, she pursued PhD studies on supply chains in non-profit environments, writing her thesis on complexity in humanitarian logistics. She earned her doctorate from Heriot-Watt University in 2017. She is currently a Senior Lecturer in Supply Chain Management at Liverpool John Moores University. Her work focuses on the interface of operations with communities, with a particular focus on remote areas and developing economies.

Damion Sturm is a Senior Lecturer and Course Leader in MSc Sports Event Management in the School of Events, Tourism and Hospitality. He joined Leeds Beckett as a Senior Lecturer in Events Management in November 2015. Hailing from New Zealand, he has an emerging specialisation in global sport media cultures, inclusive of events, celebrity, fan and material cultures. He has co-authored the book *Media, Masculinities and the Machine* with Professor Dan Fleming (University of Waikato, New Zealand), as well as recent works on fan cultures, and sports as mega/media events (Formula One, TV technologies in Australian cricket and the 2015 Cricket World Cup, and nation-building and the 2011 Rugby World Cup). Damion's current projects are probing an array of sport, media and event topics, inclusive of the aura and performance of celebrity, the global sports spectacle, affective audience assemblages, commercially laden media proliferation and complementary digital/social media platforms and their impact and influences across sport events.

Eryn White has a Bachelor of Arts (BA) in Events Management from the University of Winchester, from where she graduated in October 2017. There, she was included on the Winchester University Scholars Scheme for First Class Students, partook in the Winchester University Research Apprenticeship Programme, and won an Award for Outstanding Academic Achievement. From 2009, prior to her career in Events Management, she worked as a chef before moving on to teaching in 2013. During this time, she witnessed the mass wastage that generally accompanies the catering industry, as well as seeing first-hand a lack of education in wastage, recycling and sustainability. It wasn't until 2014 that she started her career as an Events Manager, working for a Manor House in Dorset; this led to her seeking further education and an interest in all areas surrounding events. In particular, she has a passion for investigating areas lacking standardisation, or those frequently overlooked, especially sustainability and environmental impacts surrounding organised events. It is her hope that she may actively contribute to a more sustainable future and enlighten those who may be less aware of the issues.

Anca C. Yallop is a Lecturer in Strategy at the AUT Business School, Auckland University of Technology (AUT), New Zealand. She holds a PhD in Marketing (Romania) and has completed her second PhD in Marketing Research Ethics (AUT, New Zealand). Prior to her appointment at AUT, Anca was at the Winchester Business School, University of Winchester, UK. She specialises in insight management, business strategy and business research methods. She has 15 years' experience in higher education and several years' experience working in marketing and research roles in organisations across a diverse range of sectors internationally.

Acknowledgements

The authors of Chapter 8 – Ovidiu I. Moisescu, Oana A. Gică, Monica Maria Coroş and Anca C. Yallop, extend their thanks to Mr Andi Vanca, Head of Communications, *Electric Castle* Festival, for providing useful insights and perspectives, as well as detailed information regarding the case study presented in their chapter.

The authors of Chapter 12 – Tatiana Gladkikh and Olga Andrianova – would like to thank Alexander Andrianov, a deputy CEO of the National Sustainable Development Agency, Russia, for giving his time to be interviewed and for providing insights into his field of work.

Introduction

Hugues Séraphin and Emma Nolan

The concept of sustainable development has gained much ground in the last few years as we have begun to realise how certain forces have been very damaging to the world and how the effects of globalisation have put pressure on the environment. Consequently, there has been an exponential surge in efforts to incorporate sustainable practices in both our homes and workplaces and this has been advanced by government initiatives around the world to bring sustainability practices into every aspect of our lives. Today, businesses face increasing consumer demand for sustainability and mounting pressure from environmental interest groups to introduce responsible policies. This has led to the development of theories and actions relating to sustainability as a way of trying to protect the world and limit the damage from some of these forces. As in all areas of business, sustainability has become a key trend within the sphere of tourism and event management. These two significant and interconnected industries have been actively developing and adopting sustainability principles and practices in recent years and the aim of this book is to showcase some key examples of best practice from around the world.

The most widely accepted definition of sustainable development, refined by the United Nations, is development that meets the needs of the present without compromising the ability of future generations to meet their own needs. Further attempts to define and explain sustainability have resulted in newer terminology – the triple bottom line. What this term suggests is that sustainability concerns three areas; effects on people, the planet and profit margins. Therefore the sustainable management of tourism and events means taking care of all three. Specifically there is increasing pressure for tourism and events organisations to apply sustainable targets to all elements of operations and there has been a notable focus on adopting principles of reducing, reusing and recycling. Much more consideration is now given to minimising waste and using recyclable products as well as a notable effort to move to the electronic promotion of tourism and events. The benefits of applying sustainable principles to management practices are also gaining more attention. For example sourcing food from local farmers provides healthier, more sustainable menu options and also stimulates rural economies and local culinary culture (Lee and Slocum, 2015). Additionally, the quest for quality standards in the ever-developing tourism and events industries has resulted in the call for more ways of ensuring that stakeholders provide the highest standards of service and facilities possible.

Sustainable tourism management

The tourism industry has been highlighted as an industry that can positively contribute to the economic and social development of a destination (Buckley, 2012). However, this industry can also negatively impact on a destination if poorly managed (Iniesta-Bonillo *et al.*, 2016). Among the noticed negative impacts of tourism is the over-exploitation of resources like water, minerals, oil, over-population, etc. (Sloan *et al.*, 2013). As a result, a destination is considered to be sustainable if the tourism industry does not impact negatively on the environment, on human–environment interactions and local communities; but equally, the industry needs to contribute to cultural exchange between locals and visitors and meeting the economic needs of the populations (Iniesta-Bonillo *et al.*, 2016). To this list could be added: the long-term capacity of the industry to remain 'clean' from an environmental point of view with the support of technological systems; a fair impact on all members of the population in the present and in the future; and the development of policies at local, national and international level (Sharpley, 2000). The main concern of the development of tourism is for the developing nations and their indigenous peoples, as the impacts of the industry can be either very positive or very negative (Buckley, 2012). Hence, initiatives like the Sustainable Tourism-Eliminating Poverty Program (ST-EP), initiated by the United Nations World Tourism Organization (UNWTO), are taken to use tourism to reduce poverty and increase net benefits for poor people as part of their 'Pro-Poor Tourism' policy (Holden, 2013). Destinations now consider sustainability as a competitive advantage to attract visitors, hence the growth of ecotourism, the fastest growing tourism sector globally (Iniesta-Bonillo *et al.*, 2016; Kazeminia *et al.*, 2016). Consumers are ready to pay more to spend their holidays in destinations considered as sustainable (Kazeminia *et al.*, 2016). That said, much of the tourism industry so far has failed to be sustainable (Iniesta-Bonillo *et al.*, 2016; Séraphin *et al.*, 2018), hence the reason why Sharpley (2000: 1) claimed that 'sustainable development cannot be transposed onto the specific context of tourism'. Twelve years later the United Nations (2012, cited in Iniesta-Bonillo *et al.*, 2016: 1) asserted that: 'despite efforts to promote more sustainable tourist destinations, room for improvement exists in most countries'. This seems to suggest that sustainability in the tourism industry is very hard to achieve, despite a strong will to develop policies and practices in the area (Sharpley, 2000). Liu (2003), provided a list of issues related to sustainable tourism that needed to be addressed: tourist demands in terms of sustainable products have not been taken into account; sustainability is mainly analysed from the preservation and conservation angle; the repartition of the benefits among stakeholders is poorly researched; most research focused on the fact that tourism has negative impacts on culture and the social life of the locals; research has focused on determining a threshold to tourism growth; and finally, despite the fact eco-tourism, alternative tourism, responsible tourism, soft tourism, low impact tourism and community tourism have proven not to be the way forward for sustainable tourism, writers and practitioners are still promoting these forms of tourism as being the way forward. Holden (2013) also added that there is little data that informs us of the beneficiary impacts of tourism development on the poor. In this book, we are adopting the position that 'the sustainable development of tourism requires harmonious relationships between communities, the industry and tourists' (Séraphin *et al.*, 2018; Zhang *et al.*, 2006). Equally important, the industry needs to contribute to the cultural exchange between locals and visitors and it must meet the economic needs of the population (Iniesta-Bonillo *et al.*, 2016).

Sustainable event management

The twenty-first-century event manager has a responsibility to their clients and stakeholders that requires the delivery of an event which minimises negative impacts and can endure without the overconsumption of resources (Getz, 2012). Sustainable events will have a positive impact on people, the planet and profit margins and thus help to meet the economic, sociocultural and environmental needs of event stakeholders (Ferdinand and Kitchin, 2012). Furthermore, professional event planners have an increasing ethical and legal duty to plan and deliver events that are environmentally, socially and culturally responsible (Bladen *et al.*, 2012). Responsible events are sensitive to the economic, sociocultural and environmental needs within a local host community, and are organised in order to create the best output for all involved or affected by the event (Raj and Musgrave, 2009) and in reality, for many event professionals, sustainability is now equated with survival (Brown *et al.*, 2015). This means that placing sustainability at the core of event management practices is not just important but it has become an essential part of the role, and event organisers must adopt increasingly responsible practices in order to stay competitive (Lee and Slocum, 2015).

There is conflicting evidence of the views and attitudes of event attendees towards sustainability and events. According to Ferdinand and Kitchin (2012), today people are conscious about 'green' events; part of the process of deciding whether or not to attend an event will involve weighing up how environment-friendly it is and attendees are becoming more active in contributing to reducing the impacts caused by the event. However, much research points to attendees showing a lack of appreciation towards the sustainability-related efforts of the event organiser and this can even go so far as to manifest in complaints about the inconvenience and poor quality that can result from the implementation of sustainability practices (Teng *et al.*, 2015). Nonetheless, sustainability is certainly growing as an area of concern for event attendees and increasingly the trend set by the LOHAS generation (lifestyle of health and sustainability) indicates a growing demand for organisers to implement an event sustainability policy (Heipel, 2012). Communicating with the attendees would seem to be the key to securing the support and engagement of attendees with what you are doing as a responsible event manager (Teng *et al.*, 2015). However, changing the way we plan and manage events and encouraging responsible behaviour at events is challenging and adds another dimension to the role of the event organiser.

Sustainable frameworks

In order to understand sustainability in relation to event production and to put in place a model for planning and delivering events that are sustainable, several attempts have been made at creating sustainable event frameworks. Perhaps the first attempt at creating such a framework with the involvement of the events industry is the Hanover Principles, which is the name given to a set of guidelines for the design of buildings and objects. The Hanover Principles aim to provide a platform upon which designers can consider how to adapt their work towards sustainable ends. Designers include all those who change the environment with the inspiration of human creativity. Design implies the conception and realisation of human needs and desires (William McDonough Architects (1992). The guidelines were formulated as part of the planning process for the Expo 2000 world fair, which was held in Hanover. The Hanover Principles focused on the elements and thereby included consideration of water (minimising usage), air (minimising pollution), earth (recycling) and spirit (encouraging feelings of belonging) (Ferdinand and Kitchin, 2012).

Another important milestone in the development of sustainable event management practices was the introduction of British Standard 8901. The British Standards Institution produces standards for a range of services and products and it certifies compliance with these standards. BS8901 was developed specifically for the events industry and one of the key drivers of the introduction of the standard was the 2012 Olympic Games and the desire to prove that the Olympics, as a mega event, can be delivered in a sustainable manner. BS8901 covers three key areas of events; environmental responsibility, economic activity and social progress, thereby mirroring the triple bottom line. The standard provides a benchmark for the management system, which is used to produce the event, and companies that have been awarded BS8901 have implemented the highest possible sustainability standards (Bladen *et al.*, 2012). The framework helps event managers to ensure that events demonstrate environmental responsibility, for example, by giving guidance on how to reduce carbon emissions and waste. Economic activity is central to the framework and this can be archived by using local suppliers and ensuring the event is economically viable. Social progress is also part of the framework and can be achieved by involving the community in the planning of the event, ensuring fair employment of people who work on the event.

BS8901 has since developed into a new international standard ISO20121 which was launched at the time of the London games in 2012. ISO, the

International Standards Organization, is an independent organisation based in Switzerland, which publishes standards and specifications for products, services and systems in order to uphold quality, safety and efficiency. International standards are a mark of quality assurance and thereby a basis for enhanced client or customer satisfaction (Davidson and Rogers, 2016). As such the international standard will continue to provide confirmation that an event has been planned and implemented in line with sustainability standards and these apply to the event owner, the event manager and suppliers to the event (Case, 2012). Other examples of relevant international standards include ISO9001, which applies to a management system that demonstrates quality in all areas of a business to include facilities, training, people, services and equipment. It is being adopted by many venues as a means of providing quality assurance to clients as well as motivating staff and demonstrating a commitment to ongoing development (Davidson and Rogers, 2016). Additionally, ISO14000 applies to environmentally sustainable operations and aims to reduce an organisation's environmental footprint, particularly through reducing waste and pollution. This standard is also being adopted by tourism and event organisations not only in operational management but also as a marketing tool to promote a positive image of the business (Schwarz *et al.*, 2015).

Incorporating sustainability into tourism and event operations is not without its challenges. For example, there can be a number of high and unexpected costs involved in remodelling and renovating venues in order to conform to environmental standards, and updating buildings to achieve the requirements for environmental recognition is difficult and offers uncertain benefits (Teng *et al.*, 2015). Furthermore, many managers have experienced challenges in implementing and executing sustainability policies at an operational level across a large organisation and those working in smaller enterprises have had to prioritise on one aspect of sustainable management. Additionally, many tourism and event professionals find that there is a limited number of green suppliers for them to work with, an inadequate number of green products and a scarcity of suitable resources for their needs and this has been identified as a key barrier to the success of some suitability initiatives by certain organisations (ibid.).

One area that has been particularly challenging and also where there has been much success, is within catering operations. It can be a challenge to build an effective partnership with food and beverage suppliers, particularly if they are attempting to source produce locally (Lee and Slocum, 2015) however there are a number of benefits of working with local suppliers, including supporting the local community, cutting down on food transport costs and being able to tell guests how food has been processed and where it has come from. Plus there are indications that guests are willing to pay a price premium for locally sourced food items (ibid.). However, the widespread lack of governmental regulation or industry mandate has served to limit the adoption of environmental initiatives and resulted in underdeveloped green supply chains.

The structure of this book

This book therefore serves to provide tourism and event professionals, academics and students, with examples of best practice from a variety of international events and tourism activities. Each chapter contains recent case studies highlighting some of the challenges and rewards of sustainable management in action. Part I introduces various sustainability initiatives as well as examples of sustainability in relation to the management of festivals, venues and destinations. Governance is a key feature of this section of the book, with discourse on various global government initiatives and influences on the tourism and events industries. The themes of accreditation, certification and innovation also feature heavily in this section, which includes case studies from Canada, Spain, Mexico, Brazil, the USA, Australia, Germany and Denmark.

Part II of this book focuses on sustainable music and arts festivals. Within the literature on event tourism, there is now a wealth of case studies demonstrating good practice in festival management, as much pioneering work in developing certification and benchmarking, as well as influencing consumer behaviour, has taken place in the domain of the organisation of festivals. Part II of this book therefore looks to the future and discusses priorities, trends and ambitions within festival management, drawing on examples of best practice from both the UK and Romania.

Part III of this book is devoted to sustainability and special interest tourism. The rise in consumer interest in diverse forms of tourism, as well as in exploring newer tourism destinations, is well documented and this section provides timely advice and insight into both areas. This section of the book contains two diverse chapters on the emerging trend of Ayurvedic Health Tourism and the challenges of being awarded European Capital of Culture status. The contrasting case studies from India and the Netherlands both provide insight into, and expertise on, the role of sustainability and culture within tourism management.

Part IV of this book is devoted to the topic of the green management of outdoor sites. The three chapters provide a detailed account of some of the specific tasks of managing national parks and publicly accessible locations. The importance of preserving our natural and cultural heritage is discussed, as well as the concept of ecotourism. The case studies provide fascinating examples of the challenges and achievements of managing outdoor sites, illustrated with case studies from France, Spain and Russia.

Part V of this book concludes our exploration of sustainability by focusing on sports events. Surfing and motorsport provide the backdrop to this section, which discusses the particular challenges of incorporating sustainability practices into the development of sporting competitions. Themes of consumer behaviour and financing sustainable sporting events feature in these chapters, which draw on examples of competitions taking place in Australia, Fiji and the UK.

In summary, the growing awareness of the negative environmental impacts created by individuals and businesses has led organisations to rethink their management processes and integrate environmental initiatives into their strategic planning (Whitfield *et al.*, 2014: 300). In the context of tourism and events, environmental initiatives are being used to reduce or eliminate the negative impacts associated with the production and consumption of goods and services. Tourism and event professionals are increasingly under pressure to incorporate sustainability into operations and to demonstrate the positive impact of these actions. This book therefore, provides professionals, scholars and students with a valuable account of some of the ways in which leading organisations around the world are developing innovative yet practical approaches towards the sustainable provision of tourism and events. The book includes insight into legislation, accreditation and certification as well as an overview of key developments, frameworks and guidelines for incorporating sustainable practices into the management of events, sites and destinations. The book includes a variety of examples of initiatives that have been adopted by various governments around the world and it also looks ahead to emerging trends and ambitions within the sphere of sustainable tourism and event management.

References

Bladen, C., Kennell, J., Abson, E. and Wilde, N. (2012). *Events Management: An Introduction.* Abingdon: Routledge.

Brown, S., Getz, D., Pettersson, R. and Wallstam, M. (2015). Event evaluation: definitions, concepts and a state of the art review. *International Journal Of Event And Festival Management,* 6 (2): 135–157.

Buckley, R. (2012). Sustainable tourism: research and reality. *Annals of Tourism Research,* 39 (2): 528–546.

Case, R. (2012). *Events and the Environment.* Abingdon: Routledge.

Davidson, R. and Rogers, T. (2016). *Marketing Destinations and Venues for Conferences, Conventions and Business Events* (2nd edn). Abingdon: Routledge.

Ferdinand, N. and Kitchin, P. (2012). *Events Management: An International Approach* (2nd edn). London: SAGE.

Getz, D. (2012). *Event Studies: Theory, Research and Policy For Planned Events* (2nd edn). Abingdon: Routledge.

Heipel, M. (2012). *How Are Venues Adapting To New Industry Trends?* Available at: https://michaelheipel.wordpress.com/2012/06/08/How-Are-Venues-Adapting-To-New-Industry-Trends (accessed 16 June 2016).

Holden, A. (2013). *Tourism, Poverty and Development,* Abingdon: Routledge.

Iniesta-Bonillo, M. A., Sanchez-Fernandez, R. and Jimenez-Castillo, D. (2016). Sustainability, value, and satisfaction: model testing and cross-validation in tourist destinations. *Journal of Business Research,* 69 (11): 5002–5007.

Kazeminia, A., Hultman, M. and Mostaghel, R. (2016). Why pay more for sustainable services? The case of ecotourism. *Journal of Business Research,* 69 (11): 4992–4997.

Lee, S. and Slocum, S. (2015). Understanding the role of local food in the meeting industry: an exploratory study of meeting planners' perception of local food in sustainable meeting planning. *Journal of Convention and Event Tourism,* 16 (1): 45–60.

Liu, Z. (2003). Sustainable tourism development: a critique. *Journal of Sustainable Tourism,* 11 (6): 459–475.

Raj, R. and Musgrave, J. (eds) (2009). *Event Management and Sustainability*. Walling-ford: CABI.

Schwarz, E., Hall, S. and Shibli, S. (2015). *Sports Facility Operations Management* (3rd edn). Abingdon: Routledge.

Séraphin, H., Sheeran, P. and Pilato, M. (2018). Over-tourism and the fall of Venice as a destination. *Journal of Destination Marketing and Management*, doi: 10.1016/j. dmm.2018.01.011.

Sharpley, R. (2000). Tourism and sustainable development: exploring the theoretical divide. *Journal of Sustainable Tourism*, 8 (1): 1–19.

Sloan, P., Legrand, W. and Chen, J. S. (2013). *Sustainability in the Hospitality Industry. Principles of Sustainable Operations*. Abingdon: Routledge.

Teng, C.-C., Horng, J.-S. and Hu, I.-C. (2015). Hotel environmental management deci-sions: the stakeholder perspective. *International Journal of Hospitality and Tourism Administration*, 16 (1): 78–98.

Whitfield, J., Dioko, L. and Webber, D. (2014). Scoring environmental credentials: A review of UK conference and meeting venues using the GREENER VENUE frame-work. *Journal of Sustainable Tourism*, 22 (2): 299–318.

William McDonough Architects (1992). *The Hannover Principles*. Available at: www. mcdonough.com/writings/the-hannover-principles/ (accessed 7 June 2017).

Zhang, J., Inbakaran, R. J. and Jackson, M. S. (2006). Understanding community attitudes toward tourism and host–guest interaction in the urban–rural border region. *Tourism Geographies*, 8 (2): 182–204.

Part I
Sustainability initiatives and governance

Part I

1 Strategies and best practices for greening festivals

Rachel Dodds

National context

Currently in Canada, although there have been many highlighted approaches to making meetings and events more environmentally conscious, there are no certifications or benchmarks for the greening of festivals.

There are also no federal mandates for festival sustainability practices and very little provincially. In the province of Ontario, for example, the Ministry of Tourism Culture and Sport, through the Celebrate Ontario 2015 programme, provided project-based funding to new or existing Ontario events 'to enhance programmes, activities and services and support innovations that will lead to long-term improvements, sustainability and the attraction of additional tourists'. Although there was a recognition of sustainability, Celebrate Ontario 2015 did not fund the development of best practices or provide technical and educational support to festival operators for reducing waste, energy or carbon. In 2017, there were multiple funding opportunities to have or augment events to celebrate Canada's 150 birthday through Heritage Canada, however, there was no focus on increasing environmental management or reducing negative environmental effects.

The business case for organisations going green is quite clear (Graci and Dodds, 2009; Ottman, 2011; Walsh and Dodds, 2017) and there have been some efforts by individual organisations that have highlighted the need for festivals to become more sustainable The now dismantled Icarus Foundation produced a guide in 2009, for example. Within the festival and event context, however, much of the materials are more strongly focused to Meetings, Incentive, Conferences and Events (MICE) rather than outdoor festivals (Dodds and Graci, 2012). In principle, many of the initiatives to becoming more environmentally and socially responsible can be applied to both festivals and events such as, facilities management, however, there are very few examples of best practice or adaptive management approaches that a festival organiser can adopt. There are also few examples of programming to support a festival organiser looking to adopt best practice to make their festival more sustainable.

Priority issues

Festivals of all kinds are important, both to Canada and to the economy of its many provinces, as they attract visitors both domestically and internationally. In Canada there are over 250 events that attract over 10,000 festivalgoers per event and these do not include the mega events (>one million). In the province of Ontario alone, there are over 3,000 events that happen across the province and these festivals/events contribute over $1 billion of economic impact on a yearly basis (Festivals and Events Ontario, n.d.).

Economically, these events bring thousands of visitors who contribute to the local economy and community. Socially and environmentally, however, events and festivals can be a burden on local communities if they are not managed with a sustainability mindset. Research into the environmental footprint of events show that both small and large festivals can have a negative impact on the environment and society. One example is CO_2 emissions. Emissions range from using cars to attend events, congestion, consumptive behaviour and therefore waste from food and beverage and sewage (Stone, 2009). Another example is waste, where Walzer (2014) suggests the average amount is 1.1 kg per person per day and Cierjacks *et al.* (2012) estimates that the average festivalgoer produces 2.67 kg of waste per day.

Although there is some literature on the potential benefit of greening festivals (Dodds and Graci, 2012; Mair and Jago, 2010, 2012; Gibson and Wong, 2011), there is little actual research into best practices or determining the key elements needed for achieving standards.

Trends

A number of efforts were made to provide context to this case. The first step was to conduct background research to better understand the motivations and barriers to implementing sustainability practices within the festival industry.

The second step was to undertake research on festivals globally to ascertain best practice, what a sustainable festival consisted of, and key elements needed to assist festival managers to undertake sustainability efforts. In addition to a wide Internet search of festival best practices and sustainability measures, a total of 18 semi-structured interviews were conducted with 20 festival managers across Ontario. Interviews were analysed using grounded theory to determine the significant themes or issues. Key findings outlined that while there are some notable best practices for sustainability among festivals (*Mariposa Folk Festival, Hillside Festival*, some municipal *Ribfests*), there are many festivals within Ontario that are not practising any sustainability efforts. The results show that while many festival managers are interested in incorporating sustainability initiatives into their festivals, there are multiple barriers to successfully doing so, Volunteer burnout and lack of manpower makes it difficult for many festival organisers to prioritise sustainability initiatives. Additionally, insufficient resources and funding opportunities for festivals create a strain on managers that does not support the work needed to introduce more sustainability into their festivals. Finally, there is a need for legislation or mandates from municipal, provincial and/or federal agencies to ensure that sustainability objectives become part of the overarching outcomes of festivals, as currently sustainability is not a key priority for most festivals.

The third step was to search literature and existing green festivals to determine if there were any guides, certifications or benchmarks available for Canadian festivals. The search found none but did find many international examples of festival awards although no certification or global benchmark.

The fourth step was to examine global best practices found in step two. Festivals were contacted to ask about their practices and success factors. Although the response rate from international festivals was low, there was still significant information found online about what elements constitute a green festival and what aspects festivals consider in terms of sustainability.

Government policies

From a global best practice analysis, it was found that there were few standards. In the USA, A Greener Festival (AGF, see Further resources) outlined key elements to help festivals become greener. Globally, a standard through the International Standards Organization (ISO) has developed a guideline called ISO20121. This certification provides requirements for an event sustainability management system for any type of event or event-related activity, and provides guidance on conforming to those requirements (ISO, n.d.).

Canadian examples of guides or overarching strategies for festival greening are absent. Some festival and event organisers are trying to green their events to minimise their impact on the environment, however, it is not commonplace and few efforts are funded or run by government. The former *Rideau Canal Festival* was funded by the Ontario Government to create and implement a GHG reduction approach for the management and delivery of the festival. The *Rideau Canal Festival*'s guide provided strategies, tools and expectations for three phases of the festival – planning, physical organisation and the event itself. Pride Toronto was funded by the Trillium Foundation to undertake sustainability efforts, yet success was not achieved and funding withdrawn (Dodds and Graci, 2012). In other provinces in Canada there are examples of municipal efforts and results have been positive. For example, Vancouver and Calgary both have a municipal 80/20 goal (to divert 80 per cent of its landfill by 2020). These efforts have translated into some festivals within these cities having a higher focus on environmental management from a waste diversion point of view, often achieving 90 per cent or higher diversion rates (e.g. *Vancouver Folk Festival*, Vancouver International Marathon, Vancouver Car Free day, Calgary Stampede, Calgary and Vancouver Canada Day celebrations). These municipal efforts are not commonplace, however, and did not exist in the province of Ontario.

In terms of voluntary codes in Canada, there was only one. A Canadian not-for-profit organisation, the Icarus Foundation (2008–2013), published a 'Green

Festivals and Events Guide' that provided a voluntary step-by-step approach to executing the reduction of waste, water and energy, and the use of fair trade or organic food using local suppliers and locally sourced products.

Case study: an analysis of tourist perceptions of destination attractiveness

From the literature, and reviewing global best practices, key themes were identified that contributed to a sustainable festival. These themes or elements included facilities, communications, community, energy, employee/volunteer engagement, food and beverage, procurement, transportation, venue, waste and water. Each of these elements includes key tactics to achieve greener festivals. For example, short, medium and long-term criteria are available to achieve higher levels of sustainability and best practices for each element were found. Additionally, resources and incentives do exist, however these are not necessarily easy for festival operators to adopt.

This research found multiple best practices and examples to showcase how festivals could be more sustainable (please see http://greenfestivals.ca for a full collection of case studies, resources as well as checklists to become more sustainable). This guide was then adopted by Festival and Events Ontario, a non-profit organisation representing all festivals across Ontario (www.feo.org).

The most common sustainability areas focused on by festivals is recycling and to some extent greater overall waste diversion. The next most common element is sustainable transportation initiatives such as bicycle parking or shuttle buses to reduce car traffic.

Although it is important to determine a benchmark and outline good practice, this study also sought to determine the key elements that are needed in order for festivals to achieve success. The following five key elements should be considered to ensure sustainability can be incorporated and achieved within a festival context.

1. Time and chains of command must be considered. Although festival managers may be keen to make changes, often the decisions that have the most sustainability impact also need substantial lead time and buy in. For example something simple, such as putting in place a vendor contract to ensure environmental compliance or changing cutlery to be compostable must be done at the time the vendors are first contacted which is often months before the festival date. Additionally, if a festival has an organising committee, they also must be consulted, which leads to additional lag time as these tend to meet infrequently and change must be streamlined in accordance with other priorities. Another issue for time is that changing something such as a venue requires more than just the festival organiser. For example, if the festival is located in a park, municipal recreation as well as zoning personnel must be contacted, which also leads to additional timing considerations.

2. Having a lead or key person dedicated to sustainability is essential. Although for many festivals this person may be a volunteer, passion or commitment to sustainability is imperative. This person is the one who will coordinate

and engage others to assist in sustainability initiatives and will take the time to ensure that such initiatives are implemented. A lead or dedicated person also ensures that sustainability is integrated into festival planning (Dodds and Graci, 2012). For example, thinking through how waste will be separated into recycling, compost and waste must happen before the festival takes place, as this must be outsourced or proper collection bins procured.

3. Changes must be simple and must have a return on investment. Even if festival organisers are concerned about sustainability initiatives, often there are no incentives therefore there must be some return on the investment (Cvent, 2009; Pelham, 2011).

For example, if a festival receives rebates or cost savings for recycling and composting (as it costs less to haul these types of waste compared to landfill), they are more likely to undertake waste separation. In addition, outdoor festivals that are held in parks or natural areas may have negative responses from festival-goers if the area is littered with garbage, so keeping a clean environment links to positive feedback. Festival organisers may not have designated time to devote specifically to sustainability and often this role is in addition to another organisational role or is voluntary. Therefore, for sustainability to be considered from the outset it must be simple and easy to implement. Ideas that can happen without additional money and extensive time have the most potential uptake. For example, adding a section about sustainability to the festival website could be beneficial for education, but would not require a large commitment. Car pooling and bike parking are also easy to implement and have a positive return as they are seen to address carbon impacts and lessen congestion – something festivals are often associated with (Mair and Jago, 2010; Shepard, 2007). Suggestions with more complications are not always received as favourably. For example, if a festival was not able to dispose of all types of recycling and of compostable materials through the waste provider they used, it was often viewed as a very complicated goal to try to introduce these initiatives as this would involve sourcing a new supplier, obtaining quotes and having an understanding of waste issues, which may not be within the skill set of the festival organiser. Another complication was the viability of the initiative. Solar energy, for example, is looked upon favourably by many music festivals, but the idea of a solar stage has not been tried as the reliability is questionable and solar may not provide enough power for a music stage with high intensity output.

4. Regulation or compliance is a motivator (Jones, 2014). Sustainability initiatives that are mandated have a higher likelihood to succeed. For example, if a municipality supports waste diversion, facilitation of waste streams are usually in place, thereby making it easier for festivals to comply. Additionally, regulation provides clear criteria for what must be adhered to – often something that is not set out for festivals in most municipalities.

5. Funding incentives can initiate change. With so many other areas of festival management to focus on, an incentive is a good way to encourage managers to take the initiative to make changes. Cost is often the biggest concern for festival managers and suggesting changes without an incentive can be

challenging. Many festivals rely on grants and therefore change may rely on funding agencies to require sustainability initiatives as part of funding practices (e.g. education or environmental displays because they meet the criteria of their funding). There is a need for more research that proves that making the changes to become sustainable is beneficial. For example, the *Mariposa Folk Festival* in Orillia, Ontario realised that diverting waste from landfill would reduce their haulage and tipping fees. The same festival also undertook an experiment regarding procurement and now has data to show that selling fair trade/organic festival t-shirts has a higher profit margin than standard cheap cotton t-shirts.

Similar case studies and relevant projects

There have been a number of other studies on festival sustainability. There are both academic case studies that focus on sustainability as well as some national initiatives.

National or global initiatives include a yearly conference held in the United States to discuss green events and festivals (www.agreenerfestival.com). In New Zealand there is *The Greener Events Guide* which is a national guideline produced by the Ministry for the Environment – although there is no legislation enforcing any recommendations (Grima and Nicholas, 2017). In the UK, an organisation called Sustainable Events Ltd., pushes the ISO20121 standard for large festivals as well as offering webinars, training and strategic planning services.

From an academic review, Dodds and Graci (2012) examined *Britannia Park Festival* in Ottawa and sustainable transportation initiatives such as using pedal-powered cargo tricycles for moving supplies.

Further resources

http://greenfestivals.ca – this website is based in Ontario, Canada and outlines tips and checklists for moving towards sustainability in festivals. Resources, videos and 'how tos' are also included.

www.agreenerfestival.com – this website provides information about some festivals as well as information on an annual conference for those interested in greening festivals.

References

Cierjacks, A., Behr, F. and Kowarik, I. (2012). Operational performance indicators for litter management at festivals in semi-natural landscapes. *Ecological Indicators*, 13 (1): 328–337.
Cvent. (2009). *Green Meetings Made Easy.* Available at: www.cvent.com/resources/green-meetings-made-easy.shtml (accessed 7 October 2009).
Dodds, R. and Graci, G. (2012). Greening of the Pride Toronto Festival: lessons learned. *Tourism, Culture and Communication*, 12 (1): 29–38.

Festivals and Events Ontario. (n.d.). Available at: www.festivalsandeventsontario.ca/about/background-mission (accessed April 2017).

Gibson, C. and Wong, C. (2011). Greening rural festivals: ecology, sustainability and human–nature relations. *Festival Places: Revitalising Rural Australia* (pp. 92–105). Bristol: Channel View Publications.

Graci, S. and Dodds, R. (2009). Why go Green? The business case for environmental commitment in the Canadian hotel industry. *Anatolia: An International Journal of Tourism and Hospitality Research*, 19 (2): 250–270.

Grima, J. and Nicholas, L. (2017). 'Rubbish, Rubbish Out': facilitators and barriers to waste minimization at New Zealand festivals. Presented at 3rd Global Tourism and Hospitality Conference, Hong Kong (pp. 220–224).

ISO. (n.d.). Available at: www.iso.org/standard/54552.html (accessed 23 August 2017).

Jones, M. (2014). *Sustainable Event Management: A Practical Guide* (2nd edn). Abingdon: Routledge.

Mair, J. and Jago, L. (2010). The development of a conceptual model of greening in the business events tourism sector. *Journal of Sustainable Tourism*, 18 (1): 77–94.

Mair, J. and Laing, J. (2012). The greening of music festivals: motivations, barriers and outcomes. Applying the Mair and Jago Model. *Journal of Sustainable Tourism*, 20 (5): 683–700.

Ottman, J. (2011). *The New Rules of Green Marketing: Strategies, Tools and Inspiration for Sustainable Branding*. San Francisco, CA: Berrett-Koehler Publishers Inc.

Pelham, F. (2011). Will sustainability change the business model of the event industry? *Worldwide Hospitality and Tourism Themes*, 3 (3): 187.

Stone, C. (2009). The British Pop Music Festival phenomenon. In J. Ali-Knight, M. Robertson, A. Fyall, and A. Ladkin (eds), *International Perspectives of Festivals and Events* (pp. 205–224). New York: Elsevier Ltd.

Walsh, P. and Dodds, R. (2017). Measuring the choice of environmental sustainability strategies in creating a competitive advantage. *Business Strategy and the Environment*, DOI: 10.1002/bse.1949.

Walzer, C. (2014). Assessment of the waste concept of a music festival in the case of the Tomorrow 47 Festival 2013. (In German: Bewertung des Abfallkonzepts eines Musikfestivals am Fallbeispiel 48 des Tomorrow Festival 2013). MSc. Thesis. BOKU University, Vienna. 28, 1.

2 Promoting and assessing sustainability at festivals

A case study of the 'A Greener Festival' initiative

Graham Berridge, Teresa Moore and Jane Ali-Knight

Introduction

The chapter will focus on describing the origin, documenting the process and evaluating the impact of A Greener Festival (AGF) through the eyes of festivals that have collaborated with them and undertaken their assessment scheme. Thomas and Murfitt (2011) describe how environmental management systems (EMS) tend to be voluntary internal, formalised processes that can help festivals become compliant with legislation whilst negating environmental impacts. Working towards the AGF Award, festivals are assessed on what measures they are taking to make their festival as green as possible.

The social, environmental and business focus on sustainability largely stems from the 1992 UN Conference, the commonly referred to, Earth Summit. Out of this, Agenda 21 was the main document to emerge and although not legally binding, it provided a blueprint for securing a sustainable future and a compelling practical and moral force for not only governments but also local democracies. Having a sustainable component as a significant feature of tourism developed with the emergence of the concept of ecotourism (Boo, 1990) which, with the impetus of Agenda 21, led in turn to the emergence of voluntary codes of practice as a method for promoting environmentally sound development and management (Williams, 1993). Despite entering the lexicon of practice in tourism and related activities, sustainability in the event industry has not been so well discussed (Arcodia *et al.*, 2012). Therefore, an increased understanding of evaluation tools that measure the environmental impact of events (including festivals) is important due to their potential negative environmental impacts, at both local and global scales (Collins and Cooper, 2017).

The AGF assessment process will be evaluated and challenges and best practice explored using UK and international festival case studies to demonstrate the innovative and transformational impact the scheme has on the social and environmental challenges that festivals face.

Festival trends linked to sustainability

Modern festivals can primarily be regarded as special events, which are planned to deliver various benefits, including community cohesion, place branding or financial profit (Zifkos, 2015). However, as Chernushenko (1994) explained, sports events can generate unusual amounts of environmental harm, as is the case with cultural festivals that have the potential for negative impacts on the environment. Mair and Laing (2012) discuss how, especially in the case of music mega-festivals, unintentional or not, this impact – from an economic, sociocultural, as well as an environmental perspective – is considerable. As a result of this increased awareness, locally and globally, there has been an events industry response, resulting in an increasing number of music festival organisers claiming that they can recognise and address the potential negative impacts of their events by embedding the notion of sustainability into the management of such festivals. Indeed it has been stated that expanding numbers of festival organisers around the world have been promoting sustainability and are leading the way in their efforts to reduce 'greenhouse-gas emissions, minimise waste and reduce their festival's environmental impact as well as championing positive behaviour such as educating festival audiences about the benefits of pro environmental behaviour such as recycling' (A Greener Festival, p. 2 in Zifkos, 2015). Such festivals are routinely labelled 'green' or 'sustainable' or are able to highlight their contribution to it and are seen to be meeting the demands of festivalgoers who are becoming increasingly eco-conscious (Ensor *et al.*, 2011; Raj and Vignali, 2010; A Greener Festival, Bucks New University, 2012).

The question of what and how to stage a 'green' festival was examined by Laing and Frost (2010: 262) who looked into issues related to a 'sustainable' event. They defined sustainability as 'an event that has a sustainability policy or incorporates sustainable practices into its management and operations'. They identified that a range of international festivals, such as *Glastonbury Festival*, the *Peats Ridge Festival* and the *Burning Man Festival*, were committed to improving and developing their sustainability initiatives and have this linked to the festivals' core values (*Glastonbury*'s 'leave no trace' which also features in *Burning Man*'s '10 Principles'). Further studies have shown Festivals engaging in participant education on sustainable behaviour with the example of the *Bonnaroo* festival also embedding green issues into its core values, and using marketing that conveys strong messages of environmental responsibility and sustainability (Kennell and Sitz, 2010). More recent research has considered how assessing impact via The Ecological Footprint offers a number of potential advantages to policymakers and festival organisers in terms of understanding and managing the environmental impact of festivals in the future (Collins and Cooper, 2017).

Festival accreditation

As the festival and events industry has grown and developed, awareness of the need for environmental management systems to control this growth in a sustainable way has led to the development of a range of sustainable initiatives to try and green the industry. Sustainability for events has been signposted, therefore, by several key UK and International initiatives, namely: the UK standard BS8901, which was redeveloped into the specification for a sustainable event management system: ISO20121. Other standards include international standard for event industry: ISO14001; environmental management: ISO26000; Green Tourism Business Scheme; Green Globe and Apex Green Meeting Standard. The planning and management of the 2012 London Olympics and Cultural Olympiad was underpinned by, and worked towards, ISO20121 with its industry specific guidance applied to venues, organisers and suppliers. Complementing the Olympics were initiatives such as the *Manchester International Festival* (MIF) 2008, which trialled a sustainable approach for energy use, engagement of communities and environmental impact, resulting in a sustainable development policy with sustainability now part of the MIF planning process. However, the ways and means of achieving this are not straightforward and Mair and Laing (2012) sought to explore how sustainability was implemented by understanding what are the drivers of, and constraints to, achieving a 'green' festival performance. They identified that a key indicator was the adoption of clearly articulated pro-environmental practices followed by management and monitoring focusing on, but not exclusively, waste management, transport and energy use.

The 'A Greener Festival' assessment and award

The organisation A Greener Festival (AGF) is part of this movement towards 'green festivals' and has been assessing their social and environmental impact for a decade. Founded in 2007, it followed research undertaken at a number of European music festivals which demonstrated that, whilst there were a variety of initiatives taking place at festivals there was, at that time, no systematic way of determining or rewarding their effectiveness in terms of environmental sustainability or behaviour change. Nor was there much in the way of sharing and benchmarking good practice. Festivals, by their very nature, tend to be highly resource-intensive and impactful and a more holistic approach to assessment benefiting key stakeholders as well as local communities is needed (Holmes *et al.*, 2015). AGF was formed with the aim of 'helping music and arts events and festivals around the world to adopt environmentally efficient practices' (AGF, 2017).

In order to provide support to festivals and events, AGF designed a process (see Figure 2.1) by which to assess the environmental impact of the practices and initiatives of festivals, providing external verification of the results. The scheme involves a self-registration and self-assessment process to be undertaken by festival organisers, supported by AGF staff and assessors. Assessor training

Figure 2.1 AGF assessment process.

has been more formalised with the development of a 2-day training course that has been delivered in London and Manchester. Potential assessors receive training around current trends and best practice in the environmental management of festivals and are introduced to AGF's assessment process. Assessors are given mentors to work with on their initial assessments and are able to redeem the training cost after they have completed their first full assessment. The assessment fee covers assessor travel, food and accommodation expenses and the festivals grant the assessors free access to the site but the assessors give up their time voluntarily.

Once festivals register their interest in the AGF scheme they receive support in understanding the self-assessment and are then required to complete a self-assessment form. Completion of the self-assessment provides a framework for the event's Environmental Impact Assessment. Trained assessors then visit the festival site for between 1 to 4 days, depending on the size of the event, and conduct a 'field' evaluation measured against this initial self-evaluation. This involves meeting with people from within the organisation; speaking with key stakeholders such as the traders, audience and suppliers; viewing every aspect of the festival including backstage production/infrastructure; and comparing the on-site situation with assertions and aspirations in the self-assessment. Additionally an audit of documentation supplied by the festival to support the claims made in their self-assessment document is undertaken. There is a range of areas covered by the assessment and evaluation that consider the local and global impact of the festival. These look at direct impacts for local and global systems, travel and transport, power, procurement, solid waste and recycling, water usage, waste water and sewage, legal compliance and management systems, external reach, behavioural change, and carbon analysis. Each area is graded and the festival is then given an overall sustainable rating. The festival is provided support in understanding the self-assessment, with a detailed report of both the areas to be commended and those that need further work, together with advice as to how improvements may be made. If successful in receiving the award, winners receive use of the logo, and inclusion in international media coverage. Annual awards are then presented to the festivals with the highest ratings and best practice in the UK and overseas at the end of the festival season.

In the early years the assessment process was fairly modest in its scope, however the range and focus of the assessment has evolved over time mirroring the way in which the understanding of the issues has developed and changed as the industry's approach to environmental sustainability has become more sophisticated. Over the years AGF has developed a substantial knowledge base and experience to draw upon and are able to support festival organisers by sharing the good practice found during the season. This then becomes the benchmark for the following year's assessment with the intention of continually raising standards and pushing event organisers to improve their efforts and outcomes to achieve greener and more sustainably delivered festivals.

The impact of 'A Greener Festival' award

To date over 400 festivals in 15 different countries have taken part in the scheme, including key UK festivals such as *Glastonbury*, *Secret Garden Party* and *BBC Proms in the Park* (Hyde Park) as well as festivals in Denmark (*Roskilde*), Holland (*Mysteryland*), Germany (*Das Fest*), US (*Bonnaroo*) and Australia (*Blues Fest*), with many reapplying year on year. Indeed the number of festivals reapplying year on year is now over 90 per cent (O'Neill, 2017).

To understand more about how festivals view the AGF assessment and the impact it has had on their environmental practice, four case studies have been undertaken from a cross section of festivals from the UK, Europe and Australia. Data was collected via a semi-structured interview with the senior member of the organisation responsible for implementing and managing sustainable practice onsite. The festivals range in size and scope from a very small community-based festival to a mega-festival with an audience of over 100,000. Three of the festivals, *Island Vibe*, Australia, *Cambridge Folk Festival*, UK and *Das Fest*, Germany have been assessed by AGF over a number of years and there is some longitudinal data available which provides further evidence of changes to practice. The fourth festival *Roskilde*, Denmark, was new to the AGF assessment in 2017 and is included as it provides an insight into why a festival with an impressive track record of environmental innovation and practice would choose to undertake the assessment.

Case study 1: *Island Vibe Festival*, Australia

The *Island Vibe Festival* was founded in 2006 in Australia and is situated in an area of great natural beauty, North Stradbroke Island, on the coast of Queensland. It is a very small music festival with an audience of around 2,500, with a specialist musical genre of Reggae, Dub and Electronica.

It is an event with sustainability at its core 'Every year much care is taken to make *Island Vibe* the most hospitable and comfortable festival and to keep our environmental footprint as low as possible' (Green, 2017).

The event was first assessed by AGF in 2010 and has participated annually apart from the year that A Greener Festival took out to redevelop and rewrite its assessment process. In 2013 *Island Vibe* won 'Outstanding' in the AGF Award for excellence in eight different aspects of environmental sustainability, including: Office and Event Management, Fair Trade and Ethical Purchasing, Waste, Re-use and Recycling, Water Management, Energy and CO_2 Emissions, Travel and Transport, Noise Pollution and Land Management.

The original reason for entering the award was to gain an overall idea of how the festival operated on an environmental level and direction as to where improvements could be made. The first change introduced as a result of the AGF assessment process in 2010 was the introduction of policy documents to support the environmental direction and management of the event. In the next three years the festival introduced the following:

- a dedicated space for environmental workshops;
- an annual environmental theme;
- a survey to monitor patron transport modes; and
- dedicated bike hire/tune up/locking facilities.

In addition to the above it also banned the on-site use of single-use disposable items and water sold in bottles; focused more on engagement with their audience to decide how their optional eco fee ($3 per ticket) should be spent; and marketing became more focused on eco themes, producing a dedicated page on their website.

Overall the AGF assessment has enabled the festival to crystallise current practices and formalise its future environmental aspirations. Environmental management is also embedded into the festival's operations and as a result the environmental manager now has a place on the senior management team at the top of the decision-making tree. *Island Vibe* entered the assessment and award scheme again in 2017 and is awaiting feedback from this year's assessment.

It (the AGF assessment and award) is used as a consideration point at management meetings when assessing changes to the event, it has informed all managers of their ability to operate in a greener way and certainly provides a strong marketing element as we are keen to be known as 'The Greenest festival in Australia'.

(Green, 2017)

Case study 2: *Cambridge Folk Festival*

The *Cambridge Folk Festival* (CFF), UK, celebrated its 50th anniversary in 2014 with an audience capacity of 14,000 and over 250 workshops and events over the weekend, and is widely acknowledged as a leading world folk festival. Cambridge City Council originally ran the festival until 2015 when it set up a new charity called 'Cambridge Live'. Its main ethos being '… to act as a catalyst for inspiring cultural experiences that everyone can be part of' (Cambridge Live, 2017).

Our relationship with A Greener Festival goes way back, in 2014 we won 'Outstanding' for our environmental performance and in 2016, after the award had a year's break, we were announced as a Greener Festival Associate. We are overwhelmingly happy that we have now received the Greener Festival Award at the prestigious 2016 UK Festival Awards. Winning awards alongside other great festivals such as Bestival, Download & Lattitude.

(Warwick, 2017)

The founders of CFF already had a personal interest and ethos for sustainable living but they didn't know how to put this into practice at an event. Conversations with one of the co-founders of AGF kick-started their active interest in greening the event. The concept of AGF was a good fit with their beliefs and outlook and, in 2009, *Cambridge Folk Festival* applied for the assessment. They found that the assessment provided a framework and logical structure that they could work towards and the feedback showed them how to put their ideas into practice.

Since 2009 CFF have made a series of changes and introduced new environmental initiatives year on year as a direct result of the A Greener Festival assessment feedback. These include the introduction of:

- a standard agreement with their traders and suppliers to use Fair Trade products;
- bio degradable utensils; and
- a ban on plastic carrier bags.

In addition to this they have also reviewed their transport policy to reduce audience travel emissions through the introduction of a car-share scheme and bus vouchers for a free bus transfer from the station. A more effective waste management plan, measuring and analysing power usage and measuring the event's carbon footprint, has also been introduced. This helped facilitate more effective drainage onsite and as a result the production manager improved the quality of the site plan by incorporating more accurate information on the location of the watercourse and drainage sewers. In financial terms the assessment has also had an impact, in that CFF allocate a larger proportion of the festival's budget to environmental management and, through effective cost savings, now have a paid environmental manager in place.

The impact of undertaking the A Greener Festival assessment and award is not limited to the introduction of new and improved practices; those festivals that have undertaken the assessment over several years all referred to the effect that external scrutiny can have to educate, motivate and engage both staff and other key stakeholders, such as suppliers. The scoring and the award is the tangible outcome of their efforts and is valued by the event. As CFF's Environmental Manager stated, the 'assessment provides a focal point for everyone'.

Beyond the implementation of practical changes as a result of the AGF assessment, CFF have found that both the assessment and award were a good way of showcasing and validating what they were already doing.

Case study 3: *Das Fest*, Germany

Das Fest, Germany with its 250,000 audience visits every year, is one of the biggest open-air events in Germany and has been held yearly since 1985 on the last weekend before the summer vacation. It is located in the Günther-Klotz Park in Karlsruhe, a prestigious local recreation area. Those involved are very committed to respecting that this public park is used as a festival area and great efforts are made in the run-up, in coordination with the municipal parks department, to ensure that damage to the green areas is kept to a minimum during the festival.

Since 2014, *Das Fest* has successfully achieved the 'A Greener Festival Award', as well as also earning the Green'n'Clean award in 2014. Moreover, as one of the leading festivals, it has assisted in restructuring and updating the awards by providing information and insights as an environmental officer watches over the fulfilment and improvement of criteria for retaining the award every year.

The festival has a dedicated environmental manager and they have developed a transport policy; waste and water policies; food policies, including a requirement for fair Trade products; and sustainable food, including Vegan options.

Their environmental policies were already well developed when they decided to enter the AGF scheme and were supported by management and project leaders alike. *Das Fest* felt that an important part of the assessment feedback was the sharing of information on new and future developments and their main motivation for entering the scheme was to 'learn about new innovations and technologies gleaned from other events around the world' (Varsek, 2017). Since their first assessment in 2014, *Das Fest* have introduced some changes as a direct result of the assessment and feedback and these include:

- compostable toilets;
- protection against ground pollution during the refuelling of vehicles on-site;
- bottle deposits;
- more sustainable materials used for installation (as signposting); and
- increased involvement of local companies.

Case study 4: *Roskilde Festival*, Denmark

Roskilde Festival in Denmark is probably one of the largest festivals in Europe with audience figures of 130,000. Since its introduction in 1971, the festival has grown in scale with additional visitors and more and higher profile bands. Even an accident in 2000 did not lead to a decline in attendance. Average spending amongst festival guests' has also increased over the years, reflecting growth in the economy (Hjalager, 2009) The festival has aimed to be inclusive through its support of local businesses and is widely interlinked with the social life and the economy of the area (Bærenholdt and Haldrup, 2006).

Hjalager (2009) discusses how, in the mid-1990s, environmental sustainability became a key focus of the festival. An environmental programme was developed in 1995 and the festival introduced an incentive scheme that encouraged festival participants and the providers of services to collect and sort waste, and compostable materials for cups and plates were introduced. Since then the programme has been refined and continued annually. Through the experience and knowledge gained from being an 'early mover' in this field, the festival is now able to offer consulting services on environmental management for other festivals.

Roskilde has well-developed environmental policies and practices and sets out some simple but ambitious goals on its dedicated sustainability web page. These include increasing awareness about the environmental initiatives at *Roskilde* amongst the festival guests and measuring internal sustainability awareness from 2016 and onward (Sander, 2017).

Roskilde Festival applied to the AGF assessment scheme for the first time in 2017 primarily for an independent assessment providing 'the feedback report and suggestions on how to improve' (Sander, 2017). The festival did not apply before as they were concerned that their efforts would be focused on a tick box procedure rather than making the actual changes which would have the biggest impact. The festival has clear expectations of the assessment and feedback, expecting that it will have useable suggestions that can be implemented during the next two years at the festival, thus demonstrating a desire to keep on improving and reducing their environmental impact.

Analysis/evaluation

Looking at the existing cases described above, some common themes emerge:

- The festival organisers who enter the assessment scheme are already committed to sustainability and engaged in some environmental practices. In the case of *Island Vibe*, practices that look after the environment reflect the Festival Director's personal ethics and values. This was also evident at the other festivals.
- *Cambridge Folk Festival, Das Fest* and *Roskilde Festival* all expressed a desire for improvement with increased knowledge and understanding a key driver, and a desire to want to know how to be more effective and incorporate best practice.
- The assessment process was instrumental in helping the festivals formulate environmental policies and goals for their events.
- The assessment feedback resulted in new interventions and changes to practice at each of the festivals.

These themes serve to demonstrate that A Greener Festival has had a clear and significant impact on the environmental practices of these festivals through further embedding the key principles of sustainability and signposting new approaches. Additionally, the interviews with the festivals also revealed a wider dimension to their views of the assessment scheme and award, which have consequently motivated their continued participation. These views have been collated and are summarised in Table 2.1.

A key impact dimension to the AGF assessment and award, highlighted by the festivals, was the way in which it helped to motivate staff and thus was a key feature in recruitment and sustained service delivery. This can largely be seen as an internal impact related to staff working during the festival itself. In terms of the external impact, the impact on suppliers appears less convincing in terms of their motivation to become greener. Nevertheless, the AGF awards are an external facing impact and are seen as a sense of pride and achievement as the festivals use them extensively in their PR and communications.

Conclusion

A Greener Festival is a small organisation, which provides a unique service to the festival industry. Over time it has developed an international following and reputation as 'a respected organisation' (Warwick, 2017) for its work in assessing and sharing festival environmental practices throughout the world. The evidence above reveals that A Greener Festival is having an impact on the greening of these events, succeeding in its aims to help improve and transform festivals' environmental practices to the extent that they have become embedded in the DNA of events. Festival organisers consider the environmental impact of any initiatives they introduce and, in the cases we have looked at, the role of the Environmental manager is recognised as a key part of the festivals' organisational operations.

Table 2.1 Festival motivations for engaging in AGF assessment

Festival	Size of audience	Report and feedback	Motivate staff	Motivate suppliers	External verification	Enhanced PR	Reason for continued engagement with the AGF award
Island Vibe Festival (Australia)	2,500	Yes	Yes	No	Yes	Yes	Help develop policy and assess incremental changes
Cambridge Folk Festival (UK)	17,000	Yes	Yes	Yes	Yes	Yes	Introduce new measures and check existing practices
Das Fest (Germany)	250,000	Yes	Yes	No	Yes	Yes	Recognise and improve on weaknesses
Roskilde Festival (Denmark)	135,000	Yes	Not known yet	No	Yes	Not known yet	N/A

It is also clear that the impact of A Greener Festival goes beyond the assessment process itself and is used by the events in a number of other ways, motivating staff, providing a focal point for change and improvement as well as a marketing tool to substantiate their own green claims. It has played a role in persuading some suppliers and traders to change their practice, although it has to be said that this is an impact that is not yet fully acknowledged by the festivals and as such is one area of impact where further improvement is needed.

Key to all of this is the externality of the assessment process, which provides a sense of authenticity to the festivals' communications and dealings with the various stakeholders involved in the event. 'It is more acceptable coming from an outside party' (Warwick, 2017). 'The evaluation process helps the festival to recognise weaknesses' (Varsek, 2017) as well as its strengths and it is possibly for this reason that these festivals can use the AGF assessment scheme to 'motivate staff and other suppliers' (Warwick, 2017) to make changes which would otherwise be more difficult to achieve. The most important benefit of the AGF is that the assessment and feedback it provides came from an external third party and 'it wasn't just the environmental manager saying it' (Warwick, 2017).

One further aspect to the impact of A Greener festival is its awards, which are presented annually and are based on the outcomes of the assessment process. The case study festivals all commented that they felt a sense of achievement and recognition through the awards and communicated news of the awards on their websites and through social media. Varsek (2017) said that it helped to 'sensitise the audience to environmental issues' and further motivate and inspire their staff and stakeholders alike. There is a sense that A Greener Festival has created a family of like-minded festivals that want to be part of the group of 'role model festivals' (Varsek, 2017) winning AGF awards.

Acknowledgements

The authors would like to acknowledge the following for giving their time to be interviewed and for their great insights.

Amie Green, Environmental Manager, *Island Vibe* Australia.
Liz Warwick, Environmental Manager, *Cambridge Folk Festival*.
Sven Varsek, Festival Manager, *Das Fest* Germany.
Mikkel Sander, Environmental Manager, *Roskilde Festival*.

References

A Greener Festival/Bucks New University (2012). New survey highlights fans' concerns about the environmental impact of live events. Available at: www.agreenerfestival.com/wp-content/uploads/pdfs/Bucks-AGF_AUDIENCE_RESEARCH_2012.pdf (accessed 15 July 2017).

Arcodia, C., Cohen, S. A. and Dickson, C. (2012). Accrediting sustainable event practice. In E. Fayos-Solà (ed.), *Knowledge Management in Tourism: Policy and Governance Applications* (pp. 209–218). Bingley: Emerald.

Bærenholdt, J. and Haldrup, M. (2006). Mobile networks and placemaking in cultural tourism. Staging Viking ships and rock music in Roskilde. *European Urban and Regional Studies*, 13 (3): 209–224.

Boo, E. (1990). *Ecotourism: The Potentials and Pitfalls. Volumes 1 and 2*. Washington DC: World Wildlife Fund.

Cambridge Live. (2017). *About Cambridge Live*. Available at: www.cambridgelive7trust. co.uk/about (accessed 6 July 2017).

Chernushenko, D. (1994). *Greening our Games: Running Sports Events and Facilities that Won't Cost the Earth*. Ottawa: Centurion Publishing.

Collins, G. and Cooper, C. (2017). Measuring and managing the environmental impact of festivals: the contribution of the ecological footprint. *Journal of Sustainable Tourism*, 25 (1): 148–162.

Das Fest. (n.d.). Available at: www.dasfest.de/index.php?article_id=12&clang=1 (accessed 5 June 2017).

Ensor, J., Robertson, M. and Ali-Knight, J. (2011). Eliciting the dynamics of leading a sustainable event: key informant responses. *Event Management*, 15 (4): 315–327.

Green, A. (2017). Email interview. 1 August 2017.

Hjalager, A. M. (2009). Cultural tourism innovation systems – The Roskilde Festival, Scandinavia. *Journal of Hospitality and Tourism*, 9 (2–3): 266–287.

Holmes, K., Hughes, M., Mair, J. and Carlsen, J. (2015). *Events and Sustainability*. London: Routledge.

Island Vibe (2017). Available at: www.islandvibe.com.au/sustainability (accessed 5 June 2017).

Kennell, J. and Sitz, R. (2010). Greening Bonnaroo: exploring the rhetoric and the reality of a sustainable festival through micro-ethnographic methods. Paper presented in July at the Global Events Congress IV: Festivals and Events Research: State of the Art, Leeds Metropolitan University, Leeds. Available at: http://gala.gre.ac.uk/3950/1/ KENNELL_SITZ_FINAL.pdf (accessed 2 July 2018).

Laing, J. and Frost, W. (2010). How green was my festival: exploring challenges and opportunities associated with staging green events. *International Journal of Hospitality Management*, 29 (2): 261–267.

Mair, J. and Laing, J. (2012). The greening of music festivals: motivations, barriers and outcomes. Applying the Mair and Jago Model. *Journal of Sustainable Tourism*, 20 (5): 683–700.

O'Neill, C. (2017). Email correspondence. 27 May 2017.

Raj, R. and Vignali, C. (2010). Creating local experiences of cultural tourism through sustainable festivals. *European Journal of Tourism, Hospitality and Recreation*, 1 (1): 51–67.

Roskilde. (n.d.). Culture and awareness. Available at: www.roskilde-festival.dk/more/ sustainability/culture-and-awareness (accessed 5 June 2017).

Sander, M. (2017). Email interview. 27 July 2017.

Thomas, I. and Murfitt, P. (2011). *Environmental Management: Processes and Practices for Australia* (2nd edn). Annandale, NSW: Federation Press.

Varsek, S. (2017). Email interview. 2 August 2017.

Warwick, L. (2017). Telephone interview. 4 July 2017.

Williams, P. W. (1993). Environmental business practice: ethical codes of conduct for tourism. *Hospitality Trends*, 7 (1): 8–11.

Zifkos, G. (2015). Sustainability everywhere: problematising the 'sustainable festival' phenomenon. *Tourism Planning & Development*, 12 (1): 6–19.

3   The tourist centres' image

Rita R. Carballo, María M. Carballo and Carmelo J. León

Introduction

The empirical study was conducted in the Centres of Art, Culture and Tourism (CACT) on the island of Lanzarote, Canary Islands, Spain. Lanzarote is a destination that has focused on environmental conservation with an artistic profile.

The CACT are an internationally renowned tourist model consisting of a network of spaces designed to excite through art, nature and sustainability. The relationship between art and tourism on the island has enabled the preservation of the landscape and has become a social, cultural and economic vector for Lanzarote. The progenitor of this philosophy was local artist Cesar Manrique (1919–1992) who was a strongly influential figure in the early stages of tourism development of the island. These actions and interventions aimed to turn the landscape and the island's natural attractions to value, with a view to generating a new international image and portrayal that would form part of Lanzarote's adaptation to the tourist economy. His new aesthetic ideal, called art-nature/nature-art, integrated different modes of artistic expression visible in Manrique's landscape art.

There are seven centres in the CACT network, each featuring some of the specific natural and cultural characteristics of the island. In their group, the seven Centres, represent a synthesis of the island's natural and cultural values; Cueva de los Verdes (1964), Jameos del Agua (1968), Monumento al Campesino (1968), Mirador del Río (1973), Museo Internacional de Arte Contemporáneo (MIAC) (1976), Jardín de Cactus (1990) and Timanfaya National Park. Collectively, they receive more than 2.5 million visits per year. Cesar Manrique endowed these interventions, intricately associated with the tourist industry, with economic and social functionalism unprecedented in Spanish artistic culture. All these works are imbued with the artistic principles he held most dear: respectful dialogue between art and the natural medium and between local architectural values and modern conceits.

Priority issues

Over the last few years there have been important developments in the literature regarding the influence that cognitive (functional) and affective (emotional) aspects have on the perception of the tourist destination's image. However, the analysis of specific aspects of the tourist image has not been overtly explored, and only recently have specific aspects of a destination been explored, for example, environment (Northcote and Macbeth 2006; Ryu *et al.*, 2012) and art (Buckley, 2011; Carballo and León, 2017).

As culture is utilised as a means of social and economic regeneration, the cultural tourism market has become flooded with new cultural attractions and heritage centres (Smith, 2005; Richards and Wilson, 2006). Cultural itineraries can also be a means of linking together creative enterprises and events, stimulating visitors to see a number of different activities in a specific region (Richards, 2011c). Tourists often consume the creative lifestyles of others (Richards and Wilson, 2007). Tourist experiences usually emphasise active involvement in local culture, rather than the highlights of global culture (Richards, 2011b).

Creativity has become increasingly important for the development of tourism in cities and its image in recent years (Smith, 2005; Richards, 2012) since it enhances certain atmospheres which both locals and visitors appreciate (Lindroth *et al.*, 2007); it can also help to make places more distinctive for visitors, and tourism promotion of cultural attractions can become a tool for the regeneration and the revitalisation of culture resources as well as a means of developing more sustainable models of tourism (Richards and Marques, 2012).

Trends

The destination image is based on the individual image attributes of a destination (Prayag, 2009). Some researchers have considered the influence of the cultural attractions such as the built heritage, the museums and the monuments, on the image of the tourist destination (Richards and Wilson, 2007). The image of a place is mainly 'represented by its cultural heritage' (MacKay and Fesenmaier, 2000), since the cultural identity of a place is an important part of its identity (Mazilu, 2012). In the same way, natural assets can be artistically recreated in order to enhance the tourist experience. This involves the use of creative and artistic resources that are combined with natural resources in order to generate new attractions, even green events.

Creativity requires the right environment and sufficient time resources, and it is seen as a key component in destination management strategies. In relation to creative resources, it has been found that cultural tourism is a growing demand, with more travellers increasingly ranking arts, heritage and other cultural activities as one of their main reasons for travelling (Constantin and Mitruţ, 2009). Mazilu (2012) found that elements such as art and local culture can increase the value of a destination and create an artistic image favourable to the tourist choosing the destination. Many destinations are now using 'creativity' as a development strategy (Richards, 2001; Prentice and Andersen, 2003; Richards and Wilson, 2006). The ability of a tourism destination to compete depends on 'its ability to transform the basic inherited factors into created assets with a higher symbolic or sign value' (Richards, 2011c).

Relevant regional legislation

Lanzarote is a destination that has focused on environmental conservation with an artistic profile. Due to its environmental efforts, Lanzarote has been granted various environmental certifications. Since 1993, a Biosphere Reserve was created (UNESCO Biosphere Reserves), and in 2015 it received the UN declaration of Geopark (UNESCO Global Geoparks), in recognition of its environmental management.

In addition, in 2015 Lanzarote received the Biosphere Responsible Tourism Certification recognised by the Global Sustainable Tourism Council (GSTC), a body under the World Tourism Organization. The GSTC acknowledges the trajectory followed by the island in advancing sustainability. The award also recognises social responsibility, economic development, environmental compliance, cultural protection and the involvement of the tourist at the destination.

Cesar Manrique had a powerful influence on the planning regulations in Lanzarote, recognising the dangers of tourism, but also its potential for conservation and the economy of the island: he effectively lobbied for the long-term and sympathetic development of tourism. That influence was, and is, responsible for restricting the development of high-rise hotels on Lanzarote, and the use of traditional colours and building styles in tourism-related construction. His ideas inspired a tourism product combining art and nature, together with the definition of standards for the physical infrastructure, such as the use of the colour white and low-rise accommodation facilities. The mission of the Centres of Art, Culture and Tourism is to conserve and defend the values of the island, which has been declared a Biosphere Reserve and Geopark by UNESCO, as well as to inspire and generate environmental awareness through its actions.

Case study: an analysis of tourist perceptions of destination attractiveness

The main goal of this study is to analyse how the tourist perceives the image of the natural resources of a destination as tourist-attractive. For this aim, a confirmatory factorial analysis (CFA) was used to establish what factors contribute to the Cognitive and Affective image of the CACT.

The survey instrument for this study was developed using a mixed methodology approach as recommended by Jenkins (1999). The questionnaire was developed as the survey instrument including all constructs of the proposed model to investigate the CACT Image.

The questionnaire was designed in Spanish and translated into German and English and was administered personally to the visitors of the CACT, during the months of June and August 2013, to ensure an adequate collection of tourist samples in the island. A total of 453 usable questionnaires were collected.

To measure the cognitive dimension of the CACT image 27 attributes formed the basis of a seven-point Likert-type response format (1=*Very bad*; 7=*Very good*), and the measurement of the affective dimension with an 8-item, 7-point bipolar semantic differential scale.

Results

Data were processed with SPSS 20 statistical packages. Following the usual procedure, there are two stages in the data analysis. Initially, an exploratory analysis of scale reliability (EFA) was performed to the multi-attribute dimension of the cognitive image. On the basis of the result of the EFA and theoretical background, CFA was performed on the measurement model to confirm the structure found in EFA (Noar, 2003; Carballo *et al.*, 2017; see Tables 3.1 and 3.2).

The application of EFA to the 27 attributes of the cognitive component of the CACT Image led to three factors. Twelve attributes were eliminated due to their low standardised coefficients.

The application of the CFA to the cognitive component of the CACT image showed an acceptable fit (Hu and Bentler, 1998). So, the results show that the cognitive image of the CACT is formed by three factors: Cognitive Image 1 (Expositions and exhibitions), where creative and cultural factors are valued; Cognitive Image 2 (Environmental conditions), which make references to the conservation of the environment and biodiversity; and Cognitive Image 3 (Infrastructures) refers to those factors that make references to the infrastructure of the Centres.

Summary

Creativity and art are important elements that bring in opportunities for the differentiation and specialisation of tourist destinations, since they are increasingly demanded by tourists and can contribute to destination image formation. This study has addressed the contribution that the creativity factors make to the image of the natural resources at the destination.

The results show that creativity through the enhancement of the artistic value of natural assets can make a contribution to the image of the Art Centres or artistic attractions. Thus, the creation of artistic attractions – such as the Art Centres in the case of Lanzarote – can be a useful opportunity to create a profile of the image of tourist destinations.

It has been found that when there are important artistic attractions at the destination, as those that belong to Cognitive Image 1 (artistic creativity, exhibition's variety and exhibition's quality), this factor can contribute on a higher level to the formation of the CACT image, followed by Cognitive Image 2. Finally, Affective image is the factor with lower importance in the formation of the CACT image.

Table 3.1 CFA results

Items	Cognitive Image 1 Expositions and exhibitions	Cognitive Image 2 Environmental conditions	Cognitive Image 3 Infrastructures
Artistic creativity	**0.765**	0.286	0.329
Exhibition's variety	**0.746**	0.094	0.208
Exhibition's quality	**0.738**	0.251	0.112
Additional programme	**0.714**	0.265	0.390
Interpretational material	**0.712**	0.274	0.435
The Centres know how to use the new technologies to make a visit more interesting	**0.701**	0.251	0.349
Reception of the Centres	**0.697**	0.252	0.489
Discounts for special groups (children, senior citizens)	**0.663**	0.518	0.138
The Centres' image and reputation	**0.643**	0.263	0.572
The tourist's guide explanations have been very clear	**0.617**	0.509	0.111
The Centres' decoration	**0.604**	0.478	0.298
The visitors receive enough information to make their experience more pleasant	**0.565**	0.481	0.138
Ticket price	**0.550**	0.474	0.163
Sensitive architecture	0.383	**0.791**	0.230
Nature/environmental conservation	0.133	**0.787**	0.416
Flora and fauna biodiversity	0.398	**0.778**	0.240
Good recycling system	0.327	**0.749**	0.280
Use of alternative energies	0.102	**0.685**	0.548
Staff's kindness	0.465	**0.660**	0.153
The Centres' timetables	0.489	**0.648**	0.329
Centres are easily accessible for handicapped and elderly people	0.170	0.557	**0.721**
The Centres provide good services (bar, restaurant, souvenir shop)	0.313	0.572	**0.718**
Maintenance of the Centres	0.290	0.408	**0.705**
External architecture of the Centres	0.314	0.357	**0.698**
Guiding system inside the Centres	0.230	0.350	**0.687**
Signage or directions inside the Centres	0.308	0.236	**0.379**
The Centres provide good resting areas for the visitors	0.303	0.221	**0.308**
Eigenvalue	**16.0**	**1.9**	**1.4**
% of total variance	**27.4**	**25.6**	**18.5**
Cronbach's Alpha	**0.945**	**0.906**	**0.924**

Kaise Meyer Olkin measure of sampling adequacy: 0.92
Bartlett's test of sphericity: $X^2 = 1024.8$, $df = 488$; $p < 0.000$)
Total variance explained: 87.2%

Table 3.2 EFA results

Scale and item	Factor loadings
Cognitive Image 1: expositions and exhibitions	
Artistic creativity	0.81
Exhibition's variety	0.80
Exhibition's quality	0.78
Additional programme	0.70
Interpretational material	0.64
Cognitive Image 2: environmental conditions	
Sensitive architecture	0.91
Nature/environmental conservation	0.90
Flora and fauna biodiversity	0.86
Use of alternative energies	0.81
Good recycling system	0.75
Cognitive Image 3: infrastructures	
Centres are easily accessible for handicapped and elderly people	0.90
Maintenance of the Centres	0.88
The Centres provide good services (bar, restaurant, souvenir shop)	0.80
Guiding system inside the Centres	0.76
External architecture of the Centres	0.72

Notes
GFI = 0.906; AGFI = 0.952; CFI = 0.944; TLI = 0.903; IFI = 0.975; RFI = 0.964; NFI = 0.900; RMSEA = 0.043; RMSEA = 0.04)

The implication is that creativity and art creation based on natural resources play a more important role in image formation than more conventional practice. Thus, whereas the CACT image can be improved by affective factors, there is more scope for image formation by working through the application of creative solutions that increase the value of natural assets. That is, natural assets can be recreated through artistic innovations in a way that tourists can visit them and get in touch with them, thereby enhancing the tourist experience and satisfaction, contributing to the improvement of the CACT image.

Further research should look at the contribution that artistically recreated natural assets can make to the tourists' satisfaction and visiting intentions. In addition, more evidence will be welcome regarding the relationships between creative activities and the natural resources image.

Literature review

While other factors of tourist destinations may be imitated or improved, the specific characteristics of location, nature, history, culture, art and so on, are always differential attributes of each destination. When a destination has a differential development of these specific tourism resources it will achieve greater competitiveness (Waitt *et al.*, 2003). It has been recognised that destinations are not created equal (McCartney *et al.*, 2008); some have an abundance of resources and comparative advantages, while others have limited natural resources and infrastructure to support tourism development. Ritchie *et al.* (2000) discussed whether tourist destinations can be created or whether they are just born. Yet 'a destination that is deficient in resources but uses the little it has more effectively could be more competitive than a destination endowed with a wealth of resources'.

The creative management of natural resources can lead to the differentiation of the destination with competitive advantages (Mazilu, 2012), similarly to the forms of branding based on cultural and creative resources (Evans, 2003). In this sense, culture and tourism has become one of the most attractive development options for countries and regions around the world. There is no doubt that tourism and culture are inextricably linked, and that cultural tourism is a major segment of global tourism (Richards, 2011c). In value terms, the contribution of cultural tourism is even greater, since cultural tourists are estimated to spend as much as one-third more on average than other tourists (Richards, 2007).

Therefore, since tourism utilises nature as an integral part of its products and experiences (Buckley, 2011), both artistic and natural resources are suitable for becoming creative tools for the image of destinations (Richards, 2012). Natural assets are distinctive attributes that can be specific to destinations and can serve as a basis for differentiation and image creation. Further, it has been recognised that their creative management can be a 'win–win' option for conservation and sustainable development (Naidoo and Adamowicz, 2005). Tourist destinations may take advantage of their specific natural assets to differentiate their tourist experience, so natural resources, local culture and artistic activities become relevant attracting factors.

The image of destinations can be based not just on physical and tangible assets but also on experiences built around creativity and 'living culture' (Richards and Wilson, 2006; Richards, 2012). Since tourism utilises nature as an integral part of products and experiences (Buckley, 2011), both artistic and natural resources can become creative tools for developing the image of destinations (Richards, 2012). Creativity and living culture have been shown by Romero-Padilla, Navarro-Jurado and Malvárez-García (2016) to have a range of positive side effects for city development in general and especially on supply and demand factors for tourism.

Many activities that tourists undertake at a destination depend on natural resources. Thus, the consideration of environmental conditions in the image of destinations becomes relevant (Dolnicar and Leisch, 2008). That is, destinations can improve their image by working towards improving their environmental quality (Logar, 2010).

Tourists have preferences for the environmental aspects of destinations, and therefore form a cognitive image based on these aspects which influence their decisions about what destinations to visit and what services and experiences to enjoy at the chosen destinations (Hamilton and Lau, 2005; Fridgen, 1984). Thus, destinations can increase their attraction by promoting an image based on environmental factors and activities related to their use of nature and its conservation (Akama, 1996). There are useful instruments available to do this, such as the implementation of a 'green branding' approach, which helps destinations to position themselves in a more competitive environmental profile (Mihalič, 2000).

The ways destinations manage their environmental profile through actions and recognition can have an influence on their tourist image (Ryu *et al.*, 2012). That is, destination images can be improved with the application of ecological marketing that builds on the new interest in quality environments (Chen and Tsai, 2007). For instance, there have been developments in the operationalisation of environmental certifications focusing on practices of sustainable tourism or ecotourism (Font and Harris, 2004; Font, 2002; Buckley, 2002). The Sustainable Tourism Certificate was developed to improve the image of a country as a tourist destination through the certification of sustainable accommodation (Font and Harris, 2004). There is sound evidence that environmental and sustainability certifications enhance the image of tourist destinations (Capacci *et al.*, 2015; Bartley, 2010; Lozano and Vallés, 2007).

Further resources

César Manrique Foundation

Initially founded by César Manrique in 1983. According to its charter, César Manrique Foundation's mission includes: conserving and studying César Manrique's artistic legacy and enhancing its visibility; fostering exhibitions, studies and initiatives on the relationship between art and nature; organising activities that contribute to environmental conservation and the sustainability of land use and the transformation of the natural medium, in particular on Lanzarote and the other Canary Islands; and furthering intellectual and creative activity and critical thinking.

The José Saramago Foundation

It is a private cultural institution located in the Casa dos Bicos, in Lisbon (Portugal). Founded by the writer in June 2007, its main institutional principles are to defend and spread the Universal Declaration of Human Rights, the promotion of culture in Portugal as well as in all the countries, and particular concerns about environmentalism. The house where the writer and his wife Pilar del Río lived until his death in 2010, called just A Casa (The House), is also open to visitors in Tías, Lanzarote (Spain).

References

Akama, J. S. (1996). Western environmental values and nature-based tourism in Kenya. *Tourism Management*, 17 (8): 567–574.

Bartley, T. (2010). Transnational private regulation in practice: the limits of forest and labor standards certification in Indonesia. *Business and Politics*, 12 (3): Article 7. Available at: www.degruyter.com/view/j/bap. 2010.12.3/bap. 2010.12.3.1321/bap. 2010.12.3.1321.xml?format=PAIN (accessed 28 April 2017).

Buckley, R. (2002). Tourism ecolabels. *Annals of Tourism Research*, 29 (1): 183–208.

Buckley, R. C. (2011). Tourism and environment. *Annual Review of Environment and Resources*, 36: 397–416. doi:10.1146/annurev-environ-041210–132637E.

Capacci, S., Scorcu, A. E. and Vici, L. (2015). Seaside tourism and eco-labels: the economic impact of blue flags. *Tourism Management*, 47: 88–96.

Carballo, R. R. and León, C. J. (2017). The influence of artistically recreated nature on the image of tourist destinations: Lanzarote's art, cultural and tourism visitor centres and their links to sustainable tourism marketing. *Journal of Sustainable Tourism*, 1–13.

Carballo, R. R., León, C. J. and Carballo, M. M. (2017). The perception of risk by international travellers. *Worldwide Hospitality and Tourism Themes*, 9 (5): 534–542.

Chen, C. F. and Tsai, D. (2007). How destination image and evaluative factors affect behavioral intentions. *Tourism Management*, 28 (4): 1115–1122.

Constantin, D. L. and Mitruţ, C. (2009). Cultural tourism, sustainability and regional development: experiences from Romania. In L. Fusco Girard and P. Nijkamp (eds), *Cultural Tourism and Sustainable Local Development* (pp. 149–166). Surrey: Ashgate.

Dolnicar, S. and Leisch, F. (2008). Selective marketing for environmentally sustainable tourism. *Tourism Management*, 29 (4): 672–680.

Evans, N. (ed.). (2003). *The Non-Pama-Nyungan Languages of Northern Australia: Comparative Studies of the Continent's Most Linguistically Complex Region (Volume 552)*. Canberra: Pacific Linguistics.

Font, X. (2002). Environmental certification in tourism and hospitality: progress, process and prospects. *Tourism Management*, 23 (3): 197–205.

Font, X. and Harris, C. (2004). Rethinking standards from green to sustainable. *Annals of Tourism Research*, 31 (4): 986–1007.

Fridgen, J. D. (1984). Environmental psychology and tourism. *Annals of Tourism Research*, 11 (1): 19–39.

Hamilton, J. M. and Lau, M. A. (2005). The role of climate information in tourist destination choice decision making. In S. Gössling and M. C. Hall (eds), *Tourism and Global Environmental Change: Ecological, Economic, Social and Political Inter-relationships* (pp. 229–250). London: Routledge.

Hu, L.-T. and Bentler, P. M. (1998). Fit indices in covariance structure modeling: sensitivity to underparameterized model misspecification. *Psychological Methods*, 3 (4): 424–453.

Jenkins, O. H. (1999). Understanding and measuring tourist destination images. *The International Journal of Tourism Research*, 1 (1): 1–15.

Lindroth, K., Ritalahti, J. and Soisalon-Soininen, T. (2007). Creative tourism in destination development. *Tourism Review*, 62 (3/4): 53–58.

Logar, I. (2010). Sustainable tourism management in Crikvenica, Croatia: an assessment of policy instruments. *Tourism Management*, 31 (1): 125–135.

Lozano, M. and Vallés, J. (2007). An analysis of the implementation of an environmental management system in a local public administration. *Journal of Environmental Management*, 82 (4): 495–511.

MacKay, K. J. and Fesenmaier, D. R. (2000). An exploration of cross-cultural destination image assessment. *Journal of Travel Research*, 38 (4): 417–423.

Mazilu, M. (2012). *Sustainable Tourism of Destination, Imperative Triangle Among: Competitiveness, Effective Management and Proper Financing*. Sustainable Development Chaouki Ghenai, IntechOpen, DOI: 10.5772/28062. Available at: www.intech open.com/books/sustainable-development-policy-and-urban-development-tourism-life-science-management-and-environment/sustainable-tourism-of-destination-imperative-triangle-among-competitiveness-effective-management-an (accessed 2 July 2018).

McCartney, G., Butler, R. and Bennett, M. (2008). A strategic use of the communication mix in the destination image-formation process. *Journal of Travel Research*, 47 (2): 183–196.

Mihalič, T. (2000). Environmental management of a tourist destination: a factor of tourism competitiveness. *Tourism Management*, 21 (1): 65–78.

Naidoo, R. and Adamowicz, W. L. (2005). Biodiversity and nature-based tourism at forest reserves in Uganda. *Environment and Development Economics*, 10 (2): 159–178.

Noar, S. M. (2003). The role of structural equation modeling in scale development. *Structural Equation Modeling*, 10 (4): 622–647.

Northcote, J. and Macbeth, J. (2006). Conceptualizing yield: sustainable tourism management. *Annals of Tourism Research*, 33 (1): 199–220.

Prayag, G. (2009). Tourists' evaluations of destination image, satisfaction, and future behavioral intentions – the case of Mauritius. *Journal of Travel & Tourism Marketing*, 26 (8): 836–853.

Prentice, R. and Andersen, V. (2003). Festival as creative destination. *Annals of Tourism Research*, 30 (1): 7–30.

Richards, G. (2001). The development of cultural tourism in Europe. In G. Richards (ed.), *Cultural Attractions and European Tourism* (pp. 3–29). Wallingford, Oxfordshire: CABI Publishing.

Richards, G. (2007). Global trends in cultural tourism. In G. Richards (ed.), *Cultural Tourism: Global and Local Perspectives* (pp. 1–24). New York: Haworth Press.

Richards, G. (2011a). Creativity and tourism: the state of the art. *Annals of Tourism Research*, 38 (4): 1225–1253.

Richards, G. (2011b). Tourism development trajectories: from culture to creativity? *Tourism & Management Studies*, (6): 9–15.

Richards, G. (2011c). Creativity and tourism: the state of the art. *Annals of Tourism Research*, 38 (4): 1225–1253.

Richards, G. (2012). Tourism, creativity and creative industries. Presented at the Creativity and Creative Industries in Challenging Times Conference, Breda, The Netherlands.

Richards, G. and Marques, L. (2012). Exploring creative tourism: editor's introduction. *Journal of Tourism Consumption and Practice*, 4 (2): 11–12.

Richards, G. and Wilson, J. (2006). Developing creativity in tourist experiences: a solution to the serial reproduction of culture? *Tourism Management*, 27 (6): 1209–1223.

Richards, G. and Wilson, J. (eds) (2007). *Tourism, Creativity and Development*. Abingdon: Routledge.

Ritchie, J. R. B., Crouch, G. I. and Hudson, S. (2000). Assessing the role of consumers in the measurement of destination competitiveness and sustainability. *Tourism Analysis*, 5 (2/4): 69–76.

Ryu, K., Lee, H. R. and Gon Kim, W. (2012). The influence of the quality of the physical environment, food, and service on restaurant image, customer perceived value, customer satisfaction, and behavioral intentions. *International Journal of Contemporary Hospitality Management*, 24 (2): 200–223.

Smith, M. (2005). Tourism, culture and regeneration: differentiation through creativity. In J. Swarbrooke, M. K. Smith and L. Onderwater (eds), *Tourism, Creativity and Development*. Arnhem: ATLAS.

Waitt, G., Lane, R. and Head, L. (2003). The boundaries of nature tourism. *Annals of Tourism Research*, 30 (3): 523–545.

4 The power of knowledge in the struggle for sustainable tourism

The case study of El Nevado de Toluca, Mexico

Maribel Osorio García, Ericka Amorim and Maximiliano Korstanje

Introduction

In recent years, specialists have been raising the alarm on the risks climate change poses for both underdeveloped and developed economies and for tourism worldwide. In fact, climate change seems to be a major threat that needs to be combatted through the international cooperation of all nations (Wall, 1998; Nicholls, 2004; Scott *et al.*, 2008). Although the notion of sustainable tourism has become fashionable, often used to fill papers, books and conferences, it has led to an inevitable proliferation of literature, which obscures more than it clarifies (Ashworth, 1992; Hjalager, 2000; Sofield, 2003; Korstanje and George, 2012). Therefore, the main focus of this chapter is to explore the interest in sustainability that has been generated by the Brundtland Report and which has been emerging since the 1980s. The Brundtland Report, which was entitled the 'World Commission on Environment and Development' (WCED), signalled the risks that could arise should nations not cooperate towards a more sustainable world. Originally chaired by Gro Harlem Brundtland, the board of investigation, which was supported by the United Nations, concluded that the emissions of carbon into the atmosphere should be radically reduced. Consequently, developed nations began to adopt rational models for consumption in order to avoid the exhaustion of local resources and this theory of development would go on to play a crucial role in educating the group of experts who help policymakers to curb the material asymmetries in undemocratic nations (McMichael, 2016). On closer inspection, the tourism industry or, in this case, the sustainable tourism industry, was posited as a valid means for underdeveloped economies to mitigate not only the effects of climate change but also to improve the lifestyle for its citizens (Timothy *et al.*, 2002).

Against this backdrop, this chapter investigates two cases: the protected area known as APFFNT (Area de Proteccion de Flora y Fauna Nevado de Toluca) the former Parque Nacional Nevado de Toluca (National Park of Nevado de Toluca), located in Toluca, Mexico. The problems found in El Nevado are sharply contrasted to two success stories in Brazil: El Bonito and the Island of Fernando de Noronha. In the concluding section of this chapter, we outline some interesting observations regarding the implementation of good practice in terms of eco-tourism for Latin American destinations.

The rise of green tourism

Environmental awareness has emerged as a method for expanding policies oriented towards protection (Stabler and Goodall, 1997). Jones (1987) describes green tourism as intertwined with ecology, which means that communities must manage rural activities in a sustainable way not only to benefit the local community but to protect the environment. Gibson *et al.* (2003) have since developed the concept of urban green tourism to show how a city may promote sustainable tourism as a generator of outstanding experiences. Doubtless, their belief is that green tourism is associated with nature, but also that ecology should be embraced as one of the key values of the next generation in order to make the world a safer and better place in which to live. Similarly, Romeril (1989) points out that the adverse effects on the environment means that it has become imperative to consider the nature of tourism alongside ethics as the pressure to adopt sustainable policies, which leads to ecotourism, has the potential to generate further profits for investors and local stakeholders.

It is tempting to say that green tourism is a term that has been coined to denote sustainable practices in the field of tourism, but the adoption of this term has led to the creation of a number of misconceptions. The notion that profit is the main vehicle to progress has led practitioners and academics to lose sight of what can be achieved through the adoption of green ecological programmes. Tourism is not only an agent of development and imagined social thought processes, but sometimes humankind is imagined as an external entity separated from nature (Bramwell and Lane, 1993).

In Latin America, the paradigm of sustainability, and its application in the field of tourism, has been split across two contrasting academic viewpoints. On one hand, the above-cited examples illustrate the positive experience of European destinations (mostly in Portugal and Spain) while, on the other hand, a new radical practice has emerged from English-speaking cultures which has denounced tourism as a tool for alienation and colonisation.

Orjuela's (2013) extensive review of various case studies in Europe contrasts with those from Latin America, and this indicates the limitations of some scholars who cite green tourism as the toolkit that eradicates all evils. In Spain, success has been as a result of international investment into low-cost opportunities, while in France and England tourism has been used as a platform for revitalisation and rebuilding after the obliteration caused by the Second World War. Furthermore, from 1963 onwards France created National Parks (Missions Interministerielles) to promote a respect for nature and in parallel to this development, although rural tourism was never made a national priority, it did lead to economic help from the private sector for farmers. Interestingly, across Latin America, from Mexico to Argentina, no unified policy for green-tourism could be agreed upon, although there are some points of convergence that will be discussed in this chapter.

The case of Brazil is worthy of some attention as many studies of tourism and its impacts in the Amazon region have not been published by Brazilians but by English-speaking scholars. For example, Wallace and Pierce (1996) studied 'ecotour lodges' in Amazonia by means of a questionnaire administered to visitors, front desk staff and tourists. Their investigation focused on the gap between the ideals of eco-consumers (based on their demands) and the principles of ecology (based on what Amazonia offers). In spite of the fact that tourists are in search of nature and wish to have an 'authentic' experience, this had a limited influence on the education of local people. Lastly, Hiernaux (2002) validates the belief that steps to success in managing green tourism depend upon how stereotypes, allegories or even hopes, are incorporated into social illusions and the way a sense of happiness can be profitably exploited. As an industrial activity, linked to myth-production, Hiernaux confirms tourism is based on the four following pillars: (a) the quest for eternal happiness; (b) the need to escape; (c) the discovery of otherness; and (d) the return to a lost virgin paradise and this infers the need to return to a natural environment.

The challenges of sustainability are not new as, from its inception, industrialisation has been symbolically pitted against the natural world, but now this problem seems to have reached a level that is of great alarm to environmental specialists. Quite aside from this, not all experts agree that what we are currently doing is the best method for protecting our planet, although, unlike deniers, they acknowledge and agree on the indicators of climate change

Case study: Nevado de Toluca, Mexico

The protected area of APFFNT (Area de Proteccion de Flora and Fauna in Nevado Toluca) (the former National Park Nevado of Toluca) is located in the central district of Mexico, almost 117 miles from Mexico DC. Geologically speaking, the zone was formed by a stratovolcano that has been inactive for 3,300 years. This volcano has a large crater in which two important but shallow lakes were formed by the residue of falling rain: Lago del sol y de la Luna.

It is unfortunate that the weather conditions caused by urban pressure from the growth of the metropolitan area of Toluca have seriously affected not only the flora and fauna here but also the hydrologic system. On the one hand, many different insects decimated hundreds of trees, while deforestation paved the way for a process of degradation as never seen before. Furthermore, the lack of regulation in APFFNT has led to individuals and corporations destroying land in the Toluca valley. These problems forced the ANP, which works jointly with CONANP (Comisión Nacional de Áreas Naturales Protegidas), the commission for natural areas and protected parks, to award El Nevado de Toluca a new status. By doing this, El Nevado de Toluca became a National Park in 1936 and this led to the creation of the *Area de Proteccion de Flora y Fauna* in 2013 or the Protected Area of Flora and Fauna. This new status enabled the promotion of new policies to protect the zone but also the proposal of a sustainable programme of development (CONANP 2016). However, the change of status triggered a fierce debate as, paradoxically, some of the illegal yet widespread practices that had taken place for years became legitimised within this new discourse of ecology and sustainable growth. Some academics theorised on the limitations of sustainable programmes in El Nevado as pathways towards more exploitative uses of the land. Officials and policymakers considered the influx of investment for business purposes and tourist projects instead of seeking the views of all of the stakeholders. As a consequence, one of the main concerns voiced by locals is about the level of uncertainty that exists in relation to some of the changes that have occurred as a result of gentrification. Although officials professed their efforts to preserve the zone beyond the hegemony of mass tourism, it still remains to be seen whether or not these promises will be met.

Why top-down planning does not work

In 2006, CONANP, in collaboration with other governmental departments, published a resolution document called the Estrategia Nacional para un Desarrollo Sustentable del Turismo y la Recreación en las Áreas Protegidas de México (the National Strategy for the Development of Sustainable Tourism in the Mexican Protected Areas). The resolution delineates the defining contours of a model to classify what type of tourism will be permitted in the area. The type of desired tourism can be classed as the subtypes of *planned tourism*, *predatory tourism* and *administered tourism*, and the resolution explains how tourism would be consolidated in the area and how successful the agency would be in managing ecological issues. Following the publication, tourism in El Nevado de Toluca became rapacious, which caused serious ecological and economic damage to the destination, and sustainable tourism experts found that APFFNT and ANP had lacked any precautionary platform to anticipate such ecological damage. This unfavourable verdict prompted researchers from the Universidad Autonoma del Estado de Mexico (the Autonomous University of the State of Mexico), to conduct fieldwork not only to expand the current understanding of the ecological problems in El Nevado, but also to confirm to what extent the site can be adapted under the premise of a sustainable paradigm. The report was written in 2009 and was later updated in 2014 and 2016 as researchers devoted their efforts and resources to compute the key variables that contribute to the ecological degradation of El Nevado de Toluca.

The original outcomes of the research reported by fieldworkers evinced that there were consolidated routes and tours that extend from the Mexican city of Toluca to the crater and the lakes. On these tours, visitors can make three stops at La Puerta, Las Raices and el Parque de los Venados, where makeshift and ad hoc shops and markets offer visitors numerous ethnic foods and products. Furthermore, the research mapped out 19 natural resources as potential tourist attractions including La Peñuela, the Crater and the lakes, emphasising their embedded value due to their features, but with significant deficiencies in terms of their accessibility and infrastructure, which means that the site is inappropriate for wider use (Franco *et al.*, 2009). Interestingly, studies published by Osorio

Garcia *et al.* (2011) depicted the socio-psychological profile of the visitor to El Nevado, noting two types of mass tourist activity: outdoor recreation and sport-tourism, both creating land degradation. Also of note was that the socio-demographic profile of these visitors overlapped with local residents coming from the city of Toluca in the quest for a recreative and novel experience against the backdrop of a natural landscape. The locals who chose to visit El Nevado as their primary option were not interested in the services available at the site and they were very much accustomed to the problems of accessibility that character-ises El Nevado. Neither are these visitors familiar with the concept of green tourism or ecological paradigms, nor are they are emotionally committed to limiting the ecological disruption caused by the saturation of visits (Osorio Garcia *et al.*, 2011). Many of them ride or bike to the site and pass through routes around the volcano that are uncontrolled (Osorio Garcia *et al.*, 2016). Paradoxically, as local stakeholders have had limited involvement in the national park, the profit generated by tourism is not entering into the local economy. As a result of this, a vicious circle has been created due to the lack of investment and even though the site was given national park status, it has become a reproduction of an anarchic state in which the access routes to El Nevado are inundated with visitors, particularly during the winter season.

Ultimately, in recent years, unplanned tourism practices have pushed eco-systems to unsustainable conditions and some Mexican ejidos (community net-works) are experiencing volatile migration as their main economic activity is generated through farming and agriculture. Two of these communities that have been studied, Raices and San Juan de las Huertas, showed high levels of political instability, which appears to be generated by mass tourism and by the interven-tion of special interest pressure groups. In some cases, these groups conversed directly with the government, thereby paving the way for a climate of critical instability. To some extent, the residents that were interviewed and consulted demonstrate a lack of coherence or cohesion in the policies they promote, and they lack any familiarisation with the benefits of sustainable tourism (Ramírez *et al.*, 2011). This social disorganisation plays a key role in undermining the cred-ibility of the institutions in these areas. As the theory of governance amply shows, the lack of coherence at the micro-level steered residents into a general-ised climate of apathy towards their governments, which impedes policies ori-ented to social change. In consequence, corruption acts as a conduit in the communication process between the different stakeholders, removing opportun-ities to take a more corrective course of action (Ramírez *et al.*, 2011).

As a case study, El Nevado shows how even if a site is designated as a pro-tected zone or a protected park, this is not enough to maximise its potential. El Nevado, far from being a successful example of green tourism, is a reminder of the importance of the role of the state in organising a territory. The dilemma here lies in the fact that local residents rejected external investment as well as the use of regulated real estate agents due to their claims for a more sustainable habitat, but paradoxically the lack of regulation and interest from corporations has made El Nevado a grim place, now left to its fate (Perez *et al.*, 2009). Successive projects in the region were faced with the fury of farmers, who publicly protested their opposition to a liberal market, combined with the lack of interest from investors to consult with locals as part of government negotiations. Instead of bringing these projects to a safe haven, the state retained an ambiguous position with regards to the rising conflict and the ongoing differences between those involved. On one hand, the government, under pressure from local residents, has not allowed the development of property businesses but on the other hand, the government has not created a plan of mitigation that could be applied to the area. One might conclude that this case study validates the previous assumption formulated in this chapter, that the complexity of sustainability operates beyond the hegemony of lawmaking. In sharp contrast with El Nevado, Brazil proffers interesting examples of good practices in sustainable tourism.

Case study: Brazil – the evergreen destination

Brazil is well known as an exotic destination. Despite its great prominence, helped by hosting the recent Football World Cup and the Olympic Games, the country has not seen a notable increase in recent tourist arrivals. Almost 6 million visitors were registered by official agencies, which places Brazil in 29th position in the WTO global ranking of destinations (Ministério do Turismo, 2017a). However, the Brazilian government (Governo do Brasil, 2014) notes that one out of five foreign tourists are choosing to visit Brazil in the quest of ecotourism. One of the main reasons for this is the fact that Brazil has a great variety of attractions on offer, ranging from cultural heritage sites to the Amazon, the planet's lung. Brazil also offers many case studies of sustainable destination management that are worthy of attention. For example, the city of El Bonito, located in the state of Mato Grosso, was designated as the best sustainable tourism destination by World Travel Market in 2014. This area of natural beauty is jointly administered by the private and public sectors in order to develop El Bonito as a leading ecotourism destination. To achieve this, a novel electronic system of surveillance helps to monitor the impact on the environment and the city is assessed by the number of tourists who visit the area without generating a negative impact. The information is generated through an electronic voucher that each tourist carries, which also records their name and the attractions that they visit (Governo do Brasil, 2014). This software provides policymakers and local authorities with an all-encompassing view of the interactions that take place between tourists and the environment. The voucher is managed by local travel agencies in exchange for a payment and this therefore ensures that the government is involving stakeholders and rewarding their participation in the responsible protection of El Bonito (Viegas, 2015). This type of shared control contributes to the economy and to the quality of services in the city. As a case study, El Bonito illustrates that it is possible to implement good practice in the protection of tourist destinations.

Another example of good practice in ecotourism is Fernando de Noronha, which was named as a natural heritage site in 2001 (UNESCO). It is part of a volcanic archipelago located on the northeast coast, which comprises a geological formation of 21 protected islands. Fernando de Noronha is one of these islands and it is one of the most visited destinations in the region (Ministério do Turismo, 2017b). Unlike El Bonito, the local government in Fernando de Noronha keeps a strict control over the influx of tourists through the use of a tax that limits the length of each visit. The infrastructure and accessibility of the island is maintained by the government and this includes a limit to the number of permitted flights to the island per day (currently three). Each tourist must also pay a conservation tax of €20 per day and they cannot stay for longer than 30 days and the tax increases after the fifth and tenth days. This has two important effects on the behaviour of tourists. First, the gradual imposition of the tax ensures that tourists stay for a limited number of days, and the tax boosts the state's economy and is invested in the destination. Second, the lack of a unilateral (top down) set of restrictive policies – as in the case of El Nevado – means that the visitor does not feel mistreated. Some psychological studies in the behaviour of tourists evinced that people tend to express negative feelings when they feel controlled or constrained by those in authority, yet the use of economic regulations (e.g. tax) does not create any obvious discontent. Therefore, these two examples of good practice in ecotourism suggest three significant recommendations:

- Local governments, supported by the private sector, play a leading role in the formation of sustainable destinations. Not only through the regulation of access but also in the implementation of taxes that discourage mass tourism.
- Second and most importantly, top down or centralised programmes, which are sometimes monopolised by experts, should be discouraged. All stakeholders should be engaged in the discussion and negotiation of sustainable plans.
- Last but not least, taxes can be reinvested locally towards the implementation of new programmes and the maintenance of infrastructure, which is vital for success. In terms of eco preservation, impressive enterprises or models are not necessary, instead pragmatic steps can be taken which should be monitored, revised and reversed when necessary.

Conclusion

This chapter investigated the rise and evolution of specialised literature in the sphere of green tourism and included the contemporary case study of El Nevado de Toluca and contrasted this to two successful case studies in Brazil: El Bonito and the Island of Fernando de Noronha. These remind us of the importance of synergy and commitment between all of the community stakeholders, and they emphasise the role of external investment that has been commented upon in literature. Unlike examples of successful destinations, in El Nevado the growth of tourism has been disorganised and chaotic, to the point of compromising local resources. This prompted a drastic conflict between farmers and those who wanted to promote tourism. Paradoxically, in many cases the intervention of the private sector or the state has led to the worsening of environmental problems, and we have seen what happens when residents are reluctant to consider the possibilities and benefits of a regulated version of tourism. The role of research and science in creating a platform for discourse and synergy allows stakeholders to work together in the sphere of ecological tourism consumption. In many ways, this chapter provides a contribution towards the formation of a green conscience as the most important element of sustainability in tourism, committing to the introduction of ethics as the centrepiece of the entire system.

References

Ashworth, G. J. (1992). Planning for sustainable tourism. *Town Planning Review*, 63 (3): 325.
Bramwell, B. and Lane, B. (1993). Sustainable tourism: an evolving global approach. *Journal of Sustainable Tourism*, 1 (1): 1–5.
Comisión Nacional de Áreas Naturales Protegidas (CONANP). (2006). *Estrategia Nacional para un Desarrollo Sustentable del Turismo y la Recreación en las Áreas Protegidas de México [en línea]*. Disponible en www.conanp.gob.mx/pdf_publicaciones/ TurismoEstrategia.pdf (accessed 4 March 2017).
Comisión Nacional de Áreas Naturales Protegidas (CONANP). (2016). Nevado de Toluca. Disponible en: http://nevadodetoluca.conanp.gob.mx/ (accessed 5 March 2017).
Franco, S., Osorio, M., Nava, G. y Regil, H. (2009). Evaluación multicriterio de los recursos turísticos. Parque Nacional Nevado de Toluca, México. *Estudios y Perspectivas en Turismo*, 18: 208–226.
Gibson, A., Dodds, R., Joppe, M. and Jamieson, B. (2003). Ecotourism in the city? Toronto's green tourism association. *International Journal of Contemporary Hospitality Management*, 15 (6): 324–327.
Governo do Brasil. (2014). *Bonito (MS) é eleita melhor Destino Sustentável do Mundo.* Available at: www.brasil.gov.br/turismo/2013/11/bonito-ms-e-eleita-melhor-destino-sustentavel-do-mundo (accessed 28 January 2018).
Hiernaux, D. (2002). Turismo e Imaginarios. In D. N. Hiernaux, A. Cordero and L. Duynen Montijn (eds), *Imaginarios Sociales y turismo Sostenible* (pp. 7–35). San Jose: FLACSO.
Hjalager, A. M. (2000). Consumerism and sustainable tourism. *Journal of Travel & Tourism Marketing*, 8 (3): 1–20.
Jones, A. (1987). Green tourism. *Tourism Management*, 8 (4): 354–356.
Korstanje, M. E. and George, B. (2012). Global warming and tourism: chronicles of apocalypse? *Worldwide Hospitality and Tourism Themes*, 4 (4): 332–355.
McMichael, P. (2016). *Development and Social Change: A Global Perspective*. London: Sage Publications.
Ministério do Turismo. (2017a). *Brasil recebeu 6,6 milhões de turistas estrangeiros em 2016.* Available at: www.brasil.gov.br/turismo/2017/01/brasil-recebeu-6-6-milhoes-de-turistas-estrangeiros-em-2016 (accessed 28 January 2018).
Ministério do Turismo. (2017b). Fernando de Noronha registra aumento de turistas em 2016. Available at: www.brasil.gov.br/turismo/2017/01/fernando-de-noronha-registra-aumento-de-turistas-em-2016 (accessed 28 January 2018).
Nicholls, S. (2004). Climate change and tourism. *Annals of Tourism Research*, 31 (1): 238–240.

Orjuela, D. E. M. (2013). Turismo rural y gobernanza ambiental: conceptos divergentes en países desarrollados y países en vías de desarrollo. *Turismo y Sociedad*, 14: 215–235.

Osorio Garcia, M., Franco, S., Ramírez, I., Nava, G., Novo, G. y Regil, H. (2011). El Visitante del Parque Nacional Nevado de Toluca, México. Análisis del comportamiento en un área natural protegida. *Investigaciones Geográficas*, 76: 56–70.

Osorio Garcia, M., Vallejo, B. y Vega, J. (2016). Propuesta para el desarrollo turístico sustentable del Área de Protección de Flora y Fauna Nevado de Toluca. Toluca: Universidad Autónoma del Estado de México (En edición).

Ramírez, I., Osorio, M. y Nava, G. (2011). San Juan de las Huertas y Raíces: dos comunidades en el Parque Nacional Nevado de Toluca (PNNT) y sus posibiliades de turismo sustentable, en Castillo, M. y Tamayo, L. (Coords.). Entorno del Turismo, vol. 4, México: Universidad Autónoma del Estado de México.

Romeril, M. (1989). Tourism and the environment – accord or discord? *Tourism Management*, 10 (3): 204–208.

Scott, D., Amelung, B., Becken, S., Ceron, J. P., Dubois, G., Gössling, S., ... and Simpson, M. (2008). Climate change and tourism: responding to global challenges. *World Tourism Organization, Madrid, 230*.

Sofield, T. H. (2003). *Empowerment for Sustainable Tourism Development* (Vol. 7). Oxford: Emerald Group Publishing.

Stabler, M. J. and Goodall, B. (1997). Environmental awareness, action and performance in the Guernsey hospitality sector. *Tourism Management*, 18 (1): 19–33.

Timothy, D. J., Sharpley, R. and Telfer, D. J. (2002). Tourism and community development issues. In R. Sharpley and D. J. Telfer (eds), *Tourism and Development: Concepts and Issues* (pp. 149–164). Clevedon: Channel View.

UNESCO (2001). *Ilhas Atlânticas Brasileiras: Reservas de Fernando de Noronha e do Atol das Rocas* Available at: www.unesco.org/new/pt/brasilia/culture/world-heritage/list-of-world-heritage-in-brazil/brazilian-atlantic-islands-fernando-de-noronha-and-atol-das-rocas-reserves/#c1467461 (accessed 28 January 2018).

Viegas, Anderson (2015). Bonito, MS: quando ir, o que fazer, o que visitar. Available at: http://g1.globo.com/mato-grosso-do-sul/noticia/2015/07/bonito-ms-quando-ir-o-que-fazer-o-que-visitar.html (accessed 28 January 2018).

Wall, G. (1998). Implications of global climate change for tourism and recreation in wetland areas. *Climatic Change*, 40 (2): 371–389.

Wallace, G. N. and Pierce, S. M. (1996). An evaluation of ecotourism in Amazonas, Brazil. *Annals of Tourism Research*, 23 (4): 843–873.

World Tourism Organization. *UNWTO Tourism Highlights 2017 Edition*. Available on: www.e-unwto.org/doi/pdf/10.18111/9789284419029 (accessed 28 January 2018).

5   Greening in the MICE industry

Judith Mair and Deborah Popely

Introduction

Whilst climate change and environmental issues are becoming increasingly important for all sectors of the economy, the MICE sector (meetings, incentives, conventions and exhibitions) is at particular risk due to the amount of international and domestic travel associated with it, thus contributing to greenhouse-gas emissions, and the high resource use associated with large-scale events (Rittichainuwat and Mair, 2012). Business travel is particularly vulnerable, given that it can be considered as a discretionary activity, potentially replaceable in some cases by technology such as Skype, video conferencing and virtual meetings. It is very difficult to approximate the economic importance of this sector on a global level, but the global economic significance of business tourism is not in question. Therefore, it is vital for the sector to look at ways to improve its environmental sustainability credentials, in order to maintain business in the long term. The MICE industry is taking this challenge seriously – a recent report on the sustainable practices of 30 international convention centres found that 90 per cent of them either achieved, or are actively seeking, a sustainability-related certification (Simons and Unterkofler, 2015).

Understanding the role of sustainability within event management is an important avenue of research, given the size of the events industry and its potential to negatively affect communities and the environment (Gibson and Wong, 2011; Laing and Frost, 2010). All stakeholders are demonstrating concern for the environmental credentials of business events, including the supply side (Mair and Jago, 2010), delegates (Park and Boo, 2010) and meeting planners (Tinnish and Mangal, 2012; Draper *et al.*, 2011). As Laing and Frost (2010) note, many types of events are now adopting environmentally sustainable practices, particularly in relation to energy water and waste. However, there is a dearth of detailed research on the investment in pro-environmental facilities and services within the business events or MICE sector (Mair and Jago, 2010).

The existing research suggests that there is a range of drivers and barriers to 'greening' in the business events context (Mair and Jago, 2010). Competitive advantage, image enhancement, supply chain/customer corporate social responsibility policies and consumer demand have been identified as significant drivers of greening, with lack of time, resources and knowledge being considered to be barriers (Mair and Jago, 2010). A range of considerations in the micro and macro environments were also proposed to be influential in how much time and resources were spent on pro-environmental efforts. Additionally, Mair and Jago (2010) proposed that the presence of an eco-champion was a vital catalyst in determining how much effort would be put into greening in a particular business events organisation. Popely and Tinnish (2015) described the impact of eco-champions specifically on the greening of meetings and events. All are relevant to the case study highlighted in this chapter.

Case study: greening in the MICE industry

McCormick Place Convention Centre Chicago is the largest convention centre in North America and one of the world's leading meeting facilities.[1] With 600,000 square feet of meeting rooms, 2.6 million square feet of exhibit halls, more than 170 meeting rooms, and one of the largest ballrooms in the world, McCormick Place attracts up to 3 million visitors per year. The sprawling campus consists of four buildings: the North and South Buildings, the West Building and Lakeside Center, all of which are connected by pedestrian skybridges and walkways. Some of North America's largest and most sustainable conventions find a home at McCormick Place. Noteworthy green meetings include the American Wind Energy Association (AWEA), Solar Power International (SPI), and the Green Meeting Industry Council (GMIC).

Sustainability is an important aspect of McCormick Place's mission. The facility has been recognised by the city, the state, and the national government, as well as by the Meetings and Conventions Industry, for its innovative sustainability policies and procedures related to energy and water efficiency, air quality, waste management, local and sustainable food service, and community partnerships.[2] The centre's environmental policy states that sustainability is one of five strategic priorities in the centre's business plan. The commitment to being a green facility includes energy, air quality, water, procurement, waste management and community partnerships. McCormick Place is also a hub for sustainable innovation, highlighted by its 2.5 acre rooftop garden, Electro Chemical Activation (ECA) cleaning system, Green Angels recycling programme, campus-wide GreenSeal® certification of food and beverage services, and APEX/ASTM food and beverage certification. Through a mix of innovation, inspiration, and committed staff and leadership, McCormick Place represents an ideal case of best practice for sustainability in the convention industry.

Policies, legislation and codes

Chicago is recognised as a sustainable city. It ranks 11th overall and 8th for energy efficiency on Siemens' Green City Index (www.siemens.com/press/greencityindex). The Sustainable Chicago Action Agenda engages businesses and citizens in a citywide effort to enhance sustainability and prepare for a changing climate. In connection with the plan, the city government encourages sustainable development through green building codes, tax incentives, and voluntary energy efficiency and carbon emissions reduction initiatives. Not surprisingly, Chicago is one of the leading centres for Leadership in Energy and Environmental Design (LEED®) certification.[3] LEED® is a programme that rates and third-party certifies buildings as environmentally and energy efficient. When the new McCormick Place West Building was built in 2007, earning LEED® certification for new construction and maintenance and operations was a priority.

In 2013, McCormick Place collaborated with the City of Chicago government to establish the city as a sustainable destination for meetings and events. Chicago was the first top-tier North American destination to achieve destination certification under APEX-ASTM.[4] APEX-ASTM is a voluntary international standard for sustainable meetings and events. The certification recognises destinations that offer a robust selection of green hotels and venues, low-impact transportation options, use environmentally responsible suppliers, and provide green meeting and event amenities. Around the same time, McCormick Place earned Level One APEX-ASTM venue certification, a designation also achieved by its food service provider SAVOR...Chicago. Recently, SAVOR...Chicago also achieved GreenSeal® GS-55 certification for all catering and food service concessions across McCormick Place's campus[5] GreenSeal® GS-55 is a rigorous, third party certification for retail restaurants and institutional food service operations. Having a complete package of a certified green destination, convention centre and food service provider makes Chicago a very attractive location for green meetings and events.

Findings

The primary informant for this study was Kevin Jezewski, Director of Food & Beverages and Sustainability for SAVOR...Chicago, McCormick Place's catering contractor. Mr Jezewski was interviewed by one of the researchers for the purposes of this case study. Mr Jezewski was initially asked about the Centre's motivations for investing in sustainable practices and facilities. Subsequent questions concerned the current sustainable practices and facilities in the Centre, supply chain and procurement issues and innovative new practices that are coming online.

Motivation

In relation to the question of why the Centre is investing so much in sustainability, Jezewski was clear: 'As the largest convention centre in North America, we have a huge footprint,' he said. 'We feel motivated to do as much as possible to reduce the potential negative impacts of our operations.' This has strong links with the greening motivations found in previous studies (e.g. Mair and Jago, 2010). Jezewski noted that as a publicly owned facility, state and city government sustainability policies have an impact on the Centre's operations.

McCormick Place is influenced by being in Chicago, which has a strong emphasis on sustainable development. Customer demand has played a role as well. Hosting the American Wind Energy Association (AWEA) pushed McCormick Place to invest in Renewable Energy Certificates (RECs) to offset 100 per cent of its electricity throughout the campus. Although it was a small conference, the Green Meeting Industry Council encouraged McCormick Place to adopt additional best practices that ultimately enhanced the Centre's green capabilities.

The influence is also reciprocal, according to Marissa Ritter, CMP, Assistant Director: Convention Operations & Registration Services for the Radiological Society of North America (RSNA). RSNA has held its annual convention at McCormick Place for the past 15 years. With 51,000 healthcare professionals, it is one of the largest annual conventions in Chicago. 'McCormick Place would encourage us to enhance our sustainability initiatives by bringing us good ideas and generating trend data on different projects' (personal communication). With the help of the SAVOR...Chicago team, RSNA has increased recycling overall and engaged exhibitors in recycling, encouraged the use of refillable water bottles, reduced the use of consumable plates and utensils, promoted local and sustainable food (especially produce from the rooftop garden) and facilitated food donation.

It seems that McCormick Place is having an impact in terms of spreading the word about the importance of sustainable practices, and encouraging sector-wide improvements. According to Jezewski, clients go to other centres and notice that they are not doing what McCormick Place is doing. By increasing customer expectations, other convention centres are being challenged to increase their efforts.

As well as their efforts to be environmentally sustainable, McCormick Place takes pride in their community partnerships too. Because of the large number of meals prepared on a daily basis, McCormick Place is in a position to reduce food waste while performing an important community service by donating leftover food to local homeless shelters and soup kitchens. 'We can have as many as 2000 box lunches leftover from an event that would otherwise go in the trash. Why not donate them to local charities who can distribute them to people in need?' said Jezewski. So far, McCormick Place has donated over 37 tons of food to local charities. In addition, SAVOR...Chicago employees have spent more than 2,500 hours volunteering their time in the local community since taking over food service operations at McCormick Place, including volunteering at local shelters to feed the homeless.

Sustainable practices and facilities

In relation to the question of what sustainable practices and facilities are being implemented at McCormick Place, Jezewski pointed to four key areas – energy, air quality, water and waste management. Each will be discussed in turn.

Energy

The cornerstone of McCormick Place's energy efficiency programme is the LEED®-certified West Building. LEED buildings are documented to save energy and water and generate less waste. Energy efficiency initiatives take place in other parts of the facility, including retrofitting energy efficient lighting, powering down escalators when not in use, and identifying opportunities for retro-commissioning and preventative maintenance. In order to reduce reliance on non-renewable fuels, McCormick Place has committed to purchasing Green-e Wind Energy-certified Renewable Energy Certificates (RECs) to offset 100 per cent of the facility's energy usage.

Air quality

Located outside the city centre, McCormick Place has made a priority of reducing its transportation footprint by facilitating the use of public transportation and other low-impact modes. In 2015, the City of Chicago made it easier for convention-goers to take rapid transit from the airport and other downtown destinations by establishing a new McCormick Place stop on the Chicago Transit Authority (CTA) Green Line. More recently, a $30 million bus transit lane was established to help event planners coordinate shuttles for attendees staying at hotels outside the convention centre district. McCormick Place encourages cycling with bike rack locations for two-wheeled commuters. They also enforce anti-idling and non-smoking policies.

Water

Although Chicago is blessed with an abundant water source from Lake Michigan, conserving water and maintaining its quality is a top priority. McCormick Place employs a highly efficient irrigation system consisting of timed sprinklers, moisture sensors, and drip irrigation tubes, which reduce the use of potable water for landscape irrigation by 50 per cent. Approximately 55 million gallons of storm water is diverted from city sewers per year, by means of a 3,100-foot-long storm water tunnel, located 150 feet below ground. Given the large potential water footprint from such a high-use facility, the centre has targeted reducing potable water use by encouraging the shift from bottled water to refillable water bottles and by providing water dispensers, water stations for meeting rooms and public spaces, as well as water service to head tables.

Waste management

McCormick Place has achieved an overall 63 per cent waste diversion rate through recycling, composting and donations. According to the 2017 Green Venue Report,[6] the average waste diversion rate for convention centres is 48 per cent, with a high of 100 per cent and a low of 7 per cent. McCormick Place has achieved this through changes in packaging and bulk condiments, recycling all food grease to bio-diesel, adopting a cork re-harvesting programme, and many other efforts, including a unique recycling support programme and robust food donation initiative.

To enhance participation by event attendees in post-consumer recycling, McCormick Place has developed a unique programme called the 'Green Angels'. The programme involves having SAVOR…Chicago staff monitor waste stations to help take the guesswork out of what can be recycled or composted and what must be thrown away. SAVOR…Chicago estimates that Green Angel monitored events recycle and compost 1–2 per cent more than other events at the Centre.

Sustainable procurement

SAVOR…Chicago is the food service contractor for McCormick Place. They operate in approximately 150 convention centres across the US. According to Jezewski, when SAVOR…Chicago arrived in 2011, there were limited practices in place for sustainable procurement of food and beverages. Jezewski reached out to other green venues to find information, assistance and support. He also looked to SAVOR…Chicago's sister properties, such as San Francisco's Moscone Centre. Moscone was known for being a sustainable property, heavily influenced by the chefs and local government.

Sustainable procurement, especially in the food and beverage area, has numerous challenges. For one, it can be difficult to find local sustainable food producers who can satisfy McCormick Place's volume requirements – for example, providing enough antibiotic-free chicken to support a major convention. It can often require cobbling together multiple small producers. Networking was helpful to McCormick Place in this area. Jezewski reached out to local non-profits working in sustainable food and food service, such as the Green Chicago Restaurant Coalition[7] and Family Farmed.[8] He also attended the annual Good Food Festival to identify potential vendors who could help achieve local and sustainable procurement goals. 'We initially set modest goals, such as purchasing 15 per cent local and sustainable food. Thanks to the relationships we have formed, 33 per cent of all food purchased at McCormick Place is local, organic or environmentally preferred,' said Jezewski. In addition, 80 per cent of all seafood purchased is sustainable, all coffee served on McCormick Place campus is green-certified. On the non-food side, McCormick Place does not use styrofoam or polystyrene products for catered events, and instead features biodegradable flatware, straws, serving dishes and cups. In addition, post-consumer recycled paper is used in order to reduce waste.

Other innovations

In addition to those already introduced above, Jezewski was keen to mention a range of other initiatives that McCormick Place is involved in, including the cutting-edge rooftop garden and an innovative green cleaning system.

Midwest's largest rooftop garden

Chicago is home to more than 300 green roofs installed to reduce the urban heat island effect, but the McCormick Place Rooftop Garden is among the most dramatic and innovative. At 2.5 acres, it is one of the largest in the Midwest, producing seasonal harvests of 8,000 lbs of beets, kale, carrots, lettuce, peppers, beans, tomatoes, cucumbers, zucchini, herbs and other produce used for McCormick Place catering and restaurant operations, including 'Windy City Harvest' menu items served in the 23rd Street Cafe & Market. They also maintain 20,000 bees in three hives producing 50 lbs of honey a year and 2,000 Red Wiggler worms that create 200 lbs of vermi-compost a year. In addition to providing edibles for SAVOR…Chicago's food service programme, the green roof confers energy efficiency benefits by insulating the West Building from heat and cold. It also helps manage storm water run-off from the large structure. The garden is maintained by participants in the Chicago Botanic Gardens' Windy City Harvest programme,[9] which trains ex-offenders for agricultural careers, thus also providing a social benefit.

The rooftop garden only fills about 0.25 per cent of McCormick Place's total food needs, but the fruits, vegetables, and herbs grown on-site play a prominent role in promoting sustainability in the facility and the community. SAVOR… Chicago has developed a Rooftop Garden package for meetings and events that highlights a Rooftop Salad and other locally grown, organic and environmentally preferable items. During the growing season, SAVOR…Chicago staff attend the South Loop Farmers Market every Thursday, offering samples of rooftop yield and recipe cards to encourage healthy eating. McCormick Place also offers frequent Rooftop Garden tours to students, sustainable food enthusiasts and meeting professionals.

McCormick Place recently added 50 hops plants producing the ingredients for McCormick Place Everyday Ale, the venue's signature beer. The beer is the result of a partnership with a local brewery and represents the first branded ale brewed for a convention centre using locally sourced ingredients. The beer is featured in green meeting packages, sold in the event centre and distributed through several local beverage outlets.

Innovative green cleaning system

McCormick Place set out to reduce the amount of harsh chemicals used in the facility. After finding it difficult to obtain green cleaning products in sufficient bulk, they discovered an innovative, scalable non-toxic sanitising system: Electro Chemical Activation (ECA). This technology generates two end products on-site for the user: a sanitiser/disinfectant and mild detergent using only purified salt, tap water and electricity. It is registered with the EPA as a hospital grade disinfectant and is compatible with cleaning contractor equipment and routines. From an environmental viewpoint, the system improves air quality, reduces pollution and reduces the carbon footprint of shipping cleaning products to the facility. 'It was really exciting to partner with GreenSeal® to certify the process,' noted Jezewski. In addition to being a green product, it is also very economical. Although ECA cannot replace every cleaning product, McCormick Place has already saved $40,000 with the system in the first year while also reducing the use of toxic chemicals and McCormick Place's carbon footprint at the same time.

Future opportunities and challenges

Despite their substantial efforts to date in providing a sustainable convention centre, McCormick Place are aware that the future will continue to bring challenges. For example, a massive new basketball and entertainment arena and a 1,200-room hotel being built adjacent to McCormick Place (connected by skybridges) are scheduled to open in the autumn of 2017, effectively expanding the campus. Jezewski hopes to imbue the new structures with the same sustainability standards, but notes that this may not always be a straightforward task. He would also like to expand the types of food growing on the Rooftop Garden and possibly add a greenhouse to permit year-round growing. 'We are always looking for new ideas and innovations that can be implemented at McCormick Place and SAVOR...Chicago operations across the country,' he said.

There are challenges as well, especially with respect to staff training and motivation. 'To make sustainability stick, you have to change the institution's culture and that takes time. We've only been at this about five years and some employees have been here 20 to 30 years. We have to keep pushing as a team towards continuous improvement by raising the bar through new initiatives and innovations,' said Jezewski.

Maintaining the GreenSeal certification is challenging, particularly managing all the paperwork and monitoring compliance over time. 'It is almost easier to manage campus-wide certification versus trying to separate data between sustainable and non-sustainable operations,' Jezewski continued. Another challenge is enforcing sustainability standards with independent retailers that provide concessions. 'We modeled our approach on the airport, which pushed out their green standards by embedding it in contracts,' he said.

Finally, the cost and availability of local and sustainable food and supplies is a continuing challenge. 'The large demand from a facility like ours is helping increase supply and drive down costs. For instance, a few years ago, compostables were hard to find and the price was high. Now you may pay more for the non-compostables. We also see that trend in food service, too, as the supply of sustainable produce and meat has come a long way. By collaborating with other large Chicago institutions, we hope to use our combined demand to transform the supply chain,' said Jezewski. McCormick Place is also seeking to partner with a farmers' collaborative that could aggregate sustainable produce from different farmers and deliver it directly to the Centre.

Comparison between McCormick place and other industry benchmarks

The Green Venue Report[10] is an industry benchmarking initiative that annually tracks and reports the sustainable practices of 44 convention centres around the world, including McCormick Place. Comparing the report's findings with this case study data, we found that McCormick Place was generally on a par with common practices (those that have a 75 per cent or more adoption rate), aligned with many emerging practices (25 to 74 per cent adoption rate), and an innovator (less than 25 per cent adoption rate) in several key areas. For instance, turning underutilised space into a green roof is an emerging practice that is growing at a rate of about 30 per cent year-over-year, while the number of centres with on-site gardens has increased by approximately 25 per cent per year. McCormick Place's rooftop garden stands out as a model of what can be accomplished by combining food and beverage production with the energy efficiency of green roof techno-logy. McCormick Place compares favourably on other emerging practices such as sustainable food and beverage procurement, waste diversion and reporting, food donation, providing refillable water stations, communicating sustainability pol-icies to customers and the public, and committing staff to oversee sustainability. McCormick Place is among the top innovators in renewable energy procurement, offsetting 100 per cent of energy use by purchasing Renewable Energy Certifi-cates (RECs). Only 25 per cent of centres reported purchasing RECs to offset at least 50 per cent of energy usage in the Green Venue Report. Sustainable certifi-cations are another area of innovation for McCormick Place. While one certifica-tion is common practice, and two certifications qualifies as an emerging trend, McCormick place is among the innovators (21 per cent) that have three or more certifications (LEED®, APEX-ASTM, and GreenSeal®). Finally, we found no other convention centres that had developed innovative green cleaning systems, such as ECA, or that had developed a hands-on recycling and composting sorting programme such as the Green Angels.

Conclusion

Despite the acknowledged challenges of investing in sustainable practices and facilities, McCormick Place provides an excellent case study of best practice in the convention centre sector. Their willingness to not only meet, but also signifi-cantly exceed industry standards demonstrates their commitment to sustain-ability. Having a champion like Kevin Jezewski has no doubt facilitated this process, and McCormick Place is a trailblazer in the field of sustainability. Other convention centres, and other facilities in the tourism industry, can learn valu-able lessons from the innovative practices discussed in this case study.

Notes

1 www.mccormickplace.com/index.php
2 www.mccormickplace.com/green-initiatives.php

3 www.usgbc.org/LEED/
4 www.gmicglobal.org/?page=APEX
5 www.greenseal.org/
6 https://greenview.sg/green-venue/
7 www.greenchicago.org/
8 www.familyfarmed.org/
9 www.chicagobotanic.org/education/windy_city_harvest
10 https://greenview.sg/green-venue/

Further resources

- ECA Cleaning Technology: www.ecologicsolutions.com/eca-technology/
- Green Venue Report: https://greenview.sg/green-venue/
- GreenSeal®: www.greenseal.org/
- Chicago Green Restaurant Coalition: www.greenchicago.org/
- Family Farmed: www.familyfarmed.org/
- Windy City Harvest: www.chicagobotanic.org/education/windy_city_harvest
- Julie's Bicycle: www.juliesbicycle.com/
- A Greener Festival: www.agreenerfestival.com/
- Sustainable Living Festival: www.slf.org.au/

References

Draper, J., Dawson, M. and Casey, E. (2011). An exploratory study of the importance of sustainable practices in the meeting and convention site selection process. *Journal of Convention & Event Tourism*, 12 (3): 153–178.

Gibson, C. and Wong, C. (2011). Greening rural festivals: ecology, sustainability and human nature relations. In C. Gibson and J. Connell (eds), *Festival Places: Revitalising Rural Australia* (pp. 92–105). Bristol: Channel View Publications.

Laing, J. and Frost, W. (2010). How green was my festival? Exploring challenges and opportunities associated with staging green events. *International Journal of Hospitality Management*, 29 (2): 261–267.

Mair, J. and Jago, L. (2010). The development of a conceptual model of greening in the business events tourism sector. *Journal of Sustainable Tourism*, 18 (1): 77–94.

Park, E. and Boo, S. (2010). An assessment of convention tourism's potential contribution to environmentally sustainable growth. *Journal of Sustainable Tourism*, 18 (1): 95–114.

Popely, D. and Tinnish, S. (2015). The role of champions as organizational catalysts for sustainable events. *Conference Proceedings: International Conference on Events, September 12–15, 2015* (pp. 183–196). Macau, China: Institute for Tourism.

Rittichainuwat, B. and Mair, J. (2012). An exploratory study of attendee perceptions of green meetings. *Journal of Convention and Event Tourism*, 13 (3): 147–158.

Simons, A. and Unterkofler, C. (2015). Green Venue Report 2015: the state of convention and exhibition center sustainability. San Francisco, CA: Greenview and Twirl Management.

Tinnish, S. M. and Mangal, S. M. (2012). Sustainable event marketing in the mice industry: a theoretical framework. *Journal of Convention & Event Tourism*, 13 (4): 227–249.

Part II

Sustainable music and arts festivals

6 Sustainability and festivals

An objective still to be achieved

Eryn White and Hugues Séraphin

National context

The topic of sustainability is a current issue not only in the event industry, but also in the tourism industry. Indeed, both sectors are closely related and sometimes referred as 'event tourism' (Getz, 2012). Over the summer 2017, anti-tourism movements arose in many leading tourism destinations in Europe, amongst these are Spain, Italy and the UK. Amid the main reasons for the 'grapes of wrath' are the number of visitors (considered way too high by locals); the lack of respect for local culture and environment; and the disruption of the locals' habits (Coldwell, 2017; Tapper, 2017). This wave of anti-tourism movements in Europe clearly shows that sustainability is something that the tourism industry (and to some extent the event sector) has not yet achieved. On the basis that events are important pull factors in terms of tourists' motivations to visit a destination (Getz, 2012), it is legitimate to wonder if events are next on the list for anti-tourism activists. In this line of thought, it is important to investigate what the event sector is doing in order to limit its negative impacts on the environment and local population. In other words, how sustainable or green is the event industry? In order to address this research question, this book chapter is going to investigate the event sector in the UK with emphasis on a specific festival, namely, *Love Saves The Day*.

In the UK, the event industry is fairly prominent and is currently worth £42.3 billion (Booker, 2016), set to increase to £48 billion by 2020 (Fletcher, 2012). As a destination, London is the main UK city in terms of meetings and events activities. As this chapter is going to focus on an outdoor event, it is important to indicate that over 7,000 major outdoor events are organised each year in the UK. This number of events held each year is continually increasing with *Glastonbury* being the largest festival, admitting over 100,000 attendees. That said, among the many festivals running in the UK, *Love Saves The Day* stands out, due to the many initiatives in action, aimed at minimising its impacts on the environment and more particularly in reducing the greenhouse-gas emissions. In order to continually push towards sustainability and protection of the environment, listed amongst the initiatives of this event could be: reusable cups, ethical procurement policies, recycling and alternative transport methods. Being the key focus of this chapter, it is also worth noting that, as a music festival, *Love Saves The Day* is relatively new. It started in May 2011 in the city of Bristol, to celebrate all that makes it a great city.

Love Saves The Day is not the only festival (or even event) aiming to be sustainable from an environmental point of view. Being 'green', is now a buzzword in the event industry and in other industries. Other sectors related to tourism and events are following this path. The hospitality sector is one of them. For instance, *Cavendish Venues* are leading the way in conference, meeting and event sustainability. As part of their procedure, they are the first in London to have introduced a bespoke carbon calculator for the events they hold; they offer subsidies to organisers who commit to recycling all their promotional material; they are committed to composting all food waste; their menus are redesigned to offer more choice and less food waste; they have recorded reductions in all inputs (energy, water, etc.) in the centres; and they choose local suppliers to minimise the carbon footprint. *Cavendish Venues* are also accredited as landfill neutral.

In the hospitality, tourism and event sectors for instance, it has been evidenced that customers are quite sensitive to the effort put in place by companies to reduce their negative impacts on the environment. That said, all the strategies currently in place (briefly mentioned earlier in this chapter) are more reactionary and exploitation actions. In this chapter we will claim that exploratory actions would be more sustainable. We will also suggest a strategy to put in place. A variety of examples will be used, with *Love Saves The Day* the main one.

Priority issues

When talking about green tourism or green events, first it is important to have a clear understanding of what it means to be 'green' and second, to know how to implement green strategies. At the moment there is a variety of definitions and strategies available regarding what can cause confusion and difficulties in assessing the performance of the strategies in place. More importantly, the following data clearly show that events, and more specifically festivals, have a major impact on the environment. Indeed, annually, 23,500 tonnes of waste are generated from the UK music festival industry; 5 million litres of fuel are consumed; 19,778 tonnes of CO_2 are produced (excluding travel); and recycling rates are lower than 32 per cent (Powerful Thinking, 2015). Also, the unintended and unplanned effects of festivals on the environment often include (but are not limited to): traffic congestion; increase in litter; and the disruption to local flora and fauna. A reactionary approach would be to collect the litter or to find alternatives to limit congestion and related side-effects, etc. An exploratory approach would consist in a more radical and in-depth approach. On that basis, it becomes important to educate those people attending events, Destination Marketing Organisations and event organisers, on how to mitigate the negative impact of their behaviour and activity on the environment. Taking the example of tourists travelling to post-colonial, post-conflict and post-disaster destinations (basically destinations with a negative image), Séraphin *et al.* (2016) explained that the education of these tourists at the pre-visit stage contributed to improving their perception of these destinations. Taking the example of food festivals, Pilato *et al.* (2017) explained that these events have the potential to improve the people's perception of a destination. Education is basically a proactive approach that can mitigate and sometimes prevent negative outcomes. Similarly, it appears that the more eco-conscious an individual is, the more likely this person is to perceive the negative impacts of his actions on the environment, and the opposite is true if the individual is not eco-conscious. Education is therefore key to greening an event/destination. That said, the confusion regarding what is a green event or green tourism, and which strategies to put in place at green events and green destinations, have led some festivals to promote themselves as 'green', even when they are not (Edwards, 2010).

Trends

Séraphin *et al.* (2016) and Gartner (2000) explain that the image that we have of a destination is based upon information acquired, either by induced agents (generally controlled by sources external to the individual, such as advertisements); organic agents (acquired through personal experience and normally the most trusted source of information); or autonomous agents (media sources or popular culture such as films or documentaries). We argue that the image that people have of a festival follows the same pattern. On that basis, it is very important for an event to advertise itself as 'green' (induced agent). It is also very important for the event organisers to have a strategy in place to mitigate the negative impacts of their event and, more importantly, this strategy needs to be communicated to festivalgoers and needs to contribute positively to their experience of the festival (organic agent). Finally, it is important for this strategy to stand out so that it gets commanded and shared as good practice (autonomous agent).

From the above examples, it is quite obvious that events need to have a communication strategy in place and more importantly, a sustainable strategy that can help them to stand out and gain competitive advantage. *Cavendish Venues* built part of their image and competitiveness based on this strategy. The benefits that can be reaped from a green strategy have led to the development of green marketing. This form of marketing, or cause-related marketing, which is 'binding the sale of a product to a particular cause' (Sloan *et al.*, 2013: 191), has been influenced by 'the four Ps' of sustainable development, namely: People, Planet, Profit and Progress (Sloan *et al.*, 2013). This form of marketing is also supposed to market products that are claimed to be environmentally safe and that can improve the quality of the environment (Sloan *et al.*, 2013). That said, it is important to say that the purpose of green marketing 'is not to incite consumers to consume less, but to consume better' (Sloan *et al.*, 2013: 192). What are events, and more specifically festivals like *Love Saves The Day*, doing in terms of green marketing? If we consider the fact that the branding (logo and slogan) of an organisation is supposed to tell the narrative of this organisation, *Love Saves The Day* is branding itself as being respectful to and loving of the world.

In the event industry, environment sustainability is regarded high up on the agenda when planning and delivering events. Pretty much all events have a strategy in place regarding sustainability. Some events also have a social agenda (as sustainability can also be viewed from a political, economic, social and technological angle). For instance, in 2017 Boomtown made a substantial contribution to the local community. Indeed, the event raised £32,000 for charities and projects in the local area.

Government policies

As discussed in the previous section, it is important for destinations, events, venues, etc. to be known as sustainable because of the many benefits related to this form of branding. That said, having a sustainable strategy is not an obligation. There is no government policy, no regional or national legislation. However, there are many voluntary codes, standards and frameworks. At the international level, ISO is the most common one. As an example, we can refer to ISO 20121.

> [It] is a management system standard that has been designed to help organisations in the events industry improve the sustainability of their event related activities, products and services.
>
> (ISO 20121, 2017)

The UK has developed its own, namely the British Standard (BS). Among these are BS8901:

> BS8901 is the British Standard which has been developed specifically for the events industry. The standard provides a framework of good practice and defines the requirements for a sustainable event management system to ensure an enduring and balanced approach to economic activity, environmental responsibility and social progress.
>
> (Action Sustainability, 2017)

Experts in the field of event management have also developed their own framework. Among these is Megan Jones, a consultant in sustainable events. She has developed a 9-steps framework to help event organisers to reach their objectives in terms of sustainability (Jones, 2008).

This section clearly shows that the event industry is keen to limit its negative impacts on the environment and to positively contribute to society. That said, the variety of frameworks to some extent might defeat their initial objectives by causing confusion. Also, the different certifications available (ISO or BS) might be used for marketing purposes and might, in the long-term, lose sight of their original purpose and might end up not being fit for purpose. Taking the example of the certification *Investors In People*, Smith (2011) explained that this certification does not always match the expectations of HR practitioners in terms of the benefits that could be gained.

Case study: *Love Saves The Day*

The *Love Saves The Day* festival has a strong focus on sustainability. As mentioned earlier, the organisers have developed a range of strategies in order to reach their objectives, amongst these are the sourcing of products from local suppliers; finding innovative ways to reduce waste and energy consumption; providing the 'love bus' (a shuttle bus); recycling waste; using reusable cups; implementing energy-efficient management, ethical procurement policies and alternative transport methods, all whilst trying to educate the people attending the event by raising awareness of the impacts that events can have on the environment, and more importantly by informing the audience about what is done at *Love Saves The Day* to minimise the impacts of the festival on the environment (A Greener Festival, 2015).

A study was carried out at *Love Saves The Day* (based on 396 respondents who attended the festival in 2016), which aimed to examine attendee's attitudes and knowledge towards sustainability and environmental impacts at UK music festivals. Questionnaires were the primary method of data collection, not only due to their favourability amongst similar research, or because questions can be utilised from previous studies, but because of their low cost, quick response time and lack of interviewer bias. Questions pertaining to attendees' attitudes were constructed on a 5-point Likert scale, and all questions were coded so that responses could easily be analysed using SPSS. The questionnaires were made as short as possible, as individuals were unlikely to want to respond if the questionnaires were longer than 4–6 pages. When administering the questionnaires, a random sample was picked from the attendees. The sampling procedure was closest to probabilistic sampling, which is entirely based on the principle of randomness. Through the use of this sampling method, results were able to be generalised and projected upon the entire population (Franklin and Blyton, 2011). Post-questionnaire data analysis, one short interview was used in order to validate the quantitative results. This also serves as a form of methodological triangulation, limiting the research vulnerability and reducing any possible bias according to Wilson (2014). In order to validate the findings, an interview was conducted with an industry professional (IP).

The main findings revealed that attendees' attitudes towards environmental impacts and sustainability measures were positive. When presented with this information, the IP commented they felt 'reassured'; it shows that attendees are engaging with the information given to them on how to reduce environmental impacts, even if this engagement is much less than the attention other festival aspects receive. Giving consideration to the efforts of *Love Saves The Day*, the IP believes that the fact that attitudes are positive would suggest that the measures in place are working and that the audience understands their purpose. That said, it is only 56.7 per cent of attendees who are engaging with the information given to them. The IP argued that more should be done to reach those attendees who are still displaying a negative attitude. The IP felt these findings may be due to attendees' being oblivious of the considerable footprint most festivals incur, resulting in a lack of consideration and concern relating to the environmental impacts at festivals, and sustainability measures that have to be put in place. Statistics also showed that attendees at *Love Saves The Day* had little knowledge of the environmental impacts of festivals. Given that there is such a clear lack of knowledge, changes should be made to better educate festival attendees. The IP felt that by adopting a strategic approach through integrated marketing communications, the information on festival impacts and sustainability measures could be fed to attendees over an extended period of time. Additionally, there has been recent research into future trends and how to reach attendees, which confirm the IP's opinion; Robertson *et al.* (2015) believe technology will become increasingly important at festivals and used as a way to reduce environmental impacts and educate attendees through online platforms containing official festival materials. Velt *et al.* (2015) also found that attendees would like festivals to be themed or crafted around their mobile devices.

Similar case studies and relevant projects

Glastonbury Festival was founded in 1970, long before people started to become concerned about climate change. *Glastonbury Festival* has always been the first to host 'alternative' solutions to environmental concerns. The motto/slogan of the festival is now: 'Love Worthy Farm... Leave No Trace', the objective being to achieve the best possible balance of nature and resources. The Festival also commits to maintaining the rich and diverse environment that has evolved through alternative land usage. The festival has developed its own green policies (*Glastonbury Festival*). Information from the website has been split into three categories:

Before:

- We want people to think about their journey to the Festival: to use public transport or, if coming by car, to share transport with others and maximise the carload.
- 'Limit what you bring, and clean up behind you'. The Festival commits to continuing its policy of reducing the percentage of waste that goes to land-fill, by placing controls on what is brought onsite by staff, contractors, sponsors and traders and by emphasis on their responsibility not to bring items that will end up as landfill.
- 'A tent is for life not just for a festival'. We want people to not just buy the cheapest tent, spend a little extra and buy yourself a tent that is going to last you a lifetime of camping experiences rather than just a festival or summer.

- All the wood used by the Festival is locally sourced and wherever possible, FSC-assured.

During:

- The festival is committed to minimising the amount of waste, and managing the on-site collection of that waste efficiently, 'reduce, reuse and recycle'. We want all Festivalgoers to think 'zero waste' and to take home what they bring onto the Festival site.
- There are teams of volunteers that contribute hugely to the sustainability of the Festival. There are 1,300 recycling volunteers.
- We're taking energy directly from the sun to the stage. We've introduced solar power and green technology to the Theatre & Circus and Shangri-La areas. All of the cafés' stalls and stages above the old railway line in the Green Fields are powered by the sun or wind; there are no diesel generators. Even the showers are solar powered.
- Hybrid Generators. This year we have hybrid generator sets that can integrate solar, wind, mains grid and battery storage.
- No plastic bags! All our Festival programmes come in 100 per cent organic unbleached cotton bags, printed with vegetable dyes. Our official *Glastonbury Festival* T-shirts are printed using water-based (non-PVC) inks and dyeing is also carried out using vegetable dyes.
- Compost loos. We have the largest number of compost toilets anywhere in the world. This year we will have over 1,200 compost toilets which, after a year, produce wonderful compost that is brought back onto the festival site and used within the permaculture field and different areas of the site.
- We only allow compostable or reusable plates and cutlery.
- Don't pee in the river.
- *Glastonbury* stainless steel water bottles. We are encouraging everyone to bring a reusable water bottle or to purchase a 100 per cent food grade stainless steel water bottle.
- We're recycling like mad. In 2014, half of all waste generated by the Festival was recycled.
- What we need to do now is start seriously reducing the volumes of waste that are created by the Festival and the only way to do this is to 'Reduce, Reuse, Recycle'.
- We're reducing road delivery. We've built two reservoirs and have an on-site wholesale market so food and water delivery will be hugely reduced.

After:

- WE LOVE TREES. Since 2000, we've planted over 10,000 native trees and hedge plants in the local environment. We've just planted an orchard of special variety apple and pear trees near the farmhouse. *Glastonbury* works hard to protect vulnerable habitats like badger sets, ponds, streams, hedges and ditches, by creating nature reserves and non-public zones.

To summarise, we could say that the strategy developed by this festival covers:

- transport;
- waste management;
- involvement of the local community;
- the use of alternative (and clean) sources of energy; and
- a contribution to the environment.

Further resources

The UK Green Film Festival – is the UK's annual environmental film festival, which takes place each year over a single week, up and down the country, the festival screens some of the very best films from around the world, exploring some of the big environmental issues of the day. *The UK Green Film Festival* has a nationwide network of film lovers and green thinkers. *The UK Green Film Festival* only takes place each year thanks to its generous support and partners. Not only do they play a key role in bringing green films to the UK, but they also contribute to raising awareness regarding environmental issues. Amongst the partners of the festival is *BWB Consulting Limited.* This company ranks high amongst the UK's leading development consultants, providing environmentally responsible engineering and environmental solutions for complex and challenging projects.

References

A Greener Festival (2015). *Love Saves the Day and Protects the Environment* [online]. Available at: www.agreenerfestival.com/2015/02/love-saves-the-day-and-protects-the-environment/ (accessed 5 May 2017).

Action Sustainability. (n.d.). Available at: www.actionsustainability.com/news/198/BS-8901-Make-your-event-sustainable/ (accessed 5 May 2017).

Booker, B. (2016). *An Introduction to the UK Event Industry in Numbers, Eventbrite* [online]. Available at: www.eventbrite.co.uk/blog/uk-event-industry-in-numbers-ds00/ (accessed 22 March 2017).

Coldwell, W. (2017). First Venice and Barcelona: Now Anti-tourism Marches Spread Across Europe [online]. Available at: www.theguardian.com (accessed 2 July 2018).

Edwards, R. (2010). Festivals like Glastonbury and Leeds need to curb their carbon emissions. *Guardian* [online]. Available at: www.theguardian.com/environment/green-living-blog/2010/may/05/festivals-glastonbury-leeds-carbon-emissions (accessed 13 November 2015).

Fletcher, M. (2012). Valuing the events industry for economic growth. *Raconteur* [online]. Available at: www.raconteur.net/business/valuing-the-events-industry-for economic-growth (accessed 22 March 2017).

Franklin, A. and Blyton, P. (2011). *Researching Sustainability: A Guide to Social Science Methods, Practice and Engagement.* Abingdon: Earthscan.

Gartner, W. C. (2000). Image. In C. Cooper and M. Hall (eds), *Contemporary Tourism: An International Approach* (pp. 223–229). London: Elsevier.

Getz, D. (2012). *Event Studies. Theory, Research and Policy for Planned Events.* Abingdon: Routledge.

Glastonbury Festival. (n.d.). Available at: www.glastonburyfestivals.co.uk/ (accessed 8 October 2017).

ISO 20121. (n.d.). Available at: www.iso20121.org/ (accessed 5 May 2017).

Jones, C. (2008). Assessing the impact of a major sporting event: the role of environmental accounting. *Tourism Economics*, 14 (2): 343–360.

Powerful Thinking (2015). The Show Must Go On: Environmental Impact Report and Vision for the UK Festival Industry [online]. Available at: www.powerful-thinking.org.uk/site/wp-content/uploads/TheShowMustGoOnReport_LR.pdf (accessed 5 May 2016).

Robertson, M., Yeoman, I., Smith, K. and McMahon-Beattie, U. (2015). Technology, society, and visioning the future of music festivals. *Event Management*, 19 (4): 567–587.

Séraphin, H., Butcher, J. and Konstanje, M. (2016). Challenging the negative images of Haiti at a pre-visit stage using Visual Online Learning Materials. *Journal of Policy Research in Tourism, Leisure and Events*, doi: 10.1080/19407963.2016.1261146.

Sloan, P., Legrand, W. and Chen, J. S. (2013). *Sustainability in the Hospitality Industry: Principle of Sustainable Operations*. Abingdon: Routledge.

Smith, S. M. (2011). The Relevance and Sustainability of Investors in People. Doctoral thesis, University of Central Lancashire. Available at: http://clok.uclan.ac.uk/2930/ (accessed 4 April 2017).

Tapper, J. (2017). As touting for punt trips becomes a crime, is tourism overwhelming Britain's cities. *Guardian* [online]. 30 July. Available at: www.theguardian.com (accessed 2 July 2018).

Velt, R., Benford, S., Reeves, S., Evans, M., Glancy, M. and Stenton, P. (2015). Towards an Extended Festival Viewing Experience. Presented at the TVX'15 ACM International Conference on Interactive Experiences for TV and Online Video, 3–5 June 2015, pp. 53–62, Brussels.

Wilson, J. (2014). *Essentials of Business Research: A Guide to Doing Your Research Project* (2nd edn). London: Sage.

7 Sharing the music

Shanti-Fest – a humanitarian festival?

Sarah Schiffling

The event organisers: Lincs2Nepal

Established in 2009, Lincs2Nepal is a charity based in Lincoln, England, which works with some of the poorest and most marginalised communities in Nepal. Main focus areas of their work are the provision of clean drinking water, which can have major health benefits for families and communities, and education, particularly for lower-caste and otherwise disadvantaged children. In particular, the Jeevan Jyoti School in Kohalpur, a municipality in Banke District in the Bheri Zone in mid-western Nepal, is being run by Lincs2Nepal. This school has become one of the best performing in the country since Lincs2Nepal's involvement started in 2013. The charity provides scholarships for many students through child sponsorships held by people in Lincoln and across the UK.

Lincs2Nepal is well known across Lincolnshire. Husband and wife team Garry and Tracey Goddard who are founders and trustees of the charity are very active in the local community. Regular talks in education institutions from primary schools to universities showcase their work in Nepal to ever-changing audiences. Furthermore, they run a vegetarian and vegan café in Lincoln's city centre, Café Shanti after the Sanskrit word for 'Peace'. The small café is colourfully located in Nepalese style and apart from being a popular haunt for locals and visitors alike, it also displays much information about the work Lincs2Nepal do, particularly the school they run. Profits serve to support the charity's work in addition to donations, child sponsorship, and extensive volunteer involvement. Organising a festival was a new and unexpected addition to the portfolio of activities for the Lincs2Nepal team in 2016.

The issue: fundraising for Nepal

At 11:41a.m. on 25 April 2015, a 7.8 magnitude earthquake struck central Nepal, with an epicentre located about 81km from the capital city Kathmandu. A second earthquake with a magnitude of 7.3 followed on 12 May 2015 (UNOCHA, 2015). The earthquakes resulted in the death of more than 8,000 people, injured an estimated 22,000, and destroyed or damaged up to one million houses, as well as many public facilities, such as hospitals and schools

(Sanderson *et al.*, 2016). The UN Resident Coordinator's Office in Nepal estimated that 2.8 million people needed immediate assistance. The Nepalese Government declared a state of emergency and requested aid from the international community. Over 450 humanitarian agencies responded to the call (UNOCHA, 2015).

A team from Lincs2Nepal was on the ground in Nepal within days, working in collaboration with local partners to reach remote rural communities that had been devastated by the earthquake. While the large humanitarian organisations had a significant presence in and around Kathmandu, remote areas received limited assistance as they were scarcely accessible and presented high risks to the responders. This is where Lincs2Nepal found their niche, delivering much needed emergency relief. Of course such efforts required significant funds beyond their normal operations.

There were significant fundraising efforts around the UK at the time. The UK public donated £87 million to the Disaster Emergency Committee Nepal appeal helping 13 of the UK's leading aid agencies to reach more than 1.6 million people with relief (Sanderson *et al.*, 2016). Lincs2Nepal is not a member of the Disaster Emergency Committee or any other umbrella organisation. Nevertheless, spending by the charity doubled following the earthquake, from £49,000 in 2014, to £110,000 by 2015. In the immediate aftermath, many donations were collected through crowd-funding online, but as media attention decreased, other avenues for fundraising had to be explored. Shanti-Fest – a three-day music and arts festival – was developed to ensure the continued financial support for Lincs-2Nepal's earthquake relief efforts.

Green Festivals

The UK music festival industry is a large and vibrant one, experiencing a steady growth in revenues over recent years, with the exception of an Olympics-related dip in 2012 (Mintel, 2016). However, there is a strong concentration of growth on a very limited circle of large festivals, such as *Glastonbury* and *Download*, and their operators, particularly Live Nation. As many customers attend only one event per year, small festivals, such as Shanti-Fest, often struggle. A key trend highlighted in industry research is that partnering with charity has the potential to create goodwill towards a festival, making it stand out in a crowded market of fairly similar offerings (Mintel, 2016). This is a valuable niche that Lincs2Nepal sought to explore with their Shanti-Fest.

Previous research has shown that the attitude of event organisers is a major determinant of the environmental credentials of a festival (Mair and Laing, 2012). This was certainly the case for Shanti-Fest. The ethos behind Lincs2-Nepal is one of social inclusion and environmental sustainability and the organisers aimed to display these same values in the festival they were organising. In common with other ethically conscious event organisers, they aimed to promote their values to a broader audience, creating an awareness of sustainability among visitors. However, there are suggestions in the literature that as festivals with a sustainability focus tend to attract visitors who are already conscious of such issues, there is only a very limited effect on behaviour (Mair and Laing, 2013).

Resources for Green Festivals

There are no definitive rules or regulations for organising a green music festival. However, several industry initiatives exist to track the environmental impact of the burgeoning festival industry and to encourage a reduction of the environmental impact. Not-for-profit 'A Greener Festival' are working with music and arts festivals around the world to encourage the adoption of environmentally efficient practices. They aim to provide information about how environmentally efficient methods are currently being employed at music and arts festivals and to provide information about how the impact of festivals on the environment can be limited at future events. In 2007 they set up the AGF award, which has already assessed over 350 festivals worldwide; it has been instrumental in helping festivals to adapt or refine their actions, improving resource efficiency and environmental impact.

Powerful Thinking is a think-do tank, which aims to provide clear guidance and resources to festival organisers about approaches to sustainable power and to drive a market for renewable energy supply at festivals, understanding and accounting for the business and cost restraints. Their *The Show Must Go On* report was conceived as a festival industry response to the Paris climate change talks in 2015. The report brings together all known UK research and analyses the most comprehensive datasets available on the environmental impact of festivals. While it states that environmental responsibility is important to festivalgoers, only 5 per cent of UK festivals are formally engaged with an environmental certification. Emissions are a major issue for festivals. The 279 UK summer music festivals included in this analysis had 20 kilotonnes of on-site CO_2 emissions, as well as 80 kilotonnes of CO_2 emissions on audience travel. Less than a third of the 23,500 tonnes of waste is recycled. Thus, priority areas for development have been identified as increasing recycling rates, offering more shared transport options, conserving energy and using reusable cups.

Case study: *Shanti-Fest*

Shanti-Fest was scheduled for three days in early July 2016, a little over 14 months after the earthquake in Nepal. Relief efforts by Lincs2Nepal were still ongoing and additional funds could be put to good use, both in the disaster response and the longer-term development projects. The organisers believed that their ethos of environmental and social sustainability should be embraced in the festival as well. It was highlighted in all of the promotional material that *Here at Shanti-Fest our sole aim is to change the lives of the less fortunate in Nepal.* To increase awareness for the projects in Nepal and to create actual benefits for the people there, Shanti-Fest was actually an international festival with stages in the United Kingdom and in Nepal set up simultaneously.

Organisers were keen to tie into the *International Year of Global Under-standing* that took place in 2016 and was an initiative to support a truly global outlook that fosters interrelationships between people in different parts of the world. Their approach to this was to organise Shanti-Fest in Lincoln and Kathmandu at the same time. Live streaming to and from both countries enabled visitors at both sites to party alongside each other. Technology was used to embrace unity and togetherness through music, even across a distance of 7,300 km.

Although Lincs2Nepal subsidised the festival in Nepal, they still had to charge a modest entry fee. However, wanting the festival to be accessible by as many people in Nepal as possible, a scheme called *Share the Music* was introduced. When guests in England purchased their tickets to Shanti-Fest, they were able to also by a ticket for someone in Nepal for an additional £2 fee. These tickets were subsequently distributed among Nepalese who would otherwise not have been able to afford entry to the festival in Kathmandu.

Another way to link the two festivals was through food. Every meal sold at Shanti-Fest in Lincoln included a margin that enabled Lincs2Nepal to buy 30 hot, nutritious meals for a child in Nepal. The organisers highlighted that many Nepalese children walk long distances to get to school every day, but their families lack the funds to give them a proper meal, which apart from having serious health consequences also has an effect on school attendance rates and educational success in the country. Feeding a child in Nepal a school meal for a whole month was sold as a direct benefit of consuming a meal at the festival. It was also highlighted that food would be purchased locally and employment was provided for local people as cooks in the school canteen, further increasing the benefits of what was in effect a donation to Lincs2Nepal.

A similar scheme was in operation for drinks. While visitors were promised regular pub prices for their drinks, they were also guaranteed that each drink purchased would contribute to Lincs2Nepal's ongoing effort to provide Nepal with clean drinking water. The direct link between their spending at the festival and the benefits for Nepalese recipients made the aid they were providing tangible and easily comprehensible for festivalgoers. The donations were not seen as additional expenditure. Instead, normal festival expenses doubled as donations that were linked to beneficiaries. The video links to Kathmandu – while the city is not the major focus of Lincs2Nepal's operations – provided a feeling of community and fostered a closer emotional connection with Nepal.

In the rural location of Scholey Park near Tattershall in Lincolnshire in the English Midlands, stages were set up to resemble Nepalese architecture or the emergency shelters built by Lincs2Nepal, straw was distributed to soak up the worst of the mud of an English summer, and vendors set up their stalls. Over 100 acts performed on five stages over the three-day festival, with musicians, artists and even circus groups in the line-up. Visitors could also enjoy a healing and body workshop area, children's workshops, private ships, a cocktail bus and a spectacular colour party celebration.

Residents had voiced some concerns about the noise levels from multiple festivals at the location, and these were faithfully reported in the local media.

However, the family-friendly nature of Shanti-Fest went some way to dissipate those fears. The organisers tried to remain true to their ethos locally, as well as internationally. One scheme to ensure this was called *Amazing People* and granted a limited number of free tickets to groups of people seen to be particularly deserving of them, namely nurses, junior doctors and firefighters. This was seen to help people who, like those behind Lincs2Nepal, devote their lives to helping others.

Seeing the many problems that music festivals and society as a whole have with a wasteful approach to resource utilisation, Shanti-Fest was aimed to be different. The organisers specifically asked people and organisations for their waste products to take them off their hands. In building the festival, they offered to recycle salvaged materials, including damaged wood, offcuts, old paints, pipes, tarps, fabrics etc. In the interests of the circular economy, items used at the festival site were then recycled as appropriate.

Further addressing the problem of inadequate recycling at festivals, Eco bonds were issued at Shanti-Fest. A compulsory £5 was charged on top of the ticket cost and visitors only got that money back if they returned a bag of litter to the organisers at the end of the festival. This was done to encourage everyone to clear up after themselves and to ensure that the rural festival site stayed beautiful. This system also made visitors support the organising team in an otherwise time- and labour-intensive clean-up operation.

Overall, the festival was a success. Patrons left enthusiastic reviews on Facebook, highlighting the friendly atmosphere and all around enjoyable time they had at Shanti-Fest. Funds were raised for the projects in Nepal, all while maintaining high ethical and environmental standards. Nevertheless, the festival has remained a one-off event, although originally envisioned to become a yearly occurrence. To some degree that might be attributable to the singularly large need for additional income in the aftermath of the 2015 earthquake. However, the much more pertinent reason, according to the organisers, was the extraordinary amount of work needed to put on a festival. While it was done in the spirit of the regular work of Lincs2Nepal, it still required a whole different skill set and ultimately, an event of that size was seen to detract effort from the actual cause. However, the Lincs2Nepal team have since put on smaller events in the local community that also contribute to their fundraising efforts while having a more manageable workload.

Festivals with environmental and ethical ambitions

Shanti-Fest is one of many festivals that embraces environmental and ethical aspects. As large gatherings of people, often in rural locations where much of the necessary infrastructure needs to be specifically developed for the festival, environmental issues are of considerable importance for festivals. Furthermore, the power of bringing like-minded people together for a certain cause and the potential for raising both awareness and cause, have been used by diverse festival organisers.

The most famous example of fund-raising for an ethical cause through a music festival is Live Aid. The dual-venue concert in London, England, and Philadelphia, Pennsylvania, was organised by Bob Geldof and Midge Ure in July 1985 to raise money for the famine in Ethiopia. Building on the success of the charity single *Do they know it's Christmas?* the year before, the organisers created an event that would write music history. While some see Live Aid as the biggest mega event in rock's history, demonstrating rock's compassionate spirit to a worldwide audience, others have a more critical view calling it nothing more than a glamorous charity gambit (Ullestad, 1987).

Debate of Live Aid has been highly polarised. Many praise the magnitude of this global charity event, which united many of the greatest names in music at the time for a common purpose. However, other voices see Live Aid as a sign of the commercialisation of music, regarding it as nothing more than a self-aggrandising celebration of elite musicians. Various statements and rumours seem to support this, with Queen reportedly unwilling to perform at first because they did not want to make a political statement, but ultimately agreeing because they saw Live Aid as a unique opportunity to outperform all the competition at once. Others still, see not only the aid, but also the music and the musicians at Live Aid as secondary to the main purpose of creating a media spectacle of unri-valled dimensions (Ullestad, 1987).

The very notion of charity that was embodied by Live Aid has been criticised as being a post-colonial idea that privileged Brits are feeding the world (Davis, 2010). Live Aid and the underlying charity Band Aid, which united many of the music industry's leading voices at the time, also provided the media something to focus on. Something much more aesthetically pleasing and appealing to the public than images of starving people or even worse, the political intricacies that had resulted in and now exacerbated their situation. For better or worse, Live Aid became the pinnacle of the 1984–1985 famine relief effort, raising an estim-ated US$70 million over the course of a weekend (Shuker, 2001). Much more far-reaching, according to the critics, were the positive effects on the host cities' economy and tourism industry, and the individual artists' profiles (Davis, 2010).

Despite the criticism, large-scale concerts remain a popular way of galvanis-ing public support for a cause and encouraging the public to donate. A recent example is the One Love Manchester concert, which took place at Old Trafford Cricket Ground on 4 June 2017. The concert was created by Ariana Grande in response to the 22 May bombing after her concert in Manchester, which killed 22 people and injured many more. One Love Manchester was attended by more than 50,000 people, over three times as many as the original Ariana Grande concert. Fundraising for the victims was considerable. The We Love Manchester Emergency Fund, administered by the British Red Cross, received £2.35 million in donations during the three-hour concert, bringing the total to more than £10 million.

Organised within just two weeks, One Love Manchester managed to field an impressive bill of diverse artists, with many reported to drop plans to perform elsewhere to be present at the event. The immediacy of the event added to its appeal, with a strong sense of place further contributing to a unique event that captured the emotions of many. With the London Bridge terror attack taking place barely 24 hours earlier, some had questioned the timing of the event, but after a flawlessly executed and often uniquely moving event, media commentators largely praised it (Parkinson, 2017). One Love Manchester had demonstrated the ability of music to unite people, to generate a feeling of community and continuity in the face of adversity, but also the ability of a music event to raise considerable funds for a cause, much like Live Aid more than 30 years earlier. However, this concert was executed with a much stronger link to the fundraising campaign it was supporting, with many of the attendees of the attacked concert in attendance. Media coverage of the concert fitted in with and prolonged the attention given to the attack, particularly in the wake of yet another terror attack in London that weekend, rather than detracting attention in the way that Live Aid has been accused of in relation to the Ethiopia famine.

Considerations for greening music festivals are also prevalent across much of the industry, as evidenced by bodies such as the not-for-profit A Greener Festival that aids festivals around the world in adopting environmentally efficient practices. Such practices can be found in many prominent industry examples. In the UK, *Glastonbury*, with its rural location, is often highlighted as a champion of green music festival operations, but other examples exist globally.

The Wacken Open Air, the world's largest heavy metal festival takes place every summer in the small village of Wacken in northern Germany. Growing from humble roots to more than 80,000 visitors per year, the festival soon outgrew the infrastructure of its rural location. Intense efforts in recent years have concentrated on limiting the impact on the environment. In 2017, a four-mile beer pipeline was installed in an effort to make the event more eco-friendly by eliminating the need for road transport. On average, each visitor is estimated to consume about nine pints of beer during the three-day festival, making the beer pipeline a worthwhile investment for the organisers. Attracting significantly less media attention, a system of water pipes was also installed at the same time. The benefit for the environment is much the same, as heavy trucks do not need to churn up the fields every day and road congestion is eased, with less emissions expected as a result.

The Wacken organisers have a long track record of trying to limit the environmental impact of the festival. As early as 2009, their vehicles were running exclusively on bio-ethanol fuel. There are far-reaching initiatives to avoid, gather, and recycle the rubbish created by the vast crowds. In 2011, the Wacken Open Air received Yourope's Green'n'Clean Award. This initiative guarantees that measures in the fields of sustainable management, transportation, waste management, energy efficiency and power, catering as well as purchasing are implemented. Furthermore, communicating the need to be responsible to sponsors and audiences is a key element of Wacken's efforts to protect natural resources.

They seem to have spread their message well. The official festival organisers are not the only ones propagating a greener event. The non-profit Wacken

Foundation, which is independent of the Wacken Open Air, conducts several activities with the aim of supporting emerging heavy metal musicians. These include an annual collection of plastic bottles and cans at the festival. Volunteers collect the recyclables from the revellers and return them to recycling stations, collecting the proceeds from the German 'Flaschenpfand' (bottle deposit) system that yields up to €0.25 per bottle that is returned into the extensive recycling system.

While the ethical credentials of music events can be in doubt as they are often complemented, or potentially even overshadowed, by the workings of a highly competitive industry, there are many efforts to make music festivals more environmentally friendly. Various working groups and awards exist and many festival organisers are keen to communicate their efforts for a greener festival, recognising their significant impact on natural resources, as well as on educating the public on environmental matters.

Further resources

A Greener Festival (www.agreenerfestival.com) is a not-for-profit company committed to helping music and arts events and festivals around the world adopt environmentally efficient practices.

Julie's Bicycle (www.juliesbicycle.com) is a London-based charity that supports the creative community to act on climate change and environmental sustainability. Julie's Bicycle believe that the creative community is uniquely placed to transform the conversation around climate change and translate it into action.

Powerful Thinking (www.powerful-thinking.org.uk) is a think-do tank which brings together festivals, suppliers and environmental organisations to explore ways to reduce the costs and carbon through increased efficiency and alternatives, and share findings to promote a lower carbon industry.

Yourope (www.yourope.org) is an important Association of European Festivals including dedicated groups dealing with health and safety (YES Group), green operations (GO Group) and marketing and communication (EMAC Group).

References

Davis, H. L. (2010). Feeding the world a line? Celebrity activism and ethical consumer practices from Live Aid to Product Red. *Nordic Journal of English Studies*, 9 (3): 89–118.

Mair, J. and Laing, J. (2012). The greening of music festivals: motivations, barriers and outcomes. Applying the Mair and Jago model. *Journal of Sustainable Tourism*, 20 (5): 683–700.

Mair, J. and Laing, J. H. (2013). Encouraging pro-environmental behaviour: the role of sustainability-focused events. *Journal of Sustainable Tourism*, 21 (8): 1113–1128.

MINTEL. (2016). *Music Concerts and Festivals (UK)*. London: Mintel Group Limited.

Parkinson, H. J. (2017). One Love Manchester: pop's healing power rises from the dregs of depravity. *Guardian*. 5 June.

Sanderson, D., Rodericks, A., Shresta, N. and Ramalingam, B. (2016). Nepal earthquake appeal response review. DEC/HC. Available at: www.dec.org.uk/article/nepal-earthquake-appeal-response-review-0 (accessed 21 June 2017).

Shuker, R. (2001). *Understanding Popular Music* (2nd edn). New York: Routledge.

Ullestad, N. (1987). Rock and rebellion: subversive effects of Live Aid and 'Sun City'. *Popular Music*, 6 (1): pp. 67–76.

UNOCHA (2015). Nepal Earthquake Humanitarian Response April to September 2015. United Nations Office for the Coordination of Humanitarian Affairs. Available at: http://reliefweb.int/sites/reliefweb.int/files/resources/nepal_earthquake_humanitarian_response_report_lr.pdf (accessed 21 June 2017).

8 Green strategic trends in the Romanian music festival industry

Ovidiu I. Moisescu, Monica M. Coroş,
Oana A. Gică and Anca C. Yallop

National context

Before 1990, communist Romania was an unappealing tourism destination for various reasons, such as the lack of ease of movement, security issues, lack of economic development and poor infrastructure. After the fall of communism, Romania embarked on a process that sought to improve its negative image, a process that involved the development of a new tourism product, one that was more suitable for Romania's post-socialist image (Coroş *et al.*, 2017).

The country's rebranding was built around its unique rural heritage and traditions (Mitrache *et al.*, 1996), as well as on its pre-socialist past, which survived the socialism era (Light, 2001). In line with this rebranding strategy, cultural festivals were encouraged and fostered as an alternative form of tourism due to their power to attract tourists and their positive economic impact and contribution to the preservation and promotion of Romania's cultural identity. In the last decade, as part of their development strategies, several Romanian cities and regions have organised various types of festivals focused on music, theatre, film, art, food or traditions, resulting in a significant growth of such events. During the last years, a number of these festivals have gained an international reputation – such an example is the *Electric Castle* (EC) music festival, the case study discussed in this chapter.

From a social and environmental perspective, *Electric Castle* is one of the largest and most successful of the Romanian music festivals, which proves itself greener than many of its competitors in Romania. Amongst the greenest festivals in Europe, EC was recently shortlisted for the *Green Operations Award* (one of the most significant awards for green programmes in the music industry). Initiated in 2013, EC is an international music festival that takes place every year in July, on the spectacular domain of the renaissance *Bánffy Castle* of *Bonţida*, a village located 30 km near Cluj-Napoca, the largest city of Transylvania, Romania. The festival offers participants a unique experience, combining various genres of music (rock, indie, hip-hop, electronic, reggae, etc.) with high-tech and alternative arts. Food services and on-site accommodation consisting mostly of camping facilities are also provided to festival attendees by the festival's organisers.

Established in 1070 along the Someş River, *Bonţida* is a rural locality (commune) consisting of four villages and with a population of nearly 5,000 inhabitants. The territory is low, with fertile soils that are exploited in agriculture. In 2017, the commune was granted the title of *Cultural Village of Romania*. Yet, similar to other Romanian rural areas, one of the commune's most important challenges relates to its infrastructure, roads and public transport in particular.

The *Bánffy Castle* (also known as the *Transylvanian Versailles*) represents the most important and valuable cultural attraction of the commune. A noble family of Transylvania built the castle between 1437 and 1543 – since then, the castle has undergone various renovations, its architecture including baroque, neoclassic, neogothic and romantic elements. In 2000, a decade after the fall of communism in Romania, given the poor state of the castle, *Transylvania Trust*, a local Romanian NGO, managed to include the castle's site on the list of *One Hundred Most Endangered Sites* of the World Monuments Fund as 'Site No 69'. In 2009, the NGO initiated the castle's rehabilitation process after signing a 49 years' concession contract with the Romanian state.

Priority issues and strategic trends in Green Events

Nowadays, events are viewed as one of the 'fastest growing forms of leisure, business, and tourism-related phenomena' (Getz, 1997: 1). Consequently, an increased emphasis on achieving sustainability in event management is prominent in this industry. Like other sectors of our society, events need to embrace sustainability by taking into account the triple bottom line elements: planet, people and profit (Henderson, 2011). Festivals' potential for generating a negative impact on the surrounding economic and social environment – albeit unintentionally – is substantial, especially with respect to contemporary music mega-festivals (Mair and Laing, 2012). The negative impact of such events on the environment is a consequence of the large number of participants and the local communities' capacity to provide the appropriate infrastructure (Gibson and Wong, 2011). Such negative examples might include excessive waste, litter, high water usage, noise, rowdy and delinquent behaviour, excessive drinking, traffic congestion, parking problems, disruption of the normal way of life, overcrowding, high expenditure on events management rather than community needs and increased cost of living (Fredline *et al.*, 2003).

As a result of all these negative effects, event organisers are now looking for solutions to improve the event's social and environmental impact on local communities, even when existing national or local regulations do not necessarily constrain them to do so. Thus, festival organisers are becoming more responsive to the needs of the host communities, offering volunteer and employment opportunities, engaging communities with the arts (Mair, 2014), and greening their events, especially in the case of large outdoor music festivals (Mair and Laing, 2012). By promoting recycling, waste minimisation, greener forms of transport (such as public transport or cycling), and the use of sustainable materials and services, festivals send a green educational message (Gibson and Wong, 2011). Moreover, recent studies (Wong *et al.*, 2015) have shown that there is a strong relationship between festivals' green involvement and their perceived value, attendees being willing to pay price premiums for festivals or festival-related products if they are perceived as green.

Romanian legislation for sustainable development

As a European Union (EU) member state, Romania's policies regarding sustainable development and environmental protection are subject to European directives, which are set in agreement with the strategic guidelines of the EU. The Romanian government has integrated these directives into its own sustainable development strategies and policies (Government of Romania, 2008, 2013, 2017). For example, such directives and policies relate to increasing the reuse and recycling of waste materials (European Environment Agency, 2009); rationalising the use of conventional private cars in urban areas and promoting a more efficient and cleaner public transport (European Commission, 2001); and encouraging cities to adopt sustainable urban mobility plans that address public transport or cycling as environmentally friendly transport modes (European Commission, 2013). Moreover, the national sustainable development strategy of Romania, as well as the development strategies of several Romanian counties and cities, set a number of strategic objectives in the events arena too. These strategic objectives regarding contemporary creation and cultural diversity, include providing support to projects for performing arts in areas where there are no permanent artistic establishments, as well as support in organising festivals at national, regional and local levels.

Case study: *Electric Castle* (EC)

The *Electric Castle* festival was launched in 2013. The festival had 32,000 attendees in 2013, a number that grew significantly to 174,000 attendees at its latest (5th) production in 2017 (see Table 8.1). The event, which takes place in a spectacular Transylvanian location, the Bánffy Castle of Bonțida, has attracted a large number of participants from outside Transylvania, including attendees

Table 8.1 Electric Castle festival data

	1st edition 2013	2nd edition 2014	3rd edition 2015	4th edition 2016	5th edition 2017
No. of participants	32,000	79,000	97,000	121,000	174,000
No. of artists	92	142	230	250	270
Duration	3 days	4 days	4 days	5 days	5 days

Source: *Electric Castle* (2017) 5th Edition Festival Follow-Up Report.

from abroad (for example in 2017, 35 per cent of participants came from Bucharest, the capital of Romania, while 10 per cent came from abroad, mostly from the UK, Hungary, France and Germany). Recent market research studies conducted by the organisers revealed that EC participants were mostly young graduates, 19 to 29 years old, employed in medium to highly paid jobs, coming from urban areas, and from highly educated families with family incomes above the average.

Following its success, every year since its launch, EC has been nominated for the *Best Medium-Sized Festival* category of the *European Festival Awards*. In 2017, the event was awarded the *Best Festival Camping Award* at the *European Festileaks Awards*. The EC festival was also a finalist at the *FestX Awards*, in the *Best Use of Technology at a Festival* category. Due to its green policy, involvement and innovativeness, the festival won the runner-up position in the *Star Festival in Europe* category at the *EE Music Awards* in 2015, being shortlisted twice (in 2016 and 2017) for the *Green Operations Award*, amongst the greenest festivals in Europe.

The awards received attest the international recognition of the innovative and green event strategies developed and implemented by the EC festival's organisers. Since its first production, EC contributed significantly to the restoration of the Bánffy Castle of Bonţida and its surrounding domain, which were all in a poor state before the 2010s. Thus, the rent paid each year by the organisers to the *Transylvania Trust* (the NGO that has the castle in concession) for using the venue was allocated to the restoration of the castle. Moreover, for the last two

Figure 8.1 The 2017 edition of EC.

Figure 8.2 The 2017 edition of EC.
Source: photo courtesy of *Electric Castle*.

Figure 8.3 Bánffy Castle of Bonţida during the 2017 edition of EC (outside).
Source: photo courtesy of *Electric Castle*.

Figure 8.4 Bánffy Castle of Bonţida during the 2017 edition of EC (inside).
Source: photo courtesy of *Electric Castle*.

occasions, the organisers also provided participants with the necessary means and incentives to make donations for the restoration process. As a result, in 2017 the Bánffy Castle was finally able to open its doors to the public during the festival, hosting an array of exhibitions and interactive art.

In addition to the castle's rehabilitation, EC contributed to the revitalisation of the domain surrounding the castle, as well as of other areas of Bonţida, which were in a poor state prior to becoming parts of the EC's venue. The organisers spent significant resources to extend and improve the local rural road infrastructure, and for the landscape and design of the green areas surrounding the castle. The organisers have also cleaned up and transformed a local area, which had previously become an improvised garbage dump for the villagers, into a green relaxation zone and a beach-like special festival area. All these initiatives generated further new permanent jobs for the villagers, jobs needed to maintain the festival venue and other amenities during the year.

As in the case of many other outdoor music festivals, EC has a high potential of overloading and exhausting the local infrastructure of its venue, the daily number of the event's attendees being seven times higher than the local population in 2017. Acknowledging the festival's potential negative impact on the local community due to the large amount of waste generated during the event and the extra road traffic caused by the participants coming to a remote festival location, EC organisers designed and implemented a set of long-term green strategies.

Figure 8.5 Bonțida village during the 2017 edition of EC (day).
Source: photo courtesy of *Electric Castle*.

Figure 8.6 Bonțida village during the 2017 edition of EC (night).
Source: photo courtesy of *Electric Castle*.

Thus, starting from the second occasion of the event in 2014, an 'Eco Programme' was designed and implemented. In its first year of implementation, the programme involved a series of fun contests and gamified activities, generically entitled 'Eco Games'. These games were designed to motivate the participants to be greener and more responsible, to take care of the castle and its surroundings, and to educate themselves about the effects of greenhouse-gas, or inappropriate waste disposal. The 'Eco Games' have since been consistently used at every occasion of the festival, with the aim to positively change participants' attitudes and behaviours towards recycling, selective waste collection, reduced water consumption, and even challenging them to produce alternative energy through pedalling on bicycle installations – the 66 kW of energy produced in this way supplied 75 per cent of the electricity needed for the festival's ECO Charging Point (i.e. an area where attendees were able to participate in the ECO Games) and for charging 325 mobile phones (MAINOI, 2016, 2017).

In 2015, a new component of the 'Eco Programme' was introduced: the 'Eco Ambassadors'. Through this project, organisers encouraged the use of alternative means of transportation for long distances. Thus, bike-riders who pedalled more than 250 km for sustainability-related causes of their choice were rewarded with free full passes, free camping and other awards (e.g. in 2017, the 'Eco Ambassadors' campaign gathered 27 cyclists, coming from various regions of Romania, who pedalled a total of 10,000 km on their bikes to reach the festival) (MAINOI, 2017).

For the fifth production of EC (2017), a 'Zero Waste' campaign was kicked-off as a third component of the 'Eco Programme', with a long-term goal to reduce, reuse and recycle all the waste generated at the festival. Specialised staff ('eco promoters') and differentiated bins to collect waste selectively were placed all over the festival area, while rewarding participants who disposed waste properly. As a result, in 2017 the organisers recycled 39 tons of plastic, aluminium, cardboard, glass and other materials, representing two-thirds of the entire waste produced at the festival. The 'Zero Waste' campaign also involved hiring 120 local staff dedicated to recycling, as well as investing in appropriate installations (recycling stations, waste collection points, compactors, press-containers, etc.).

In order to minimise the negative impact of the air pollution and road traffic caused by the participants coming to a remote festival location, EC organisers identified a secondary road to be used as a main access route, and provided several shuttle buses for participants travelling 30–40 km away from the festival location. It was estimated that in 2017, out of the approximately 35,000 participants entering the festival's gates daily, about 23,000 were not accommodated on-site and needed daily transportation to and from the festival location. However, the 60 shuttle buses employed during the 2017 event managed to provide transportation for about 6,000 participants daily. Furthermore, a special agreement signed with the Romanian National Railways offered a temporary train station, which allowed trains to stop near the event's venue, even though the regular train schedule did not cater for such stops.

In addition to the above long-term green strategies, every year EC was also involved in various social responsibility projects. A relevant 2017 project – 'The Weather Policy' – involved EC's partnership with NN Group, an international insurance company, and consisted of 'signing' a special weather insurance policy that would provide electricity to family homes from remote areas of Romania. Fans were encouraged to post online their weather forecasts during the festival, to donate directly to the cause or to purchase festival merchandise, which would further generate donations to the cause. As a result of the campaign, 26 families received photo-voltaic installations that provided electricity to their homes for the very first time.

Another relevant social responsibility project of 2017 involved EC's partnership with Lidl, the global discount supermarket chain. The Lidl Market shop built especially for EC 2017 was transformed after the event into a state of the art sports facility that benefited the local school, which has also received new classroom furniture. Overall, Lidl invested €70,000 in the renovation and modernisation of the village's school for primary and secondary education.

Last, but not least, worth mentioning is the significant contribution that EC brings to the local economic development of *Bonţida*. Thus, besides the temporary jobs created during the festival and the permanent jobs created for maintaining the festival venue and amenities during the year, EC significantly contributes to the local budget through the taxes paid for each sold ticket. By providing accommodation to festival participants, villagers can also supplement their income streams. In 2017, EC organisers estimated that villagers accommodated about 2,000 people for the 5 days' duration of the festival at an average price of €18 per night, which means a total earning of almost €150,000 for the villagers. Moreover, for future editions of EC, organisers intend to provide opportunities to local producers to promote and sell their produce and traditional products and artefacts during the festival.

Other relevant green events in Romania

National and local government strategies in Romania generally encourage the organisation of cultural festivals. Such events are considered an effective and lucrative way of attracting tourists, while also having a positive impact on the image of the host region and community, as well as on its inhabitants' quality of life.

In line with current attitude trends perceived amongst EU citizens, a significant number of Romanians also became, especially during the last decade, more socially and environmentally conscious, as well as more interested in green events. Inherently, new green cultural events became popular in Romania, such as *FânFest, Music Outdoor eXperience (MOX)* and *Smida Jazz Festival*. *FânFest* is a multi-art activist festival (music, exhibitions, theatre, dance, workshops, debates, etc.) that has taken place almost every year since 2004 in the village of *Roşia Montana*. Initially, the event started as an initiative to stop an international corporation from developing a non-sustainable gold mine operation in the area, and continued as a tool to support and emphasise the potential tourism-based sustainable development of the village and surrounding areas.

The *Music Outdoor eXperience (MOX)* festival is another green cultural event, taking place every year since 2012 in various picturesque and spectacular Romanian mountain rural areas such as *Măguri-Răcătău* (2012, 2013 and 2014), *Buscat* (2015) or *Valea Drăganului* (2016 and 2017), gathering thousands of participants each year. Although MOX festival's core product offer is focused on electronic music, the event is primarily aimed at promoting traditional music, dance, products and crafts, as well as green forms of tourism such as those based on self-accommodation (such as camping) and hiking. The festival also helps relatively isolated local communities to become more popular as tourism destinations and to further benefit from a sustainable income from attracting visitors.

Smida Jazz Festival represents the newest green music event, which was launched in 2016 and is held annually. Similar to MOX, the festival has an overall sustainability goal, although the core motivation of the event is the gathering of jazz music fans and artists. Thus, the festival's mission includes promoting local traditions and traditional products and crafts, and supporting the local mountain community of *Smida* and its surroundings in becoming a viable green tourism destination.

In addition to all these newly launched green cultural events, the Romanians' increased interest in socially and environmentally friendly events had a significant positive impact on existing green cultural events, which developed at a more rapid pace and became more popular. A good example in this case is the *Sighişoara Medieval Festival*, a yearly medieval art event (theatre, music, dance, crafts) aimed at promoting the citadel of *Sighişoara*'s cultural heritage, in a sustainable and green manner. The festival was launched in 1992 and has developed into one of the largest in Romania, attended by tens of thousands of visitors each year. Other cultural events taking place in Romania have been influenced by the public's mindset and the shifting trend towards green events. For example, the *Transylvania International Film Festival (TIFF)* in Cluj-Napoca, introduced in 2002, started to recently use the *Bánffy Castle* of *Bonţida* as the event's location, joining efforts in the restoration of the castle with the *Electric Castle* festival. In recent years, TIFF became more involved in socially responsible projects such as creating special entertainment events for children from disadvantaged families during the festival and creating an educational platform for children.

A similar environmental input can be seen in the case of the annual *Untold Festival*, taking place in Cluj-Napoca since 2015, which is currently the largest electronic music festival held in Romania and it has built a strong international reputation in the music festival industry. Although often criticised because of the festival's negative impact (such as the location of the festival in the city centre, and the discomfort created to locals due to noise levels), the organisers have sought to minimise the noise pollution and to implement efficient waste management procedures during the event, whilst also implementing socially responsible projects each year. For example, in an effort to support the local health authorities, a blood donation campaign was initiated with donors receiving free full passes for a certain amount of blood donated.

Successful partnerships with local NGOs

As a general trend, Romanian festival organisers tend to involve and to seek support from local and, usually, small-sized NGOs in order to put into practice innovative green initiatives. *Electric Castle*, for example, has partnered with MAINOI, a local NGO, in order to implement its 'Eco Programme', and with 'Free Mioriţa', another local NGO, for implementing the 'Weather Policy' social project. *FânFest*, the multi-art activist festival, collaborated for most of their actions with Alburnus Maior Roşia Montana and other Romanian NGOs specialised in promoting green development of rural areas and fighting non-sustainable industries, such as certain types of mining or logging. In addition, in order to organise the *Smida Jazz Festival* and to implement its green initiatives, the event's initiators created a dedicated NGO (Transylvanian Cultural Development).

The Romanian cultural festivals organisers' choice for local small-sized NGOs represents a trend in the Romanian music festival industry. This trend is mainly due to NGO partners' capacity as local organisations to understand the local context in more depth, its limitations and demands. Furthermore, due to their local nature and small size, NGO event partners typically dedicate themselves exclusively to certain events. Thus, they become both more dependent and more dependable, gaining an extremely high motivation in contributing to their associated events' long-term success.

Acknowledgement

We thank Mr Andi Vanca, Head of Communications – *Electric Castle Festival*, for providing useful insights and perspectives, as well as detailed information regarding the case study presented in this chapter.

References

Coroş, M. M., Gică, O. A., Yallop, A. C. and Moisescu, O. I. (2017). Innovative and sustainable tourism strategies: a viable alternative for Romania's economic development. *Worldwide Hospitality and Tourism Themes*, 9 (5): 504–515.

Electric Castle. (2017). *5th Edition Festival Follow-Up Report*.

European Commission. (2001). Green paper. Towards a European strategy for the security of energy supply. Available at: http://iet.jrc.ec.europa.eu/remea/sites/remea/files/green_paper_energy_supply_en.pdf (accessed 2 July 2018).

European Commission. (2013). A concept for sustainable urban mobility plans. Available at: https://ec.europa.eu/transport/sites/transport/files/themes/urban/doc/ump/com%282013%29913-annex_en.pdf (accessed 2 July 2018).

European Environment Agency. (2009). Diverting waste from landfill. Effectiveness of waste-management policies in the European Union. Available at: www.eea.europa.eu/publications/diverting-waste-from-landfill-effectiveness-of-waste-management-policies-in-the-european-union/at_download/file (accessed 2 July 2018).

Fredline, L., Jago, L. and Deery, M. (2003). The development of a generic scale to measure the social impacts of events. *Event Management. An International Journal*, 8 (1): 23–37.

Getz, D. (1997). *Event Management and Event Tourism*. New York: Cognizant Communication Corp.

Gibson, C. and Wong, C. (2011). Greening rural festivals: ecology, sustainability and human-nature relations. In C. Gibson and J. Connell (eds), *Festival Places – Revitalising Rural Australia*. Bristol: Channel View.

Government of Romania. (2008). *Strategia națională pentru dezvoltare durabilă 2013–2020–2030*. Available at: www.mmediu.ro/beta/wp-content/uploads/2012/06/2012-06-12_dezvoltare_durabila_snddfinalromana2008.pdf (accessed 2 July 2018).

Government of Romania. (2013). *Strategia națională pentru siguranță rutieră 2013–2020*. Available at: www.mmediu.ro/app/webroot/uploads/files/2015-07-28_Strategie_Siguranta_Rutiera_2015.pdf (accessed 2 July 2018).

Government of Romania. (2017). *Planul național de gestionare a deșeurilor*. Available at: www.mmediu.ro/app/webroot/uploads/files/2018-01-10_MO_11_bis.pdf (accessed 2 July 2018).

Henderson, S. (2011). The development of competitive advantage through sustainable event management. *Worldwide Hospitality and Tourism Themes*, 3 (3): 245–257.

Light, D. (2001). Facing the future: tourism and identity building in post-socialist Romania, *Political Geography*, 20 (1): 1053–1074.

MAINOI. (2016). *Electric Castle 4th Edition Project Report*. Available at: http://mainoi.ro/project/eco-electric-castle-zero-carbon-footprint/ (accessed 2 July 2018).

MAINOI. (2017). *The Journey of an Eco Festival. Electric Castle 5th Edition Project Report*. Available at: http://mainoi.ro/wp-content/uploads/Raport-ECO-Festival-2017.pdf (accessed 2 July 2018).

Mair, J. (2014). Greening of events. In T. De Lacy, M. Jiang, G. Lipman and S. Vorster (eds), *Green Growth and Travelism: Concept, Policy, and Practice for Sustainable Tourism*. Abingdon: Routledge.

Mair, J. and Laing, J. (2012). The greening of music festivals: motivations, barriers and outcomes. Applying the Mair and Jago model. *Journal of Sustainable Tourism*, 20 (5): 683–700.

Mitrache, S., Manole, V., Stijan, M., Bran, F. and Istrate, I. (1996), *Agroturism și turism rural*. București: Fax Press.

Wong, I. A., Wan, Y. K. P. and Qi, S. (2015). Green events, value perceptions, and the role of consumer involvement in festival design and performance. *Journal of Sustainable Tourism*, 23 (2): 294–315.

Part III

Sustainability and special interest tourism

9 Leeuwarden cultural capital 2018

Building a sustainable event

Marisa P. de Brito and Elena Cavagnaro

European Cities of Culture

Each year, for the past 30 years, one or more cities in Europe has been awarded the title of European Capital of Culture (ECC). This event was created in 1985 to celebrate the richness and diversity of cultures in Europe, and to stimulate the sense of belonging to Europe. Indirectly it is also a stimulus to boost new energy into a city's culture and to raise its international profile. In 2018, two cities will host the title: Leeuwarden in the Netherlands and Valetta in Malta. In this chapter, the main case study is about Leeuwarden, and how it is integrating sustainability in the preparations towards the delivery of a responsible 2018 European Cultural Capital Event, in order to leave a legacy to the city, the region and future European Capitals of Culture.

The main objective of European Capitals of Culture is to promote the diversity of cultures in Europe. Additional objectives include collaboration across borders, boosting the capacity of the cultural sector, and leveraging the profile of the city internationally (see Cavagnaro *et al.*, 2016). Thus it does have a strong social dimension: to broaden the accessibility to culture by European citizens. Leeuwarden was selected to be European Capital of Culture in 2018 and in its Bid Book showed the resolution to deliver a sustainable event. This is exemplary since the guidelines from the European Commission to assess success of the event do not prescribe per se a holistic sustainability approach and, as Koefoed (2013) emphasises, more research is needed around the relationship of ECCs and sustainability. The choice of Leeuwarden is probably the result of the global movement of sustainability in events, which has both a strong presence in Europe and in the Netherlands in particular, as discussed below.

Case study: Leeuwarden-Fryslân – socio-economic and environmental challenges

Leeuwarden is the capital of the province of Frisia, one of the three Northern Provinces of the Netherlands. Frisia faces several socio-economic and environmental challenges, including an ageing population, weaker economic growth than the central area of the Netherlands and threatened bio-diversity. To quote some figures, the population of Frisia is expected to shrink on average by 6.5 per cent in 2025 compared to 2016. This loss comes at the expense of small cities in the countryside, as the capital city is still expected to grow. A similar trend is visible when looking at economic data. For example, in 2015 Frisia still registered a decrease in jobs of 0.3 per cent compared to a year earlier, while the Netherlands overall registered an increase of 0.5 per cent.

In 2016, the trend became positive in Frisia, with a 0.8 per cent increase compared to 2015. However, this increase was mostly concentrated in the major city centres, including Leeuwarden, thus enhancing the attractiveness of the bigger cities compared to the ones in the countryside (Province of Fryslân, 2016). The fragility of the ecological situation can be appreciated by considering the sharp decline in meadow birds. In line with a negative European trend attributed to modern farming techniques (European Commission, 2012), in 20 years the breeding population of two of the most iconic Frisian meadows birds, the black tailed godwit and lapwings, decreased by 60 per cent and 40 per cent, respectively, compared with 1996 levels (Postma, 2016).

Sustainability trends in events

The Director of the MCI consultants group has recently outlined the top-ten sustainable trends for events in 2020 (Bigwood, 2016). Comparing to what had been theoretically anticipated in the academic literature (Getz, 2009), sustainability trends can be distinguished at three different levels: network (macro); supply chain (meso) and the level of the event (micro), as explained below.

At macro level: an increase in stakeholder pressure from corporate sponsors, local communities, volunteers, and city or regional authorities, who more carefully select events based on the potential socio-economic and environmental value.

At meso level: partnerships for sustainable procurement and for leveraging the business case for sustainable brands, where one expects an increase in modular design, bio-materials, and cradle-to-cradle management.

At micro level: prioritising transparency and ethics, welcoming third-party certification, and bringing about holistic sustainability programmes, leading to phasing-out single-use products with sustainable menus and materials being the norm.

Notwithstanding this positive trend, sustainability remains challenging. In the Netherlands this has led to innovative forms of collaboration among festivals (Van der Voort and De Brito, 2017) such as *Green Events* and *Innofest* as discussed later in this chapter.

In addition, there are universal socio-technological trends (see Calvo-Soraluze *et al.*, 2016) regarding digitalisation of supply and demand of products, services and information. They offer many opportunities to exploit data analytics, to co-create a sustainable event with the audience, personalise green experiences and tailor for environmentally conscious niches. Festivals such as *Roskilde* in Denmark and *Boom* in Portugal have been already experimenting with this by programming educational and fun activities around sustainability. Not surprisingly, those events have several times been awarded for their high level of commitment to sustainability.

The Dutch context: government policies

With more than 700 major festivals organised annually, the Event and Festivals sector is a large sector in the Netherlands. Though events have to abide by Dutch national law on matters such as alcohol and (temporary) employment, the task to specifically regulate festivals is left to the city or region in which a festival takes place.

While sustainability has gained increasing attention, the Netherlands is still lagging behind in addressing some sustainability challenges. Consider, for example, that only 5.5 per cent of the energy consumed in the Netherlands is produced by renewable sources – the lowest percentages in Europe bar two.

To stimulate sustainability, the Dutch Government has chosen to sign non-binding agreements with specific economic sectors, including Events and Festivals. In this context in 2014 'Green Events Nederland' was created as a platform where knowledge can be gathered and shared. 'Green Events Nederland' has signed a non-binding agreement (a so-called green deal) with the Dutch Ministry for Infrastructure and Environment, aimed at reducing waste at festivals. Several major Dutch festivals have co-signed this Green Deal.

Another interesting, bottom-up initiative is *Innofest* – a platform uniting the major festivals from the north of the Netherlands, universities and innovative businesses. *Innofest* sees festivals as living labs where sustainable innovations can be tested before their introduction into the 'real' world. *Innofest* was launched in January 2015, has now partnered with Green Events and is intended to fulfil a major role in supporting sustainable innovation during Leeuwarden-Fryslân ECC 2018.

Leeuwarden-Fryslân ECC 2018, the Netherlands

The socio-economic and ecological challenges may set Frisia apart from other Dutch provinces, yet they are not unique to Frisia. In fact several European regions are confronted with similar challenges. The ambition of Frisia as European Capital of Culture for 2018 is an attempt to show how a large-scale cultural intervention can fuel innovative approaches to deal with these challenges.

In retrospect, it may be said that Frisia had begun to more fully appreciate the opportunities presented by cultural awareness, in fuelling both socio-economic development and appreciation of a healthy natural environment, in the 1980s when the *Oerol* festival was created by one visionary, Joop Mulder, on the Frisian island of Terschelling. In just a few years, *Oerol* grew from a local event to a 10-day theatre and music festival featuring international and national artists with 130,000 tickets sold annually. In the dialect from Terschelling, 'Oerol' means 'all over'. This refers to the fact that festival activities are embedded on the whole island, including natural protected areas. Acts are often developed specifically to blend into nature, and respectfully showcase its beauty. A second defining moment has been the unique event *Simmer 2000* (Summer 2000). The aim of *Simmer 2000* was to reach out to all emigrants from Frisia and to invite them to spend the summer of 2000 at home. This last was intended literally: emigrants were invited to come back to the houses they had lived in before leaving Frisia. In this case, too, the idea was developed not by policymakers or event organisations, but from a small group of Frisian citizens led by Griet van Duinen. To host the returning emigrants a major effort was asked by thousands of people who opened up their homes for them or organised events, such as a marathon all along the oldest dike in Frisia. *Simmer 2000* showed the power of Frisia citizens, in Frisian language *Mienskip* – a concept that took the central stage in the Bid Book of Leeuwarden ECC and through this engagement it is expected that the event will positively impact the social, economic and environmental sustainability of the province. To quote from the Bid Book: 'It is our goal to focus on citizen participation in each and every event of our programme' (p. 1).

To start with, Leeuwarden has partnered with the whole Province of Frisia. The official name of Leeuwarden ECC is in fact Leeuwarden-Fryslân 2018 (LF2018). With the support of the Municipality of Leeuwarden and the Province of Fryslân, the LF2018 organisation has encouraged citizens' participation by, on the one hand, reaching out to existing local cultural networks, and on the other by soliciting new initiatives while offering financial and professional support. This approach has proved to be fruitful. At the time of writing several initiatives developed by the *Mienskip* have been added to the official programme.

The programme itself is intended to explore themes that are intrinsically connected with the socio-economic and environmental challenges briefly presented above. The theme 'Nature and Culture' is dedicated to exploring and strengthening the links between bio- and geo-diversity. The threatened godwit, for example, is linked with Frisian people through songs and the (now only virtual) tradition of egg raping. One of the major projects in this line is indeed dedicated to the 'King of the Meadows', the godwit. 'King of the Meadows' is a citizens' initiative committed to design and implement economically and ecologically viable forms of farming. The network now includes farmers, artists, musicians, teachers, business people and scientists. One of the projects this network is developing for LF2018 is a series of (festival) encounters that follow the migration of the godwit from North Denmark, via Frisia and Spain to Morocco thus connecting not only the biological reality of meadow birds but also the cultural diversity of the places where the godwit stops and feeds.

The theme 'City and Countryside' aims at closing the gap between the two by underlining their interdependence and by designing spaces where the rural and the urban community can meet each other. In the project 'Feel the Night', for example, city-dwellers are invited to enter the darkness of the countryside and feel the power of a truly natural night. Through this experience they are also invited to reflect on and rethink the way cities are illuminated.

'Community and Diversity', the third and last theme of LF2018, is centred on empathy and openness towards other cultures. Culture is a deeply felt theme in Frisia, a province that is still proud of never having been conquered by the Roman Empire – contrary to the Southern and Central part of the Netherlands – and where an own language is spoken.

By integrating economic, social and environmental considerations in the choice of the main themes, the approach to sustainability by LF2018 may well be defined as integrative and holistic. As such, it goes further than simply aiming at sustainability certification of single events. Although the Bid Book promises that certification will be sought after, and events are encouraged to partner, for example, with *Innofest* in order to explore and implement specific sustainability measures, the ambition of LF2018 is laudably broader. A fragility of this approach is the intrinsic difficulty to measure the impact of so many small activities in terms of their contribution to solving the major socio-economic and environmental challenges that LF2018 wishes to address.

Similar case studies and relevant projects

In the Netherlands, more than 700 festivals are organised annually, each with an attendance of over 3,000 visitors. Overall, the festival sector stimulates the economy with revenue of about €675 million. The festival sector has therefore an important socio-economic role. In addition, and for some years, the awareness of the sector has grown regarding its environmental impact and many festivals have started a variety of initiatives to mitigate that impact.

In particular, as briefly stated above, a platform to stimulate green events was launched in 2014: *Green Events*. On this platform, nine large Dutch festivals exchange knowledge on how to make their events more sustainable: Amsterdam Open Air, DGTL, Four Days Marches Nijmegen (4 Daagse), Extrema Outdoor, Into the Great Wide Open, Mysteryland, Solar Weekend, Welcome to the Village and Zwarte Cross. Together with Green Events and Stichting Nederland Schoon[1] those events have signed a Green Deal[2] with the Dutch Ministry of Infrastructure and Environment, committing to a drastic reduction of waste. Green Events has identified several areas of focus to tackle sustainability at events, such as the composting of biodegradable waste, reducing campsite waste and mitigating littering, in general.

Another collaborative platform is *Innofest*, which was formed in January 2016 by a festival in Leeuwarden, Welcome to the Village, and seven other major Northern Dutch festivals. This initiative is co-financed by the European fund for regional development to work on innovations for festivals. *Innofest* approaches festivals as a living lab. The rationale is to test innovative solutions at festivals that can also then be scaled-up into cities or regions. The latter are complex settings, and so are festivals, where many functions come together. At the same time festivals are a controlled space, making it suitable to assess novel green solutions. *Innofest* focuses on five challenging areas: waste, energy, logistics, temporary buildings and water. Eight festivals in Northern Netherlands have already opened their terrains as living labs: *Into The Great Wide Open, Welcome to the Village, Eurosonic-Noorderslag, FestiValderAa, Noorderson, Paradigm, Oerol* and *TT Festival Assen.*

Recently, a major research project, under the umbrella of *CELTH*, the Dutch Center of Expertise for Leisure, Tourism and Hospitality, brought together the *Innofest* and *Green Events* festivals, in particular *DGTL* and *Welcome to the Village*, for further exchange of knowledge regarding sustainable strategies for events (CELTH, 2016). As put by the former Director of CELTH, Hans Dominicus,

> CELTH aims on developing and distributing knowledge about leisure, tourism and hospitality, so this domain is better able to co-drive the sustainable social and economic development of society. The foci are on future consumer behaviour, new value creation and sustainable development. Projects are carried out by Dutch knowledge institutes in collaboration with national and international industry.

For the period of 2015–2016, a CELTH project on sustainable strategies for events focused, amongst others, on two waste streams: plastic cups and cigarette butts, each culminated with interventions at a festival in 2016. *DGTL* festival chose to introduce hard-cups with a deposit/refund system (DGTL, 2016) while at *Welcome to the Village* there were interventions regarding the cigarette butts.

DGTL is a two-day electronic dance music festival, which takes place early in the festival season (around Easter) in the NDSM wharf in Amsterdam, attracting about 40,000 people. *DGTL* introduced hard-cups with a contactless wristband for deposits and refunds. The research here focused on understanding the impact of the introduction of the system on: (a) the visitors; (b) the organisation of the festival. The research was triangulated with offline and online resources, an audience questionnaire, participant observation and a focus group with staff. In general, there was a positive attitude towards the initiative by the audience, employees and volunteers. However, not everybody got the system as quickly as desired, showing that there is a need for the organisation to familiarise the audience with it. For further take-away lessons we refer to De Brito and Smorenburg (2016).

Welcome to the Village (WttV), is an open-air festival that occurs every July, in a natural lakeside setting, near the city of Leeuwarden and attracting about 7,000 festivalgoers. *WttV* chose to focus on cigarette butts. Interventions were designed in one of the festival areas to encourage the audience to not throw away their cigarette butts into the natural environment. In particular two interventions, on different days, were carried out: (1) to give portable ashtrays to people; and (2) to have boards where people could stick their cigarettes, sketching predefined drawings. The research involved collecting and counting the butts on the ground, observing behaviour and conducting mini-interviews. In general the audience (both smokers and non-smokers) received the experiments well. Some even suggested improvements, showing that there is an opportunity for co-creation with the audience. Distributing portable ashtrays had definitely an effect, reducing the butts on the ground by about two-thirds. Other results and recommendations can be found in Cavagnaro *et al.* (2017).

Summary

At the European level, *A Greener Festival (AGF)* is a platform that facilitates the exchange of best practices regarding sustainability at festivals and events. Set up in 2007, it has been auditing sustainability at festivals for many years, giving out the A Greener Festival Award for the best performer. In 2017, *AGF* also launched the Greener Event Award so that events other than festivals, or venues and arenas can also apply to be assessed. Some well-known and awarded festivals in Europe include the *Boom* festival in Portugal and the *Roskilde* festival in Denmark (see De Brito and Terzieva, 2016).

AGF not only awards festivals for their sustainability but also stimulates green behaviour throughout, spreading knowledge on innovative practices. One such instance was the campaign *Love your Tent,* in association with the Eco-Action Partnership, which stimulated festivalgoers to reuse their tents instead of abandoning them at the festival camps, a burden for festivals and the environment and unfortunately not a rare occurrence. On that topic, and in the Netherlands, two young entrepreneurs launched *KarTent*, a 100 per cent cardboard tent co-designed with Smurfit Kappa, a worldwide leader in paper-based packaging. This innovative product was granted the internationally renowned Red Dot Design Award.

Notes

1 Foundation Nederland Schoon is a Dutch organisation that fights littering by carrying out research, campaigns and providing advice. See: www.nederlandschoon.nl/.
2 Green Deals are agreements between the central government in the Netherlands and entities such as companies or civil society organisations, with the objective of carrying out innovative practices for sustainable targets. See: www.greenevents.nl/index.php/green-deal/.

References

2018 Leeuwarden (2017). 31 July. Available at: www.2018.nl/ (accessed 2 July 2018).
AGF (2017). A Greener Festival, 31 July. Available at: www.*agreenerfestival.com/* (accessed 2 July 2018).
Bigwood, G. (2016). Top 10 Sustainable Event Trends for 2020. Available at: http://live. mci-group.com/2016/08/top-10-sustainable-event-trends-2020/ (accessed 2 July 2018).
Calvo-Soraluze, J., de Brito, M. P. and San Salvador del Valle, R. (2016). The Future of Events: Towards Sustainable Business Models. In M. P. De Brito, and E. Cavagnaro (eds), *Strategies for Sustainable Events*, pp. 29–30. Available at: www.researchgate. net/publication/312938842_Strategies_for_Sustainable_Events (accessed 2 July 2018).

Cavagnaro, E. and Staffieri, S. (2016). Change as a benefit from travelling: for 'me', for 'me & you' or for 'all'? – A case study among students studying in the Netherlands, in Tourism 2016, Proceedings of the International Conference on Global Tourism and Sustainability, Lagos, Portugal, 14–16 October 2016, edited by S. Lira, A. Mano, C. Pinheiro and R. Amoêda, Barcelos: Green Lines Institute for Sustainable Development.

Cavagnaro, E., Postma, A. and Brito, M. (2017). The sustainability agenda and events. In N. Ferdinand and P. J. Kitchin (eds), *Events Management: an International approach*, 2nd edition. Thousand Oaks, CA: Sage, pp. 288–316.

CELTH (2016). Sustainable Strategies for Events. Retrieved from www.celth.nl/k/en/n738/news/view/18841/18577/project-sustainability-strategies-for-events.html.

CELTH (2017). CELTH – Centre of Expertise Leisure, Tourism, and Hospitality, 31 July. Available at: www.celth.nl/en/.

De Brito, M. P. and Smorenburg, H. (2016). Hard-cups: the case of DGTL. In De Brito, M.P. and E. Cavagnaro (2016), *Strategies for Sustainable Events*, pp. 18–21.

De Brito, M. P. and Terzieva, L. (2016). Key Elements for designing a strategy to generate social and environmental value: a comparative study of Festivals. *Research in Hospitality Management*, 6 (1): 51–59.

DGTL (2016). 16 March. Available at: https://dgtl.nl/well-use-hard-cups-and-bottles.

DGTL (2017). 31 July. Available at: https://dgtl.nl/ (accessed 2 July 2018).

European Capitals of Culture. (2017). 31 July. Available at: https://ec.europa.eu/programmes/creative-europe/actions/capitals-culture_en (accessed 2 July 2018).

European Commission (2012). Communication from the Commission to the European Parliament and the Council on the European Innovation Partnership 'Agricultural Productivity and Sustainability'. Available at: http://eur-lex.europa.eu/LexUriServ/LexUriServ.do?uri=COM:2012:0079:FIN:EN:PDF (accessed 2 July 2018).

Green Events (2017). 31 July. Available at: www.greenevents.nl/.

Innofest (2017). 31 July. Available at: http://innofest.com/.

KarTent (2017). 13 August. Available at: http://kartent.com/en-uk.

Koefoed, O. (2013), European Capitals of Culture and cultures of sustainability – the case of Guimaraes 2012. *City, Culture and Society*, 4 (3): 153–162.

Love Your Tent (2017). 13 August. Available at: www.loveyourtent.com/.

Postma, J. (2016). Widevogelmeetnet Friesland, Verslag 2015, Nijmegen: Sovon. Available at: www.sovon.nl/sites/default/files/doc/Rap_2016-03_WMF-2015.pdf (accessed 7 July 2017).

Province of Fryslân (2016). Factsheet Werkgelegenheid in de provincie Fryslân, Eerste Resultaten Werkgelegenheidsonderzoek 2016. Available at: http://fryslan.databank.nl/Jive/report?openinputs=true&id=4 (accessed 7 July 2017).

Van der Voort and De Brito, M. P. (2017). Nederlandse festivals werken samen aan afvalvrije festivals *forthcoming* – NRIT Trend Report (in Dutch).

10 A case study on prospects and emerging trends of Ayurvedic health tourism with green growth in Kerala, India

Anu Treesa George and Min Jiang

Introduction

The United Nations Environment Programme (UNEP) defines a green economy as one that results in 'improved human well-being and social equity, while significantly reducing environmental risks and ecological scarcities' (UNEP, 2010: 5). Green growth or 'greening' has been defined as the investment in sustainable practices and environmental facilities and this term also extends to sociocultural sustainability (Bowen and Fankhauser, 2011; Butler, 1999). In their vision for green growth DeLacy and Lipman (2014) discuss the duty of humans to conserve the earth's resource base for the future by ensuring inclusive and sustainable growth and as such green growth would become an asset for the well-being of the whole ecosystem. Essentially, the multifarious concept of 'green growth' means being more resource-efficient, cleaner and more resilient (Hallegatte *et al.*, 2012).

As tourism is one of the world's most promising industries, in terms of its ability to enrich the sustainable growth of the world economy, it has a key role to play in driving forward the trend of transitioning to a green economy (Blanke and Chiesa, 2013; Lipman and Vorster, 2011). Furthermore, as the tourism industry has close connections to numerous sectors at local and international levels, even small improvements in sustainability practices will create important impacts (Ekins, 2002). In 2010, UNEP together with the World Tourism Organization (UNWTO) stated in the Tourism in the Green Economy Report that an approach to sustainability should

> aspire to be more energy efficient and more climate sound, consume less water, minimise waste; conserve biodiversity, cultural heritage and traditional values; support intercultural understanding and tolerance; generate local income and integrate local communities with a view to improving livelihoods and reducing poverty.
>
> (UNEP, 2010: 2)

However, in transitioning to a green economy, the ever-emerging global tourism industry faces several challenges. Although tourism contributes significantly to economic growth, sociocultural integrity and environmental sustainability, further efforts by the industry are needed to improve energy and GHG emissions; water consumption; waste management; the loss of biological diversity and the effective management of our cultural heritage (UNEP, 2010).

Within a developing country, a focus on green growth as part of a practical and flexible strategy can lead to sustainable economic development (Law *et al.*, 2011). In India, as in many countries across the globe, green growth is now promoted, in part, to conserve natural resources. This is generating a growing body of evidence through case studies of excellent environmental practices and innovative steps taken to minimise negative impacts on the environment, and these demonstrate some of the potential for positive outcomes that can be achieved by countries and their communities (Vazquez Brust and Sarkis, 2012). This chapter provides insight into the emerging trend of Ayurvedic health tourism and presents a case study of how it is supporting economic development in Kerala, India. The potential for Ayurvedic tourism is growing and as such, careful management of this branch of tourism can form part of the development of green growth in this part of Asia and beyond.

The historical background of Ayurveda

The word 'Ayur-veda' originates from the old Indian language, Sanskrit – where Ayur means 'life' and veda means 'knowledge' and the origins of Ayurveda are thought to date back to 6000 BC (Haseena and Mohammed, 2014; Muralidhar and Karthikeyan, 2016). Ayurveda is an ancient science, considered health-specific rather than disease-specific, which is concerned with the patient's body, mind and spirit. Ayurveda is a unique and indispensable branch of medicine as it is a systematic means of detoxification. This system of medicine focuses on holistic treatment and emphasises the prevention of body ailments in addition to curing them. It is defined as the science of life (Muralidhar and Karthikeyan, 2016). Most of the principles and practices of this system of medicine were recorded in the Vedas – a body of ancient Indian scripture and records of knowledge, which consists of the Rig-veda, Yajur-veda, Sama-veda and principally the Atharva-veda. Ayurveda uses herbs and oils to heal and rejuvenate the body and to restore balance and good health.

In the eighteenth century, a number of provincial rulers across India became acutely interested in Ayurveda and began to promote its study. The first course in Ayurveda was started in the Government Sanskrit College in Calcutta in 1827 and by 1920 the Indian National Congress passed a resolution demanding the government promote the integrity of such an ancient and indigenous system of medicine. Consequently, the government established many Ayurveda colleges in India. The Maharajas of Travancore, Cochin, Jamnagar, and Mysore were particularly supportive of promoting Ayurveda and the colleges that they established are still considered to be among the best (Muralidhar and Karthikeyan, 2016) and as such the period from 1925 to1950 is considered to be a golden era for Ayurveda in the modern age. However, from the 1980s onwards, Ayurveda has become better known around the world as Ayurvedic practitioners have visited many countries, notably Italy, Germany, America, Japan and Australia, which has boosted the scope of Ayurveda and paved the way for more international awareness and acceptance.

Ayurvedic health tourism in Kerala

The integration of the health sector with the tourism sector has become a new feature of the socio-economic development of the Asia-Pacific region and this is especially true of India. Health tourism is defined as 'the organised travel outside one's local environment for the maintenance, enhancement or restoration of an individual's well-being in mind and body' (Carrera and Bridges, 2006: 447) and it is driven by familiarity, availability, cost, quality and bioethical legislation (Rosenmöller *et al.*, 2006). Health tourism in India encompasses a range of practices that includes authentic and original forms of yoga, meditation and Ayurveda, and the growing worldwide recognition and acceptance of Ayurvedic healing as an effective relaxation therapy and beauty regimen has widened the prospects of Ayurvedic health tourism.

Kerala is an evergreen state, situated on the southern tip of India, which enjoys unique geographic features and is marketed as 'God's Own Country' by the local tourist board, Kerala Tourism. Kerala has emerged as the most acclaimed tourist destination in India for the past two decades and it has been selected by the World Travel and Tourism Council as a partner state for enhancing the tourism industry. Kerala's unique selling proposition as a tourism destination is that it is 'one of the ten paradises of the world' known for its 'ABC' – Ayurveda, backwaters, culture and cuisine.

It is believed that some traditional Ayurvedic treatment methods were being used in Kerala even before the advent of Sanskrit. But with the arrival of the Sanskrit language, the Ayurveda health care system began to flourish in Kerala. Kerala Ayurvedic methodology mainly follows Ashtangahridaya and Ashtangasamgraha written by Vaghbata. Vaghbata is considered 'The Trinity' of Ayurvedic knowledge and the most influential classical writer of Ayurveda. Therefore, the history of Ayurveda in Kerala can be divided into three phases: the pre-Sanskrit arrival period, the post-Sanskrit arrival period and the modern period.

Today, Kerala's equable climate, natural abundance of forests (with a wealth of herbs and medicinal plants), and cool monsoon season (June to November) work well as part of Ayurvedic curative and restorative packages. This has led to a remarkable growth in tourism activities centred around Ayurvedic health care holidays and Ayurvedic detoxification. Branches of Ayurvedic treatment such as meditation, yoga and reiki have also triggered the growth of Ayurvedic health tourism (Gopi, 2017; Hall, 2003; Manoj, 2010). This has culminated in the development of the new concept of 'Ayurvedic tourism' and the growing global interest in Ayurveda also resulted in the convening of the World Ayurveda Congress in Cochin in November 2002.

The increase in tourism in Kerala has been phenomenal. In 1986 Kerala received 50,000 foreign tourist arrivals creating an economic impact of $2.56 million US dollars. By 2010 this had risen to 600,000 foreign tourist arrivals and $58.2 million (Department of Tourism, 2012: 2). Although the first tourism policy for Kerala was launched in 1995, the substantial increase in visitors was noted by the Kerala state government who, in recognition of the importance of the tourism sector, introduced responsible tourism initiatives in 2007. The Kerala state government also began to pay more attention to Ayurveda, not because of its immense healing powers, but due to its potential to further the growth and development of the tourism industry. The following case study is the result of an exploration of the perceived benefits of Ayurvedic tourism, which was undertaken with tourists, employees and members of the local community of Kumily, and the findings have the potential to assist the government in developing policies and marketing strategies to promote Ayurvedic health tourism in Kerala.

Case study: Ayurvedic resorts and spa centres in Kumily, Kerala

Study area and research methods

Kumily is a major tourist destination near Thekkady, Periyar Tiger Reserve, Kerala. The Periyar Wildlife Sanctuary is spread across $777\,km^2$ (300 sq. mi), of which $360\,km^2$ (140 sq. mi) is thick evergreen forest. The sanctuary can be explored by trekking, boating or jeep safari. Kumily is known as the gateway to Thekkady and as the spice capital of Kerala.

Seven of the best Ayurvedic resorts and spas in Kumily were identified and selected for this case study. The research focuses on the expectations and levels of satisfaction from the perspective of the tourist as well as the marketing environment, supporting services, community engagement and strategies adopted for Ayurvedic tourism. The study also assesses the views of tourists on how the attributes of Ayurveda can be used for promoting this branch of tourism. The study analyses the current situation of Ayurvedic tourism in Kerala and also the prospect of the green growth of this branch of tourism.

The case study was conducted via a mixed methods design incorporating surveys and interviews to understand the experience of the tourist and to explore themes that will underpin the future development of Ayurvedic tourism in Kerala. Nearly 100 questionnaires were distributed to international tourists and 10 interviews were conducted with members of the local community, and managers and employees of Ayurvedic resorts and Ayurvedic spa centres. The interviews were conducted to identify the potential cultural contribution made by the resorts to conserve cultural heritage and traditional values. A total of 60 questionnaires were completed and analysed and therefore it must be noted that the limitations of this case study are that it is based on a relatively small sample size and it has concentrated on the perceptions of tourists and the local community.

Analysis of results

Survey results from the experience of the tourist

The research reveals that in terms of marketing reach, most of the respondents came to know about Ayurveda through the Internet. Fifty-six per cent of international tourists pointed out that they were attracted to visit by both the availability of Ayurvedic treatments as well as the opportunity for sightseeing in Kerala. The majority of respondents fell into the 40–49 years age bracket and most chose to stay for less than three weeks, with no respondent staying for more than eight weeks. Most tourists were highly satisfied with their experience of Ayurveda, with only a few indicating dissatisfaction. These results are encouraging as they show that a well-designed and carefully marketed Ayurvedic tourism product could attract tourists to visit Kerala for up to 3 to 4 weeks and this illustrates that Ayurvedic tourism is in a critical growth stage. This high level of satisfaction infers that there is scope to develop the Ayurvedic tourism industry and the government should take adequate steps to promote this industry. Table 10.1 provides a summary of the profile of tourists.

The study also explored opinions of the Ayurvedic treatment facilities and respondents were asked to rank several attributes of an Ayurvedic treatment, which included: relief from stress and health problems, experienced doctors, trained masseurs, treatment space and accommodation, the attitude of management,

Table 10.1 A summary of the profile of tourists

Profiles	Categorisation	Number	Percentage (%)
Source of information	Friends and relatives	17	28.33
	Websites	30	50
	Advertisements	3	5
	Past visitors	5	16.66
	Periodicals	2	3
	Other sources	3	5
Purpose of visit	Ayurvedic treatment	4	6.66
	Sightseeing	20	33.33
	Both	34	56.66
	Other purpose	2	3.34
Length of stay	Less than 3 weeks	38	63.33
	3–4 weeks	16	26.66
	4–8 weeks	6	10
	More than eight weeks	0	0
Level of satisfaction	Highly satisfied	36	60
	Satisfied	14	23.33
	Neutral	7	11.66
	Dissatisfied	3	5
	Highly dissatisfied	0	0

Source: compilation from the primary data collected.

cost-effectiveness, quality of medicines and treatment, traditional Ayurvedic methods and social and cultural factors. A mean value analysis was conducted to examine tourists' perceptions of the various attributes of Ayurvedic tourism. A three-point scale was used for this purpose, where 3 points were given for agree, two points for neutral and one point for disagree. A 0 to 1 score shows the respondents are dissatisfied, 1.01 to 2 score shows the respondents are neutral, and 2.01 to 3 score shows the respondents are satisfied. From the analysis of the mean value, it is clear that Ayurvedic treatment facilities can really contribute to the health tourism industry. The mean values range between 2.96 and 2.83 and this shows that Ayurveda has been greatly accepted by international visitors and that they are highly satisfied with their experience of Ayurveda. The attributes which scored the highest value of 2.96 are relief from stress, treatment space and accommodation and the quality of medicines, demonstrating that a thriving Ayurvedic tourism industry is operating in Kerala. These results are illustrated in Table 10.2.

A ranking table was used to analyse the attributes that can best promote Ayurvedic tourism from the perspective of tourists, as this can help in increasing the scope of Ayurveda. The most important factor was given ten points and the least important was given one point. From the perspective of tourists, the most important attribute, in terms of promoting Ayurvedic health tourism, was the quality of medicines and treatments available, with a score of 525. This was followed by the use of traditional Ayurvedic methods, which scored 513. However, the research also reveals that tourists are concerned about the facilities provided and the quality of service. Therefore, it is critical that the government take measures to improve the quality of the provision of Ayurveda, such as through the introduction of regulations and licensing. These results are illustrated in Table 10.3.

A ranking table was also used to analyse the various weaknesses that may hinder the provision and development of Ayurvedic health tourism. The attributes considered to be the weakest in terms of promoting Ayurveda include the notion that traditional Ayurvedic methods are fading, that there is a lack of

Table 10.2 Total and mean value scores for the attributes of Ayurvedic treatments from respondents

Attributes	Total score	Mean value
Relief from stress and health problems	178	2.96
Well qualified doctors	174	2.90
Trained masseurs	173	2.91
Treatment space and accommodation	178	2.96
Attitude of management	171	2.85
Cost effectiveness	170	2.83
Quality of medicines and treatment	176	2.96
Traditional Ayurvedic methods	174	2.90
Social and cultural factors	177	2.94
Personal attention drawn	170	2.83

Source: primary data.

Table 10.3 Respondents' ranking of the strongest attributes for promoting Ayurvedic tourism

Attributes	Total weight	Rank
Quality of medicines and treatments	525	1
Traditional Ayurvedic methods	513	2
Relief from stress and health problems	463	3
Trained masseurs	440	4
Well-qualified doctors	437	5
Treatment space and accommodation	427	6
Attitude of management	404	7
Personal attention	398	8
Cost effectiveness	378	9
Social and cultural factors	315	10

Source: primary data.

well-trained masseurs, unethical practices are in use, there are some uncertified and questionable centres in operation, there is a lack of adequate infrastructure and a lack of council-driven promotion and marketing.

The most significant weakness was given seven points and the least important was given one point. Among the weaknesses, uncertified and questionable centres scored 294 points representing the greatest challenge and this was followed by unethical practices (276 points). The full results are presented in Table 10.4. Therefore, in order to help international tourists to identify and use reputable providers of Ayurveda, the official destination website should provide a list of certified centres to ensure the quality and authenticity in the provision of traditional Ayurvedic treatment.

Further results and recommendations

The results of this research indicate that Ayurvedic health tourism in Kerala has not yet developed to its zenith and has further potential. However, the involvement of

Table 10.4 Respondents' ranking of the weaknesses that may hinder the promotion of Ayurvedic tourism

Attributes	Total weight	Rank
Uncertified and questionable centres	294	1
Unethical practices	276	2
Lack of adequate infrastructure facilities	207	3
Poor marketing strategies	189	4
Lack of council driven promotion	144	5
Traditional Ayurvedic methods are fading	121	6
Lack of well-trained masseurs	97	7

Source: primary data.

unqualified personnel within the health care sector is damaging the reputation of this ancient science. Traditional Ayurvedic practitioners are of the view that the treatments offered in hotels and resorts are shorter than customary treatments and finishing treatments in less time means cutting corners. Additionally, some respondents complained about the quality of the Ayurvedic treatments and they were dissatisfied with the service provided to them. This demonstrates that the business-driven approach in use by some of the hotels and resorts can result in compromising the quality of service to customers and this is likely to damage the attractiveness of Ayurvedic tourism. It is therefore crucial for the government to take action to ensure that a quality service is maintained by imposing rules and regulations.

Ayurvedic tourism has created significant economic, social, cultural, political and environmental impacts in Kerala. Most of the resorts and spa centres employ at least one doctor and six masseurs as well as nine to twelve additional members of staff. From the interviews undertaken with employees at Ayurvedic resorts, it is clear that these organisations provide employment opportunities to local people and that local communities are involved in the supply of the medicinal plants that are required for treatments. Therefore, Ayurvedic tourism supports the local community and ensures them a good quality of life. Furthermore, the sector has the potential to expand employment opportunities to highly skilled as well as non-skilled members of society.

Ayurvedic tourism has enabled Kerala to engage in inter-cultural exchanges and it has enhanced the image of the state, increased employment and educational opportunities, modernised infrastructure and increased urbanisation. The worldwide acceptance of Ayurveda has created a growing demand for skilled manpower in the form of skilled doctors and masseurs who are an essential component of the sustainability of the industry. The establishment of various Ayurveda colleges in different parts of Kerala will continue to provide a supply of quality manpower. Ayurveda potentially encourages the conservation of cultural values and enhances Kerala's rich heritage.

As per the views of doctors, Ayurvedic treatment can deliver excellent results in the monsoon season, when the atmosphere is cool and the body is receptive to oils and therapy. Furthermore, the promotion of Ayurvedic tourism in Kerala has been focused on encouraging tourists to visit during the monsoon season as historically this has been a low season for tourism. However, the result of this research indicates that this marketing approach has not been effective as the majority of tourists visiting in order to receive Ayurvedic treatments, do so during the peak tourist season of October to March. Therefore, in the future, providing seasonal discounts to domestic tourists may attract them to visit Aurvedic centres during the monsoon months.

Key suggestions put forward by managers, employees and doctors from the Ayurvedic resorts include the following:

1   Hotels who offer shorter treatments should call themselves 'well-being centres' and not 'Ayurvedic centres'.

2   The government should reduce the significant tax on hotel rooms, and the food and liquor consumed by tourists.

3   The state government should create a council to promote tourism, and migrant workers from Kerala should be involved in the international promotion of tourism to Kerala.

4   The government should entrust local bodies to function as watchdogs to ensure a high quality of service is provided at Ayurvedic centres. A mechanism to monitor the quality of herbal products and medicines should be developed to incorporate measures for banning substandard batches of Ayurvedic medicines.

5   Ayurvedic educational institutions and courses should be developed to incorporate more research practices to include the collection, cataloguing and digitalisation of ancient Ayurvedic manuscripts. A scientifically based clinical analysis of popular medicines could draw more global attention to Ayurvedic products, and 'holistic villages' offering such facilities should be formed.

6   Ayurveda could be packaged with other heritage attractions such as the folk arts of North Kerala or the art forms *theyyam* and *thira* as this will enrich the overall tourism experience.

7   Marketing plays a prominent role in attracting tourists and there should be a greater focus on marketing via the internet, media and advertising campaigns as this has the potential to reach more tourists.

In summary, this case study demonstrates that the government should take adequate steps to support the growth of the Ayurvedic tourism industry in Kerala through the development of infrastructure, research and marketing and the implementation of regulations, subsidies and tax exemptions. However, such development should form part of a wider strategy for green growth.

The Ayurvedic tourism industry can contribute to the paradigmatic shift towards green growth by taking the initiative to positively influence tourists, contractors, suppliers and local communities (Jones 2010) but this requires improvement as the shortage of basic amenities, poor waste management and the exploitation of natural resources have so far been evident in most tourist destinations in the area.

An approach to developing Ayurvedic tourism through a strategy of green growth and corporate social responsibility (CSR) can enhance this branch of tourism. This can be achieved by conserving the cultural values of Ayurveda, reducing water consumption, using renewable sources of energy such as solar and wind power, managing waste and protecting the biodiversity of the environment. Furthermore, there is scope to increase the sociocultural benefits of Ayurvedic tourism to local communities by providing further opportunities for training and skills development for the local workforce and by developing Ayurvedic gardens that will be used to promote social inclusion. The integration of green growth with the development of Ayurvedic tourism can improve the conservation of resources and transform a tourist destination. The strategic management of Ayurvedic resorts and associations can meet the needs of local communities by, for example, offering volunteer and employment opportunities, and by engaging communities in the arts and cultural activities to encourage and influence pro-environmental and pro-social behaviour.

Conclusion

Kerala's tourism product has not yet achieved its full potential (Thimm 2017) and this chapter has explored the current provision of a branch of tourism, Ayurvedic tourism, in Kerala and the potential to develop it further. Using a case study involving Ayurvedic health tourists, managers and employees of Ayurvedic resorts and spa centres, we conclude that visitors have demonstrated that there is a wider scope for Ayurvedic health tourism. The research provides insight into the satisfaction of tourists, the current marketing environment, the effectiveness of supporting services and community engagement in the provision of Ayurvedic tourism. Based on the research, we have provided a number of suggestions for the development of Ayurvedic tourism as part of a strategy for green growth. The benefits of sustainable growth are plentiful, and for the tourism industry, the growth of a green economy is a potentially powerful tool that can assure the complimentary development of communities with both natural and built environments. Furthermore, Ayurvedic tourism can improve the sociocultural effects of tourism, which have been defined as 'any impacts that potentially have an impact on the quality of life for local communities' (Fredline *et al.*, 2003: 26). This can be achieved through job creation and the engagement of the community in the promotion and provision of Ayurvedic tourism.

However, there remain major gaps in our collective knowledge about the potential of Ayurvedic health tourism, particularly regarding whether such development will positively promote environmental sustainability. It is crucial to understand the barriers to green growth in order to overcome them. Therefore, there is the opportunity for further study of Ayurvedic tourism within the context of sustainable tourism. India is a country rich in cultural diversity, with an immense amount of resources that support tourism and it is one of the pioneer countries to promote Ayurvedic tourism. India, and Kerala in particular, has shown that Ayurvedic tourism is a promising industry and with the right government support, it has the potential to make a significant impact on the lives of local communities and it can contribute to green growth through conserving biodiversity, cultural heritage and traditional values.

References

Blanke, J. and Chiesa, T. (2013). The travel and tourism competitiveness report 2013. The World Economic Forum [online]. Available at: www.weforum.org/ (accessed 30 June 2018).

Bowen, A. and Fankhauser, S. (2011). The green growth narrative: paradigm shift or just spin? *Global Environmental Change*, 21 (4): 1157–1159.

Butler, R. W. (1999). Sustainable tourism: a state-of-the-art review. *Tourism Geographies*, 1 (1) 7–25.

Carrera, P. M. and Bridges, J. F. (2006). Globalization and healthcare: understanding health and medical tourism. *Expert Review of Pharmacoeconomics and Outcomes Research*, 6 (4): 447–454.

DeLacy, T., Jiang, M., Lipman, G. and Vorster, S. (2014). *Green Growth and Travelism: Concept, Policy and Practice for Sustainable Tourism, Volume 44*. London: Routledge.

Department of Tourism, GOK (2012). Government of Kerala Tourism Policy 2012. Available at: www.ecotourismsocietyofindia.org/file/State%20Policies/Kerala%20 Tourism%20Policy.pdf (accessed 2 July 2018).

Ekins, P. (2002). *Economic Growth and Environmental Sustainability: The Prospects for Green Growth*. London: Routledge.

Fredline, L., Jago, L. and Deery, M. (2003). The development of a generic scale to measure the social impacts of events. *Event Management*, 8 (1): 23–37.

Gopi, R. (2017). Ayurveda tourism: issues of development and gender in Contemporary Kerala. In I. K. Mitra, R. Samaddar and S. Sen (eds), *Accumulation in Post-Colonial Capitalism* (pp. 165–187). Singapore: Springer.

Hall, C. M. (2003). Health and spa tourism. In S. Hudson (ed.), *International Sports and Adventure Tourism* (pp. 273–292). New York: Haworth Press.

Hallegatte, S., Heal, G., Fay, M. and Treguer, D. (2012). From growth to green growth – a framework. *National Bureau of Economic Research* [online]. Available at: https:// openknowledge.worldbank.org/handle/10986/3670 (Accessed: 30 June 2018).

Haseena, V. and Mohammed, A. P. (2014). Sustainable tourism strategy development in kerala as a tool of growth. *Asian Journal of Science and Technology*, 5 (3): 192–197.

Law, A., DeLacy, T., McGrath, M. and Whitelaw, P. (2011). Tourism destinations in the emerging green economy: towards blending in brilliantly. Presented at the CAUTHE 2011 National Conference: *Tourism: Creating a Brilliant Blend*, p. 1171.

Lipman, G. and Vorster, S. (2011). Green growth, travelism, and the pursuit of happiness. In J. Blanke and T. Chiesa (eds), *The Travel and Tourism Competitiveness Report 2011: Beyond the Downturn*. Geneva, Switzerland: World Economic Forum. Available at: https://srecanja.files.wordpress.com/2012/05/wef_traveltourismcompetitiveness_report_ 2011.pdf (accessed 2 July 2018).

Manoj, P. (2010). Tourism in Kerala: a study of the imperatives and impediments with focus on ecotourism. *Saaransh RKG Journal of Management*, 1 (2): 78–82.

Muralidhar, S. and Karthikeyan, P. (2016). Asian research consortium. *Asian Journal of Research in Social Sciences and Humanities*, 6 (6): 1043–1052.

Rosenmöller, M., McKee, M., Baeten, R. and Glinos, I. A. (2006). Patient mobility: the context and issues. In M. Rosenmöller, M. McKee, R. Baeten and I. A. Glinos (eds), *Patient Mobility in the European Union*, European Observatory on Health Systems and Policies [online]. Available at: www.euro.who.int/__data/assets/pdf_file/0011/120332/ E88697.pdf (accessed 30 June 2018).

Thimm, T. (2017). The Kerala Tourism Model – an Indian state on the road to sustainable development. *Sustainable Development*, 25(1): 77–91.

UNEP (2010). Green Economy Report: A Preview, New York. Available at: https:// sustainabledevelopment.un.org/index.php?page=view&type=400&nr=126&menu=35 (accessed 2 July 2018).

Vazquez Brust, D. and Sarkis, J. (eds) (2012). *Green Growth: Managing the Transition to a Sustainable Economy: Learning By Doing in East Asia and Europe, Greening of Industry Networks Studies, Volume 1*. Dordrecht/New York: Springer.

World Bank (2012). *Inclusive Green Growth: The Pathway to Sustainable Development*. Washington, DC: World Bank.

Part IV

Green management of outdoor sites

11 The elusive goal of sustainable tourism

A case study of the Camino de Santiago in France and in Spain

*Frédéric Dosquet, Thierry Lorey,
Hugues Séraphin and Thomas Majd*

For more than a thousand years, pilgrims have trodden the Camino de Santiago to the tomb of Saint James the Greater in Santiago de Compostela. Despite its long cultural and religious heritage, the pilgrimage's popularity declined massively in the sixteenth and subsequent centuries, only to see a huge resurgence in recent decades. Somewhat paradoxically, the rejuvenation of a pilgrimage that is partly about a return to nature has raised a number of environmental issues. Hence, the recent influx of pilgrims is forcing the actors involved in managing this intangible asset to address the practical and pragmatic aspects of sustainable tourism.

A long transnational history

Although the first pilgrimages to the tomb of St James, in the ninth century, were entirely within the Iberian Peninsula, by the tenth century pilgrims came from much further afield. Today, the Ways of Saint James, as the Camino de Santiago is also known, cross the whole of Europe, covering several thousand kilometres as they converge upon Santiago de Compostela, the capital of the autonomous province of Galicia.

The original reason for creating the pilgrimage was to strengthen ties between the rest of Christian Europe and the Kingdom of Asturias, then under threat from the Muslim forces occupying southern Spain. It immediately fulfilled its initial, geostrategic purpose and had great politico-religious impact on both sides of the Pyrenees. In fact, Saint James would become a key figure in the building of the Spanish nation, where he is known as 'the Moor-slayer' (*Matamoros* in Spanish) because of the help he is said to have given King Ramiro 1st of Asturias in his fight against the Moors in the ninth century. According to another legend, in 813 CE, Saint James appeared in a dream to Charlemagne, the king of the Francs, and ordered him to deliver his tomb from the Moors. Charlemagne was told that the Milky Way would guide him across the Pyrenees to the apostle's tomb. Other pilgrims soon began following the route indicated by Saint James, creating a dense network of pilgrimage trails covering the whole of Europe. Four main routes across France, starting in

Tours, Vezelay, Puy-en-Velay and Arles, merged into a single route across Spain (*El Camino françés*). By the twelfth century, the pilgrimage had reached its peak in terms of fame and social standing (Péricard-Méa and Mollaret, 2010), and, in the fifteenth century, Pope Alexander VI declared it to be one of Christianity's three great pilgrimages, alongside Jerusalem and Rome. Nevertheless, by the sixteenth century the Church authorities had begun doubting whether the apostle's tomb actually was in Santiago and the pilgrimage went into decline. As a result, by the nineteenth century the original pilgrimage came close to disappearing entirely, with fewer than 40 pilgrims attending the apostle's mass in Compostela Cathedral in 1867. In the middle of the twentieth century, Franco's dictatorial government resurrected the cult of Saint James for ideological reasons, but Spain's closed borders prevented any significant revival of the pilgrimage. Only when democracy was restored to Spain, in 1975, were pilgrims from around the world once again free to visit Santiago de Compostela. However, the recent explosion in the number and type of pilgrims following the Camino de Santiago did not occur until modern society moved into its post-modernist phase at the end of the twentieth century (Maffesoli, 1988). Finally, the particularity of these Routes is to cross several European countries, especially France and Spain. It means that there are different policies and practices for management to abide by, and especially the sustainable tourism management, of these Routes of Santiago de Compostela depending on the national points of view. That is why this case study is interesting – these Routes are at the crossroads of national and international managerial policies.

Two international labels: increased protection but also increased pressure

Today, the Camino de Santiago is no longer as exclusively religious an affair as it once was. In fact, the pilgrimage constitutes a unique cultural, religious and commercial continuum within Europe, whose importance in terms of cultural heritage and tourism has been recognised through the award of two international heritage labels. In 1987, the Council of Europe named the 'Santiago de Compostela Pilgrim Routes' the first European Cultural Route in acknowledgement of their role in promoting the exchange of ideas, expertise and art, in bringing people together, and in creating a European collective memory. Ultimate recognition for the Camino came in 1998, when the 'Routes of Santiago de Compostela in France' was inscribed on UNESCO's World Heritage list. Unlike the Spanish section of the pilgrimage trail, which obtained World Heritage status in 1993, the UNESCO inscription for the French part of the routes includes monuments and buildings (churches, hospitals, bridges, etc.) along the four routes, as well as seven sections of the routes themselves. In total, 71 monuments and seven sections of the routes in ten French regions have been given UNESCO protection. The impetus provided by these two international labels has contributed to the massive rise in the pilgrimage's popularity, with an almost 4,000-fold increase in pilgrim numbers since 1970. The *Oficina del*

Peregrine recorded just 68 pilgrims arriving in Compostela in 1970, 209 pilgrims in 1980, 4,882 pilgrims in 1990 and 55,004 pilgrims in 2000. Taking a ten-year mean in order to smooth out year-to-year variations shows that, on average, 212,903 pilgrims reached Compostela every year between 2006 and 2016. However, this average masks an increase from 101,149 pilgrims in 2006 to 277,854 pilgrims in 2016, a rise of almost 275 per cent. This rapid growth in pilgrim numbers is the result of a combination of sociological factors, increased publicity and religious factors.

- Viewed from a sociological perspective, the pilgrimage to Santiago de Compostela provides two things that individuals in today's post-modern society are seeking (Maffesoli, 1988) – a life experience that is not just about consumption, and the need to be part of a group of like-minded individuals.
- Increased publicity, largely through numerous widely marketed and successful books and films about the Camino de Santiago, has also contributed to the rise in pilgrim numbers. For example, the 100 per cent increase in the number of Americans doing the pilgrimage in 2011–2012 was certainly fuelled by the release of an American film called 'The Way' at the end of 2010.
- Two religious factors have a significant impact on pilgrim numbers. First, Jubilee Years, that is, years in which St James' Day (25 July) falls on a Sunday, attract more pilgrims than other years. For example, 272,135 pilgrims visited Compostela in 2010, a Jubilee Year, compared with 145,877 pilgrims in 2009. Second, large religious gatherings in Compostela, such as visits by the Pope in 2002, 2009 and 2010, also attract large numbers of pilgrims.

Together, these factors have had an unprecedented impact on the popularity of the pilgrimage, which now attracts people from all walks of life, and have helped ensure the cultural and physical survival, at least for now, of the Camino de Santiago. However, the resulting environmental pressure is starting to raise questions about the sustainability of tourism along the pilgrim trails.

Sustainable tourism, a multidimensional concept

The present chapter adopts François-Lecompte and Prim-Allaz's (2009) definition of sustainable tourism, which 'targets the entire tourism industry, examines wilderness areas as well as rural and urban areas, encompasses the notion of cultural and architectural heritage, and encourages changes in behaviours, starting at home and not just in the countries visited'. This is similar to the Brundtland Report's (1987) definition of sustainable development, which 'must be capable of satisfying the needs of the current generation without compromising the ability to satisfy the needs of future generations'. So defined, the concept of sustainable tourism is highly relevant to the pilgrimage along the Camino de Santiago for several reasons.

- First, the Camino de Santiago is the embodiment of a heritage bequeathed by earlier generations to the current generation, which will in turn pass it on to future generations. Pilgrims feel they are experiencing, and therefore perpetuating, a feeling of belonging to a community, whether that community is spiritual, geographic or, more globally, human.
- Second, the pilgrimage routes bring together innumerable tourism-sector stakeholders in a continuous chain that stretches for thousands of kilometres. These stakeholders, which cover the entire length of the pilgrimage, are exceptionally varied, and include public bodies and private organisations, international companies and local service providers. Following the classification drawn up by Cohendet *et al.* (2010), Lorey *et al.* (2016) defined three layers of stakeholders in the pilgrimage, categorising them as 'upperground', 'middleground' and 'underground'.
- Third, the pilgrimage combines natural, cultural and architectural characteristics, as pilgrims progress through a constantly changing natural and architectural landscape and meet many other people from extremely varied backgrounds (in 2016, people from 146 different countries undertook the pilgrimage).
- Finally, because many pilgrims start the pilgrimage from their front door, it is not associated uniquely with the behaviours they produce in the areas through which they travel; it is also associated with the way they behave at home.

Moreover, as the literature (Camus *et al.*, 2010; Lozato-Giotart *et al.*, 2012; Diallo, 2014) shows, the Camino de Santiago encompasses all three classic dimensions of sustainable tourism. These dimensions are environmental sustainability, achieved by managing and conserving resources and biodiversity; economic sustainability, achieved by ensuring the viability of local business; and social sustainability, achieved by giving recognition to and respecting local cultures. UNESCO's justification for adding the Camino de Santiago to the World Heritage List also takes into account these three dimensions:

- Criterion (ii): The Route of Santiago de Compostela played a crucial role in the two-way exchange of cultural advances between the Iberian Peninsula and the rest of Europe, especially during the Middle Ages, but also in subsequent centuries. The wealth of cultural heritage that has emerged in association with the *Camino* is vast, marking the birth of Romanesque art and featuring extraordinary examples of Gothic, Renaissance, and Baroque art. Moreover, in contrast with the waning of urban life in the rest of the Iberian Peninsula during the Middle Ages, the reception and commercial activities emanating from the *Camino de Santiago* led to the growth of cities in the north of the Peninsula and gave rise to the founding of new ones;
- Criterion (iv): The Route of Santiago de Compostela has preserved the most complete material registry of all Christian pilgrimage routes, featuring ecclesiastical and secular buildings, large and small enclaves, and civil engineering structures;

- Criterion (vi): The Route of Santiago de Compostela bears outstanding witness to the power and influence of faith among people of all social classes and origins in medieval Europe and later.

Finally, the means of locomotion used by pilgrims following the Camino de Santiago leaves negligible or zero carbon footprints. Hence, as the statistics gathered by the *Oficina del Peregrine* in Compostela show, the means of locomotion that pilgrims use are highly compatible with sustainable tourism.

Table 11.1 shows the percentage of pilgrims using each mode of locomotion in 2016. These figures have been stable since 2004.

All these factors would suggest that the pilgrimage along the Camino de Santiago, with its focus on communion with nature and benevolence towards other people, would not have any sustainability concerns. Unfortunately, this is not the case and stakeholders in the Camino are having to rethink their positions and take measures to ensure the pilgrimage's sustainability.

A still fragile form of sustainable tourism

The existence of the pilgrimage as a form of sustainable tourism is being challenged by a number of issues, most of which are related to its ever-increasing popularity. One such issue is waste management. For example, unless they are made aware of the problem, the large numbers of pilgrims following the Camino will inevitably generate large amounts of litter, which damages the environment along the trails. Our experience of the pilgrimage, which we did between 2012 and 2016, showed that little action has been taken to address this problem. As a result, pilgrims dispose of their litter as they see fit, which is not always in the most environmentally responsible way. Another major issue is the damage to the pilgrimage's image due to the crowding on the trails detracting from the journey's meaning and reducing its cachet as a unique and extraordinary experience. This observation led Dosquet *et al.* (2015) to suggest 'demarketing' the pilgrimage in order to reduce pilgrim numbers.

Although officially everything possible is being done to protect the Camino, the reality is sometimes different. This is particularly obvious when the measures taken in Spain are compared with the situation in France.

Table 11.1 Means of locomotion used by pilgrims

Means	%
On foot	92.42
By bicycle	8.40
On horseback	0.12
In a wheelchair	0.04
By sail boat	0.01

Source: *Oficina del Peregrine*, Compostela, 2017.

As UNESCO noted, the Spanish section of the Camino benefits from a high level of protection:

> The Route of Santiago de Compostela is completely preserved and characterised by a high level of conservation of the route itself and of the buildings and sites along the way, making it a unique example of a medieval pilgrimage route which is still in use today. The route also illustrates the integration into the environment.

In fact, the Camino was accorded Spain's highest level of heritage protection as early as 1985, when it was listed as a 'Property of Cultural Interest' (*Bien de Interés Cultural*, BIC) under the First Additional Provision of Historic Heritage Act 16 of 25 June 1985. Further measures to protect this unique heritage have been taken by the autonomous regions through which the Camino passes. Aragon was the first region to protect its section of the Camino, creating a technical coordination committee to restore and revitalise the pilgrimage trail via Decree 96 of 24 May 1988. That same year, under Statutory Decree 290 of 14 December 1988, Navarre defined official boundaries for the Camino de Santiago, combined with a special protection regime for areas within these boundaries. Castile and León, under Decree 324 of 23 December 1999, listed a clearly defined zone around the Camino de Santiago as a 'historic ensemble' (*Conjunto Histórico*), while Rioja listed its section of the Camino as a BIC via Decree 14 of 16 March 2001, which also establishes a peripheral protection zone. Most recently, three decrees approved by Galicia in 2011 and 2012 gave further protection to the Camino in this region.

In addition to this legislative protection, UNESCO appreciates the steps that have been taken to oversee actions by the Camino's various stakeholders. The most important measure in this respect was the creation of the Consejo Jacobeo (Council of Saint James), which was set up in 1991 to coordinate cooperation between Spain's central government, especially the Education, Culture and Sport Ministries, and the autonomous regions traversed by the pilgrimage. Royal Decree 1431/2009 of 11 September 2009 restructured the Council into a central committee, an executive committee and a cooperation committee, in order to 'strengthen the functions of the Consejo Jacobeo as an entity for cooperation in relation to the management of the Camino de Santiago inscribed on the list of World Heritage Sites'.

Nevertheless, these protection measures have not resolved every problem and a number of potential threats remain, due to pressure from the growth of tourism and the number of pilgrims, and to the expansion of infrastructure such as major highways, high-speed train lines, and the natural growth of towns and cities. Hence, UNESCO has highlighted the need to enforce regulatory measures and legislation, the importance of carrying out impact studies before authorising any new construction, and the need to take into account the Camino's attributes when drawing up municipal development plans.

Problems in France are more perceptible for a number of reasons. First, France has had five years' less experience than Spain in protecting the Camino, as UNESCO did not add the French sections of the pilgrimage to the World Heritage list until 1998. Second, in contrast with Spain, where the entire Camino has World Heritage status, the Routes of Santiago in France are listed as a serial property comprising just seven sections of the four main routes, plus 71 monuments. As a result, a large, diverse and often fragmented group of stakeholders is responsible for managing the World Heritage property in France, thereby hindering the implementation of effective conservation measures for the different sites, such as the establishment of buffer zones to protect their exceptional universal value. In 2015, the French authorities (Prefecture of the Midi-Pyrénées Region) acknowledged this problem:

> [The Routes of Santiago have] the particularity of being a serial property, which means that each of its components must satisfy management conditions (…) which must be coherent for the whole: for UNESCO, the 78 components of the property form a single property. Neglecting these management obligations for just one component could lead to the entire property losing its World Heritage status.

This statement recognises the complexity of the administrative landscape surrounding the Camino, with responsibility for protecting the UNESCO properties being shared between ten regional councils, 32 *départemental* councils, and innumerable intermunicipal and municipal councils, as well as other public bodies such as the ACIR (Agency for Inter-regional Cooperation and Networking) and the European Federation of the Saint James Way. In addition, because parts of the Camino de Santiago cross private land, a number of private organisations have to be taken into account, not to mention the Church authorities and associated charities such as Webcompostella. In order to improve coordination between these bodies, in October 2014 the French government asked Pascal Mailhos, the Prefect of the Haute Garonne *département*, to head an inter-regional coordination committee for The Routes of Santiago serial property. The committee's objective is to:

> bring together landowners, managers and the 'Compostelle' inter-regional cooperation association, which is responsible for running the network. It will enable stakeholders from the different regions to share objectives and exchange good practices. It will also help create and organise local commissions that will contribute to the governance of the property. These commissions will help implement local and inter-regional management plans.

To this end, on 5 November 2015 the government signed a 3-year agreement mandating ACIR Compostelle to coordinate studies and actions aimed at guaranteeing the integrity of The Routes of Santiago. ACIR Compostelle's efforts are already bearing fruit. As the Periodic Reporting Questionnaire published by the World Heritage Centre in December 2014 noted: 'protection measures designed to maintain the exceptional universal value of the property, including the conditions needed to preserve its authenticity and/or integrity, constitute an appropriate or better basis for its effective management and protection'. Finally, the French government must create buffer zones around all 78 UNESCO-listed properties, including the seven sections of the routes. Although the 71 monuments included within the World Heritage property are already protected under current French planning and heritage protection laws, local authority action plans for developing hiking trails do not include any measures for protecting the seven sections of the routes.

In conclusion, although the foundations for developing sustainable tourism along the Camino de Santiago have been laid, there remain large differences between what has been done in Spain and what has been done in France. Spain's more global vision of the tourism economy and appreciation of its strategic value have given it a lead over France. However, France has made significant progress in recent years, as the government has understood that this unique heritage can only be preserved by carefully managing the Routes of Santiago and the development of tourism along them. The Camino de Santiago has the potential to become a paradigm of cross-border sustainable tourism, an objective all the stakeholders involved, from international organisations and government authorities to the Catholic Church, charities and the pilgrims themselves, would like to see attained. Through its very essence, the Camino de Santiago is a potential archetype for sustainable tourism; now it must live up to that promise.

References

Brundtland Report. (1987). Rapport: Notre avenir à tous.
Camus, S., Hikkerova, L. et Sahut, J.-M. (2010). Tourisme durable: une approche systémique, *Management & Avenir*, 4 (34): 253–269.
Cohendet P., Grandadam, D. and Simon, L. (2010). The Anatomy of the Creative City. *Industry and Innovation*, 17 (1): 91–111.
Diallo M.-F. (2014). Les études quantitatives sur le tourisme durable: une analyse des principaux travaux de recherché. *Management & Avenir*, 3: 204–221.
Dosquet, F., Estellat, N. and Lorey, T. H. (2015). Marketing touristique, démarketing et création de valeur. Le cas des chemins de Saint-Jacques-de-Compostelle, dans les Pyrénées-Atlantiques. 2e Conférence de l'AFMAT, EM Strasbourg, mai 2015.
François-Lecompte, A. and Prim-Allaz, I. (2009). Les Français et le tourisme durable: proposition d'une typologie. *Management & Avenir*, 9: 308–326.
Lorey, Th., Dosquet, F., Errami, Y. and Chantelot, S. (2016). La gestion du patrimoine des Chemins de St Jacques de Compostelle: la nécessaire émergence d'un nouveau leadership public. 5eme Congrès de l'Airmap (Association Internationale en Recherche de Management Public), Poitiers, juin 2016.
Lozato-Giotart, J.-P., Leroux E. and Balfet, M. (2012). *Management du tourisme durable: Territoires, offres et les strategies*. Paris: Pearson Education.
Maffesoli, M. (1988). *Le Temps des tribus*. La table ronde.
Péricard-Méa, D. and Mollaret, L. (2010). *Chemins de Compostelle et Patrimoine mondial*, La Louve Editions.

12 Clearfield

Sustainable tourism and architecture in a new eco-park in Russia

Tatiana Gladkikh and Olga Andrianova

Introduction

This chapter offers its readers a case study of Clearfield (Yasnopole). The ecological park was founded in 2015 and is situated on the banks of the river Oka, 120 kilometres outside Moscow. The area of outstanding beauty has a span of 500 hectares. Rich in its flora and fauna, it is distinguished by its forests, fields, hills, lakes and rivers. The main idea of the eco-park is to promote a healthy lifestyle through events, workshops, activity holidays and healthy eating, as well as to advance research and innovation in the field of green architecture and construction. The main philosophy of the eco-park is living in harmony with nature.

Ecotourism as a relatively underdeveloped type of tourism in Russia is discussed in the context of organisational and management differences between national parks and eco-parks in the country. Introducing ecotourism as an environmental movement with a relatively short history, the chapter focuses on the Year of Ecology in Russia in 2017, which stimulated the advancement of eco-initiatives in order to promote environmental awareness and actions. The case study of Clearfield offers an example of a successful private eco-initiative of an eco-park. The chapter concludes with a proposition that such eco-parks can become examples of good practice for promoting environmental awareness and sustainability through enhancing ecotourism in the country.

National parks and eco-parks in Russia

According to the Ministry of Natural Resources and Ecology of the Russian Federation (2018), there are 50 national parks in the country. Their aim is to promote nature conservation, advance ecological education and support research activities. The Russian network of national parks is state-regulated and is relatively young. Its history goes back only 35 years, when the first national park *Sochinsky*, near Sochi was founded in May 1983 (Sochi National Park, 2018). In comparison, the world's first national park, Yellowstone, was founded in the USA in 1872 (Yellowstone, 2018); and the first national parks in Europe originated in Switzerland in 1909 (Sveriges National Park, 2018). The Government of the Russian Federation must approve the establishment of national parks in Russia, thus national parks are the property of the State and follow Government programmes and initiatives to achieve their objectives (National Park Alania, 2018).

Eco-parks are a more recent phenomenon in the country. They are often funded by private individuals and enthusiasts and operate without government support or relevant regulatory systems. Guided by values and visions of their owners and shareholders, they are organised and managed in a multitude of ways from religious and spiritual communities to authentic settlements promoting 'natural' living. Largely known to their visitors and members through word of mouth, they are independent organisations, which are significantly different from official national parks in the country. However, despite the differences of government-led and privately initiated approaches, they both address the same ecological concerns and focus on promoting ecotourism, which became a topical issue during the Year of Ecology in Russia in 2017. Ecotourism received significant attention alongside a number of other priorities and projects aimed at improving environmental and ecological conditions and awareness in the country.

Ecotourism

Ecotourism emerged as a new type of tourism in the 1970s to 1980s, and since then has been growing in its popularity all over the world. Its aim is to provide people with access to nature where they can rest, relax and re-energise while enjoying the surrounding landscapes. Ecotourism encourages nature conservation and preservation of natural resources and usually takes place in the natural territories, untouched by urbanisation. Ecotourism can be understood in a variety of ways but generally the following characteristics could be applied to all of them:

- tourism to the natural environment
- tourism into the natural environment with the purpose of learning about the natural heritage (ecological education)
- tourism which supports nature conservation and local culture
- tourism which has a positive impact on the socio-economic development of the area of visit.

Thus, the three main components of ecotourism are environmental education, preservation of ecosystems and respect for local populations. This observation reflects multiple and varied definitions of ecotourism, which focus on fully-fledged relaxation in nearby pristine nature; a combination of recreational activities and learning about nature and local traditions; an opportunity to apply modern environmental technology; and a preservation of nature and cultural surroundings that is economically beneficial to the local population (Evstrop'eva and Korytnyi, 2016: 795). Donohoe and Needham (2006: 194) suggest that ecotourism provides a more meaningful experience than other types of tourism and offers 'more ecological sustainability, more environmental education and greater satisfaction for participants'.

Ecotourism in Russia

Ecotourism is a developing sector of the tourism industry in Russia. It emerged in the mid-1990s with the establishment of ecotourism projects in the North West and Far East of Russia with support of TACIS (Technical Assistance Programme Stimulating Partnerships between the EU and the Community of Independent States), WWF (World Wide Fund for Nature) and USAID (United States Agency for International Development).

It was recognised that, in order for ecotourism to develop according to internationally recognised principles and within the framework of sustainable development, it is essential to coordinate joint efforts, advertising and marketing policies; establish a common standard of service; and implement ecotourism in natural reserves. In order to achieve this, the Association of Ecotourism was founded in 2001 with the support of the Ecotourism Development Fund, United States Agency for International Development (USAID) and the World Wide Fund for Nature (WWF) (https://ecodelo.org) and the National Ministry of Natural Resources of Russia. The main aim of the Association is to inform, advocate and implement world practices of ecotourism in Russia.

The Association works with local authorities and international organisations in the creation of children's eco-camps, the development of ecotourism in Kamchatka, the revival of traditional skills and the regeneration of villages in Siberia, the development of birdwatching (sport ornithology), and sustainable tourism in Smolensk. *Russian Conservation News*, a journal published by the Association, is available in Russian as well as in English to attract both a Russian- and an English-speaking readership, to share knowledge and experience of nature conservation in Russia, and to inform and educate the general public on the latest developments in the field.

Lapochkina *et al.* (2016) report that ecotourism in Russia is largely evidenced in national parks and a growing dynamic can be observed through the rising numbers of tourists visiting national parks. For example, 464,000 Russian tourists visited national parks in 2005 compared to 3.1 million in 2014. Despite the growing number of Russian tourists, the number of foreign tourists remains static (36,000 people in 2005 and 36,000 tourists in 2014). The main reason for such low numbers of overseas visitors is the poor infrastructure of ecotourism, low investment, weak marketing and imaging of places to visit. However, Russia's rich natural environment and extensive and varied natural and geographic areas have every potential to attract more ecotourism. Russia's current revenue from ecotourism is estimated at $12 million (compared to $14,000 million in the USA). Increased revenues could support further development of ecotourism thus contributing to the environmental agenda of the country (Lapochkina *et al.*, 2016).

2017: a year of ecology

Environment and sustainability are the focus of the Government's priorities in contemporary Russia. Russian President Vladimir Putin officially declared the year 2017 a Year of Ecology. The idea of this initiative was to attract attention to the areas of concern and to improve environmental sustainability of the country. According to the President, sustainability and the environment are not only a topical contemporary issue, it should become a systematic everyday responsibility of the authorities at all levels.[1] The Year of Ecology brought to the public attention the country's focus on preserving its natural environment, ensuring ecological efficiency and security, developing eco-awareness across all sections of society and involving the citizens in protecting the country's natural resources. Under this initiative, 234 large-scale eco-projects have been launched, 600 all-Russian nature preservation actions have been initiated and a total of 238 billion Russian Rubles (approximately £3.12 billion) of joint funding has been allocated to support the activities (A Year of Ecology in Russia, 2017).

One of the main priorities of The Year of Ecology was the development of ecotourism. Sergey Donskoi, the Minister of Natural Resources and Ecology, stated that in 2016 more than 10 million people visited nature reserves and national parks. The growth of interest in this type of tourism demands new effective approaches towards developing this market and a number of government initiatives specifically focus on successful implementation of its ideas regarding the development of ecotourism. For example, the government's national project 'The Wild Nature of Russia: to Preserve and to See' aims at enhancing conservation, restoration and sustainable use of biodiversity and natural landscapes. This includes developing ecotourism on the grounds of the 22 protected territories of national significance.

The Russian Federal government aims at developing internal tourism and tourism for foreign visitors as part of the Conception of the Long-term Social and Economic Development of the Country. The Federal Programme of Tourism Development identifies tourism as one of the strategic priorities that will contribute to addressing social and economic issues in the country. It encapsulates its main priorities and identifies ecotourism as a strategic focus among other types of tourism popular in the country, such as recreational, health, cultural and sport tourism. However, ecotourism accounts for only 1 per cent of the tourism industry in the country at present. The main areas of ecotourism in Russia are concentrated in the Far East, the Volga Region, the Urals, the North West, North Caucasus and Southern Federal Regions. Ecotourism, if developed and improved according to the expectations of sustainable development and nature conservation, is predicted to attract 0.3 million people.[2]

Development of tourism in Russia is not only a government concern. It is also a topical issue for the Russian Geographical Society (RGS). The RGS Tourism Development Committee, which convened at the Park-Museum 'Ethno-World' ('Ethnographic World') near the city of Kaluga (150 km south west of Moscow) on 24 October 2017, discussed the current state of tourism in various parts of Russia. The meeting involved local and Federal government officials and regional representatives of the Russian Geographical Society. The Agenda included an issue of attracting tourists to the Areas of Special Protection thus enhancing the popularity of ecotourism, which is still not very well developed in

Russia due to a number of reasons: lack of coherent collaborative provision in the field of ecotourism and insufficient information about the ecotourism available; cost of transportation in the country due to the monopolistic character of travel companies and the size of the country; low service quality and high costs of accommodation and food, stemming from the inefficient taxation policy in the country; the general attitude in the country to 'free' natural resources and disrespect towards the norms of eco-legislation; the low quality of eco-infrastructure and eco-technology; and a lack of professionally trained ecotour guides. One of the actions agreed at the meeting was producing brochures with tourist routes on the protected territories in the country using the good practice of Altai and Barguzinskyi Nature Reserve to attract more visitors to other areas.[3]

Ecotourism is recognised as a new contemporary type of tourism in the country, with its socio-economic benefits and long-term impact on nature and society. At the moment it is largely being developed across the Areas of Special Protection, Nature Reserves and National Parks. The idea of ecological parks is also developing, although their number is still limited and some of them are privately organised by enthusiasts and philanthropists. Clearfield is one of them.

Clearfield: a new eco-park near Moscow

The establishment of Clearfield was influenced by its founder's desire to move away from Moscow, Russia's capital, and to settle in the countryside in order to enjoy a higher quality of life in a tranquil territory unspoilt by pollution, traffic, urbanisation and over-population. Having explored various areas outside Moscow, he found a place he liked which was far enough from Moscow and yet within a two-hour drive from the capital. Only several hectares of land were purchased at the beginning with a view to building a house for himself and his family. However, his love for the place grew bigger and eventually he bought 500 hectares, which was too large a territory for just one family and he decided to develop his land to make it a special place for sharing with others who hold similar values and who would enjoy and appreciate Clearfield's beauty and character. Clearfield is a purely private initiative funded by its founder without any additional/government funding supporting the project. The main reason for this is 'the anti-building' philosophy of the eco-park. Contrary to the government focus, it does not aim at creating numerous new workplaces or extensive infrastructure.

The idea of Clearfield with its tranquil natural beauty unspoilt by urbanisation is not influenced by official policies or government initiatives. On the contrary, it stems from a human desire for beauty, spirituality and connection with nature. It also reflects the current demand amongst the urban population to escape the traditional and new challenges of large cities, experience a better quality of life and engage with meaningful recreational activities in beautiful natural settings. This is a recognised issue in the development of society in particular and civilisation in general, which is caused by a growing population living in large cities. According to the UN World Cities Report 2016, a yearly average number of urban dwellers globally has grown from 57 million between 1990 and 2000 to 77 million between 2010 and 2015. In 1990 43 per cent (2.3 billion) of the world's population lived in urban areas, by 2015 this figure had grown to 54 per cent (4 billion). The World Population Review states that Moscow's population in 2016 was estimated to be 12.19 million people making it the sixth largest city in the world and the most populous city in Russia. However, these figures are not believed to be completely accurate as, due to illegal migration, the true figure may be between 13 and 17 million.

A growing urban population is influenced by the forces of social, technological, environmental, political and economic change and Clearfield is a natural response which addresses two important social issues characteristic for contemporary Russian society: demand for a high quality, natural environment that is lacking in large cities, and spiritual development and searching for 'right' values. Its eco-focus seeks to enhance personal development and growth through encouraging learning and intellectual development in a clear natural environment with its beautiful landscape surrounded by water, trees and beautiful views.

Alexander Andrianov, a deputy CEO of the National Sustainable Development Agency, sees Clearfield as a project that demonstrates characteristics which make it an ecotourism destination through its:

- thoughtfully designed architecture, which is considered part of spiritual life
- non-intrusion into wildlife habitat
- careful use of water resources and creation of natural water features using methods of permaculture
- encouragement of eco-culture which stimulates careful treatment of the wildlife and nature resources and protective behaviour in the territory of the park
- avoidance of religious influences and escapism, prevalent in many similar initiatives across Russia.

Clearfield differs from many current ecotourism initiatives in the country as it combines ecological farming and functional creativity of eco-architecture. Clearfield's eco-village offers diverse, comfortable and energy-efficient accommodation to its visitors, as well as meeting rooms for educational activities and restaurants for sampling locally produced organic products of the highest quality. All the buildings in the park are designed to highlight and enhance the beauty of nature. A variety of animals live freely within the park. In the centre of the park there is a manmade lake, built using the principle of permaculture.

The park operates an eco-laboratory as a collaborative event platform for architects from around the world who are involved in designing contemporary energy-efficient houses using eco-sensitive technology. The educational centre hosts seminars, conferences, developmental programmes and workshops for knowledge exchange and skills development.

The first event, which laid the foundation for all further events, was a festival of eco-living, *Ekotectonika* in 2015. This was an official opening event for

Clearfield when the eco-park was officially introduced to the public. Alexander Andrianov, the organiser of the event, remembers it as

> a very beginning … no building was taking place at the time. But the festival has set out Clearfield's direction as an eco-park with certain values for people who share these values. So, the people who came to the festival saw the place and started conversations about its development.

In summer 2016, Clearfield hosted the 2nd Russian Festival of Green Architecture and Eco-friendly Lifestyle.

> This time it was different as we by then had hotels, facilities, water, electricity … The infrastructure had been build. People who visited it could see some finished houses and a lake in the center of the park. So, they could evidence the development of the park and to see its values underpinning the development. Some officials visited this time (Ministers from Tula and Moscow, some MPs, etc.). So it was an official opening of the actual project of green architecture and eco-friendly lifestyle.
>
> (Andrianov, 2017)

The aim of the Festival was to challenge and transform the existing approaches to architectural design and construction though education in the field of eco-building. The Festival was organised around four main event platforms: 'Central Stage' which hosted presentations, expert talks, key-note addresses, Q&A sessions and award ceremonies; 'Building Workshops' for interactive presentations by industry experts, practical skills workshops and quizzes; 'Eco-Life Master Class' with talks and lectures by relevant experts; and 'Children's Workshops' which organised children's activities such as drawing, sculpture and costume-making.

The focus on children's development is another priority area of the eco-park. Experienced architects carry out educational programmes for young architects. A children's camp, which operates at Clearfield, has a strong focus on environmental education and community development. Additionally, the eco-park offers its visitors, young and old, a range of outdoor activities: horse riding, cycling and cross-country skiing can be enjoyed along a network of different routes at any time of year.

The overall strategy of the Clearfield project is built on the principle of the integration of sustainability and responsibility; the idea of creating a community of people seeking true a connection with nature forms the underlying fabric of the Clearfield project. Events and festivals such as a theatre festival, family educational holidays, children's summer schools with a focus on languages, theatre and dance, and other children's summer activities are carried out in the open air which is unusual for urban children whose educational activities in a city typically take place indoors. Visitors engage in educational ecological tourism for families and children through creative projects where they make clothes and costumes for their theatre performances, practice acting, read and discuss books, go on walking trips, collect mushrooms and study insects and plants and experience connecting with nature and their inner selves in a variety of ways.

The activities organised at Clearfield support the idea of holistic development of individuals and the community. With a focus on architecture, the eco-park places a particular emphasis on the aesthetic unity of nature and human activity, a recognition of the environmental concerns that we face, and innovation in architectural design that adheres to the challenges of sustainability of our future on this planet.

The eco-park's transformational impact on society is also evident through its contribution to the development of the local infrastructure. For example, the roads, which have been built for the visitors, can also be used for the needs of the local community. A unique feature of Clearfield's establishment and development as a non-profit initiative is its' self-funding. This is rare, considering the national context in which the eco-park is being established. Ecotourism and innovation is a relatively new industry in Russia, the country that has progressed through a period of dramatic economic, social and political transformation since the collapse of its communist regime in 1991. It is yet to develop its more sophisticated approach to addressing the social and environmental challenges that the world and the country face today. One such approach could be to focus on developing eco-cities, which is also a new and innovative idea for Russia. Concerned with sustainability of our living, eco-cities feature prominently in policy discourses worldwide and represent a topical research agenda in the field of urban studies and planning, and urban geography (Caprotti, 2014). First, grass-roots initiatives for creating eco-cities in Russia have started developing in the country (e.g. the town of Tarusa) and deserve special attention.

In summary

This chapter has considered Clearfield as an emerging destination for ecotourism and as an example of best practice in eco-event spaces and eco-venues in Russia as a post-transformational space. The chapter has demonstrated that the latest developments in the field of sustainability and responsibility, initiated by the government in Russia during the Year of Ecology, place an emphasis on the development of ecotourism in the country. However, the integration of society and innovation at the grass-roots level, such as in Clearfield, already contributes to the enhancement of ecotourism and addresses the global challenges of social and environmental change. A more collaborative approach by the government and society in developing eco-parks (and potentially eco-cities) would certainly achieve better results for the country and the global community.

Acknowledgements

The authors would like to thank Alexander Andrianov, a deputy CEO of the National Sustainable Development Agency, Russia, for giving of his time to be interviewed and providing valuable insights into his field of work.

Further resources

www.bibliofond.ru
www.ecotourism-russia.ru
https://ecodelo.org
www.welcomeurope.com

Notes

1 http://ecoyear.ru
2 www.programs-gov.ru
3 www.rgo.ru

References

A Year of Ecology in Russia (2017). Available at: http://ecoyear.ru (accessed 28 February 2018).
Andrianov, A. (2017). Telephone interview. 10 August 2017.
Caprotti, F. (2014). *Critical Research on Eco-cities? A Walk through the Sino-Singapore Tianjin Ecocity*. Available at: www.academia.edu/4660985/Caprotti_F_2014_Critical_research_on_eco-cities_A_walk_through_the_Sino-Singapore_Tianjin_Eco-City (accessed 2 July 2018).
Donohoe, H. M. and Needham, R. D. (2006). Ecotourism: the evolving contemporary definition. *Journal of Ecotourism*, 5 (3): 192–210.
Evstrop'eva, O. V. and Korytnyi, L. M. (2016). How to develop cross-border ecotourism in the Lake Baikal Basin. *Problems of Economic Transition*, 58 (7–9): 794–804.
Lapochkina, V. V., Kosareva, N. V. and Adashova, T. V. (2016). Environmental tourism in Russia: trends in development. *International Research Journal*, 5 (47).
Ministry of Natural Resources and Ecology of the Russian Federation. (2018). Available at: www.mnr.gov.ru (accessed 26 January 2018).
National Park Alania. (2018). Available at: www.npalania.ru (accessed 26 January 2018).
Sochi National Park. (2018). Available at: www.sochinationalpark.ru (accessed 26 January 2018).
Sveriges National Park. (2018). Available at: www.nationalparksofsweden.se (accessed 26 January 2018).
UN World Cities Report. (2016). *UN Habitat for a Better Urban Future*. Available at: www.unhabitat.com (accessed 28 February 2018).
Yellowstone. (2018). Available at: www.nps.gov (accessed 26 January 2018).

13 Sustainable development in regional nature parks in France

The case of the Camargue Nature Park

Erick Leroux and Thomas Majd

Introduction

Since France's regional nature parks (PNRs in French) were created, they have shown their ability to manage and protect natural areas. Sustainable development has meant that they had to inject some dynamism into the territories that come under their management. They have done this notably by marketing PNR as a brand, based on valuation strategies, which has served as a lever for local development, and also emphasised the preservation and reasonable use of natural resources under their authority. Such is the case of Parc Naturel Régional de Camargue (PNRC) which for several years has implemented a strategy of sustainable development. PNRC is famous for its biodiversity and as an exceptional wetland, and it is supported by many stakeholders (local governmental bodies, professionals, various associations, local inhabitants and companies) who provide help in the preservation of the natural environment and in the development of the area. In that sense, PNRC relies on a framework which considers the area under management as a regulatory system, mediation with the stakeholders as a cognitive principle, participation as a modus operandi, governance as a conventional setup, agreements as relational schemes and sustainable development as a common project. As a reminder, there are various approaches to sustainable development in the field of ecotourism (Lozato-Giotart *et al.*, 2012).

The first part of our work in this chapter will present France's regional nature parks and their missions, and provide a reminder about sustainable tourism. Then we will devote the second part to Parc Naturel Régional de Camargue, with its natural environment, its specific bull-rearing as well as gastronomical aspects, and PNRC's sustainable development and ecotourism strategy.

Regional nature parks in France

Regional nature parks: a public area management system

France's regional nature parks were created in 1967 and endowed with an operating mode based on concertation with a view to preserving the natural environment. Their approach has effectively relied on a sustainable development policy long before that concept emerged. Right from the time of their inception PNRs have had to ensure harmony between the preservation of the environment and the development of rural areas struggling to conserve their natural and cultural heritage. When sustainable development appeared in the 1980s, PNRs accentuated their sustainable development policy by promoting sustainable tourism, invigorating local crafts, commerce and agricultural production. Thereafter, the term 'Parc naturel regional' appeared as a brand, through which PNRs could value their activities in terms of the protection and valuation of ecosystems. The economic agents of PNR-managed areas could also value their products better as a result.

Regional nature parks were created for both the protection and the valuation of large regional areas in France. Each PNR supports a sustainable development project based on the protection of its natural and cultural heritage and the valuation of the various components of that heritage (Leroux, 2010). The founding principle is that only a predominantly rural area may receive the PNR label, subject to its natural and cultural heritage being recognised as at once fragile, specific and of outstanding quality. PNRs are therefore areas sharing a common objective of sustainable development based on the conservation of natural and cultural heritage resources. Numbering 52 to date, they cover 15 per cent of France's national territory. The latest addition was the Calanques regional nature park. Altogether they represent roughly 4,000 villages or towns and over three million people.

At the national level there is a Federation of Regional Nature Parks, which is the voice of the network of regional parks. It allows its members to share their problems – and solutions – and work together on common methods, communicate on achievements and plan for the future. In order to fulfil this multifaceted mission, the Federation relies on the following entities:

•   The Assembly ('Assemblée générale') brings together all members of the Federation and a general meeting of the assembly must take place once a year, possibly more often if necessary. It discusses and approves Federation policy, strategic direction and action programmes. It falls into three sub-groups:

    Parks: 155 representatives
    Regions: 57 representatives
    Partners: 17 representatives

•   The Bureau includes 23 members appointed at the Annual General Meeting. It is the executive branch of the Federation. The Bureau issues recommendations about new parks and about updates of the Federation's Charter, and prepares and investigates applications submitted to the Assembly. It also studies proposals of strategic direction issued by the committees and draws up partnership agreements. Current issues, the preparation of national positions, and the evolution of parks and their difficulties may be debated at the Conference of Presidents and Managers. The committees and work groups, up to 40-strong, make proposals and meet several times per year. The Park Managers Group contributes to the strategic reflection and draws up proposals about the work carried out by committees or the bureau. It is also a place where information as well as values may be shared.

• The Direction, Research and Forecasting Council ('CORP' in French) is made up of scientists, researchers and luminaries. Its role is to monitor and warn about societal issues, to contribute to the committees' reflection and give speeches during conferences and colloquiums.

Each PNR is a member of the Federation of regional nature parks. As a result, its stakeholders, such as regional governmental bodies, commit to implementing the means to ensure its continuity – for example, as regards water and waste management. Thus, despite economic crises and agricultural desertification in rural areas beset by natural disadvantages, PNRs have made possible the economic development of some areas by supporting economic sectors, by creating tourism products (thematic tours, accommodation and catering services), and by taking part in events such as fairs or trade shows.

In addition, when projects linked to urban development are being considered, the relevant regional park must be consulted and it will deliver its official opinion. The various stakeholders of each PNR are usually the governmental bodies concerned at regional, *département*, and municipal level as well as possibly chambers (e.g. chamber of agriculture), socio-professional organisations and public institutions. They take part in the management of the PNR in accordance with a Charter approved by France's national government. This Charter, lasting 15 years, sets the objectives to be achieved and the measures to be taken, notably with a view to protecting the environment and developing the Park. The Charter is later assessed. Thus, the governance and participation of each regional park is ensured by many stakeholders, and it is each park's charter which sets its specific missions, and which also determines specific objectives as well as the means to be implemented and the assessment schemes. A review of the charter and a public enquiry are also taken into account.

In this regulatory context, a so-called 'mixed syndicate' ('syndicat mixte', made up of notably all the municipalities as well as the councils concerned) works transparently, proposes a budget and takes decisions in line with thematic committees and in concertation with the various partners, including local elected representatives. Decisions and actions taken by each park are made public and available for consultation by anyone. For example, the population takes part in the parks' projects on local areas, through many community groups, public institutions and other organisations. Depending on the case, parks may mobilise people living in the area that they manage by associating them with certain activities. Furthermore, parks develop educational and awareness programmes for inhabitants as well as visitors, and solidarity initiatives in favour of certain disadvantaged groups (e.g. young people, disabled people) in the name of a more responsible and caring society. Finally, companies that are in a PNR must also commit to sustainable development (Stoll *et al.*, 2015).

The various missions of PNRs

PNRs' charters mention a number of missions, the main ones being the protection of ecosystems, the provision of support to a solidarity-based economy, and the valuation of natural and cultural heritage.

Protection of ecosystems

PNRs work towards the preservation of the areas that they manage through knowledge, and the sharing of knowledge, in order to protect biodiversity better with the help of the local population and stakeholders. Their ability to manage space efficiently is grounded in their concertation with the various economic agents, and in the areas that they manage, with regards to the species and natural spaces inventory programmes. That is the reason why biodiversity is featured in each area project and also why all the parks have adhered to the principles of the European Union's Natura 2000 network.

Social economy

In line with the objectives of sustainable development in their areas and their values, parks experiment with methods of human organisation based not only on competition but also on solidarity and participation. In partnership with agents of the solidarity-based economy, parks work towards the creation of companies or the takeover of existing ones. For example, help may be given to a co-operative. Parks also provide help to groups, connecting producers and consumers in fields linked to the defence of the environment and the area's culture, as well as to the creation of producers' organisations within an economic sector (producers, artisans and shops).

Economic valuation of natural and cultural heritage

Striving for a sustainable development based on natural and cultural heritage, PNRs help the various economic agents operating in the areas under PNR management to adhere to their charter by signing agreements. Thanks to the schemes, they aim to value their image notably by publishing books (e.g. the Encyclopaedia of the Camargue), by improving natural and cultural resources economically, and by seeking quality standards for their area. They also carry out other activities such as leading production, maintaining and developing artisanal know-how, and promoting the products and services inherent in the PNR brand. Finally, some PNRs also award prizes to the groups and governmental bodies involved in the valuation of the area.

Reminders on sustainable tourism

According to the World Tourism Organization, the number of tourists keeps on rising and should reach 1.6 billion by 2020. Most of the destinations favoured by tourists are located in developing countries, which welcome the ever-growing numbers of tourists. Those countries endowed with, sometimes fragile, nature sites are going to have to better manage their growing tourist influx. In order to curtail the risk of degradation of tourist sites, sustainable tourism can ensure wealth distribution between developed and developing countries by meeting the three main requirements of sustainable tourism:

- Environment: minimal and sustainable use of renewable resources.
- Social and societal aspects: equal opportunities between North and South, respect for the cultures of visited sites, promoting employment and health.
- Economy: wealth creation, fair distribution of income.

As tourism grew by leaps and bounds from the 1970s, it led to social and environmental problems and raised the question of how to respect the local communities and the environment. The WTO therefore recommends sustainable tourism, defined as 'Tourism that takes full account of its current and future economic, social and environmental impacts, addressing the needs of visitors, the industry, the environment and host communities'.

Several forms of sustainable tourism exist: ecotourism, rural tourism, fair tourism and participatory tourism.

In 2002, during the World Ecotourism Summit in Quebec, an official declaration recognised the relevance of the various ecotourism approaches to make tourism in its different forms more sustainable. Ecotourism is thus the best solution, as it is able to ensure that economic development, the well-being of communities, and the protection of ecosystems are combined. According to Ceballos-Lascurain (1987), ecotourism is:

> [t]he form of tourism that involves travelling to relatively undisturbed or uncontaminated natural areas with the specific object of studying, admiring and enjoying the scenery and its wild plants and animals as well as any existing cultural aspects (both past and present) found in these areas.

Several categories of indicators may be chosen: environmental, human, economic, heritage and cultural (Leroux and Pupion, 2015).

The stakeholders at the service of the sustainable development strategy of Parc Naturel Régional de Camargue

In this second part we focus on the geographical aspects of PNRC, its stakeholders and its strategic choices as regards sustainable development and ecotourism through local governance.

The Camargue: geographical aspects and tourism

The Camargue stretches over 110,000 hectares (271,815 acres) where over a hundred species of migratory and nesting birds may be observed, among which the most famous is the pink flamingo. The PNRC is situated in the River Rhône

Delta, in the *département* of Bouches-du-Rhône, thus in the Provence-Alpes-Côte d'Azur region, and was created in 1970. It includes the whole town of Saintes-Maries-de-la-Mer and part of the city of Arles. This nature park features notably a vast lagoon, the *étang de Vaccarès*. The scenery of PNRC is remarkably varied.

According to the Observatoire départemental des Bouches-du-Rhône, the PNRC is attracting growing interest from tourists, who visit the Park Information Centre (Maison du Parc), and the sites of Marais du Vigueirat, la Capelière, and Domaine de la Palissade on a regular basis. According to the survey of the PNRC (2009), the profile of visitors to the Camargue differs depending on the time of the year with short stays in the Camargue (63 per cent of tourists stay less than three days). The main reasons for visiting the PNRC are as follows: (a) hiking and horse riding, (b) mountain biking and bicycle touring, (c) hunting (d) fishing (e) water-related activities. Events such as bull-fighting and other bull-related activities, and a photography exhibition in Arles known as the Rencontres Internationales de la Photographie are other reasons cited.

The Bull: at the heart of Camargue traditions

The presence of bulls makes the Camargue an attractive area. The Camargue bull represents one of the greatest traditions of the region. In fact in addition to bull-fighting, which does exist in the Camargue but is not specific to it, there are three types of local bull traditions: Camargue bull races (where rosettes placed on the bulls' foreheads and horns have to be removed by brave young men, and the bulls are not slain at the end), street traditions (the escorting of bulls by cowboys on horseback through streets, while members of the public try to distract the bulls) and *ferrade* (catching and branding of young bulls). The bull race is of course a show but also a sport taking place in a bull-ring and officially recognised as such. Bull races take place during so-called bull days each year between March and September.

Currently there are about 150 bull farms, which compete between each other and make little profit. As a result the farms have diversified their activities in order to remain profitable and welcome visitors, offer catering facilities, or renting out their bulls for village fêtes. They have also developed event organisation activities by renting rooms for wedding receptions. As for the production of meat, it allows farms to make up for a loss of money from cattle rearing – capitalising on the AOP (Appellation d'Origine Protégée) quality label that it benefits from. Finally other food products are sold such as sausage, bull terrine, Camargue rice, and *fleur de sel* (very pure fine salt).

Camargue gastronomy and the quest for quality labels

The Camargue is an attractive area whose reputation relies on agricultural and food products, which have improved over time to become sought-after products. The annual harvest of Camargue rice, and wine from vineyards under controlled irrigation, are produced in small quantities.

The Camargue has developed know-how based on the scarcity of basic products. The transformation of products for consumption, including wine and cold cooked meats, is carried out by artisanal practice giving an image of authenticity backed by quality and/or authenticity labels (AOC, AOP, IGP). In the cultural field, tourists in the Camargue appreciate labelled products because they are entirely coherent with heritage resources such as the Nature Reserve, UNESCO Biosphere Reserve and Parc Naturel Régional de Camargue.

Typical Camargue dishes are: *aïoli* (fish, seafood and boiled vegetables together with a strongly garlic-flavoured mayonnaise), *gardianne de taureau* (bullmeat stew with rice) and *poutargue* (a sort of caviar made with mullet egg pouch).

Camargue gastronomy attaches great importance to traditional dishes, which must be reproduced in the ancestral way. Camargue cuisine is based on poor people's dishes that draw on local resources. The success of Camargue tourism, as far as visits and gastronomy are concerned, relies on concepts of life close to nature, suiting those seeking to discover the Camargue ecosystem.

In the end, Camargue culture connects together various parts that we have mentioned previously: culinary tourism, cultural tourism and sustainable tourism. Many economic agents play a role in this: bull farmers and horse farmers, community groups and governmental bodies, as well as tourist offices.

Parc Naturel Régional De Camargue's sustainable tourism strategy

A nature park's sustainable development policy requires some long-term choices, implying an agreement between all the stakeholders, always with a view to preserving the natural site. The park may have to face politicians who may harbour short-term views, notably for electoral reasons. However, within a system of area governance a single strategic agent cannot, on his or her own, impose their vision and must obtain agreement by the majority of the area's stakeholders. Otherwise conflict is likely.

The strategic orientations taken by the PNRC between 2003 and 2009 were revisited for the period from 2010 to 2015 by the stakeholders, and the resulting discussions led to a new sustainable development strategy based on four pillars, as follows:

1   A tourist offer based on the interconnection of the area's economic agents within a network, including agriculture and tourism, in an attempt to value the park's scenery and develop tourists and professionals' awareness of the preservation of the park's natural sites.
2   Ensuring the quality of the tourist offer by taking into account the environmental aspects of the park, providing solutions to the issues of insufficient accommodation and improving accessibility to the whole park area.
3   Better distribution of the tourist activities over the whole park area, taking into account tourist flux and trying to distribute tourists better on the various sites and over time (developing tourist activities in the off-peak season).

4   Working on the PNRC's image so that it is in line with the park's policy of environmental protection, respect and understanding of the cultural identity of the Rhône Delta's communities.

When it revised its charter (2010–2022), the Mixed Syndicate of the PNRC (SMPNRC) put into place a 'sustainable tourism forum' and authorised all the stakeholders to take part in discussions in accordance with the principles of the European Charter of Sustainable Tourism.

This forum was highly successful since it led to solutions on many subjects and to strategies to continue the park's sustainable development policy, namely:

- Improving ecosystems' capacity of resilience against climate
- Maintaining police and surveillance
- Developing communication
- Managing problematic species
- Limiting site pollution due to waste
- Limiting the impact of motorised traffic
- Stewarding work on the Reserve
- Asserting itself as an inescapable authority of water management in Camargue
- Establishing a management of water which may be closer to how a natural lagoon works

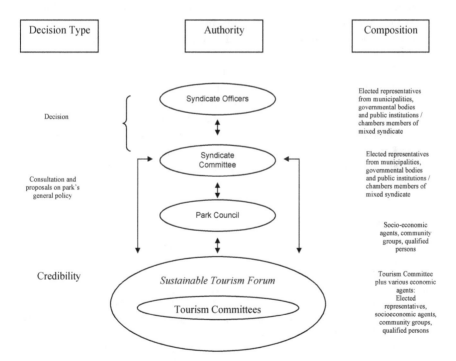

Figure 13.1 Diagram of the SMPNRC Sustainable Tourism Forum.

- Improving water quality
- Limiting the impact of fishing
- Restoring lawns
- Limiting disturbance on the dunes and beaches
- Reducing pollution originating from the sea and potential risks
- Restoring and maintaining the water systems of the specific sites of La Capelière and Salin de Badon
- Managing the environments of La Capelière and of Salin de Badon
- Improving knowledge of the Reserve's network of ponds
- Improving knowledge of the evolution of the wasteland near the Amphise site and defining how it should be managed
- Carrying out administrative and financial activities in relation to Reserve management
- Meeting the training and management needs of personnel
- Carrying out management and maintenance of equipment and infrastructure.

Conclusion

Thus, with its new sustainable development strategy, the PNRC and its stakeholders are playing a strategic role as they take an active part in the protection and development of the Camargue nature site. Outside of the field of tourism, the French government, over several decades, has tried to encourage neighbouring villages and (small) towns, generally referred to as 'communes', to come together to share some of their tasks and activities (e.g. space management and economic development) and called this process 'intercommunality' ('*intercommunalité*') – with contrasting results. In that sense the way the park area is organised is comparable to a cluster of such 'communes' for political reasons. The creation of a Sustainable Tourism Forum has allowed the park to bring together the stakeholders and harmonise the various points of view towards a common goal, while taking into account the power struggles which are part of its local and area governance, with a view to building a viable sustainable development strategy. Over the years Parc Naturel Régional de Camargue has consolidated its sustainable development strategy.

References

Ceballos-Lascurain, H. (1987). *Estudio de Prefactibilidad Socioeconómica del Turismo Ecológico y Anteproyecto Arquitectónico y Urbanístico del Centro del Turismo Ecológico de Sian Ka'an, Quintana Roo*. Étude réalisée pour SEDUE, Mexico.

Leroux, E. (2010). Stratégie et Développement Durable: du concept de l'Optimum Ecotouristique à la pratique, *Management & Avenir*, 34 (4): 306–317.

Leroux, E. and Pupion, P.-C. (2015). Management du tourisme et des loisirs (2014), Edition Vuibert, 304 pages *Labellisé FNEGE*.

Stoll, A., Carteron, J. C. and Séraphin, H. (2015). France. In W. Visser (ed.), *The World Guide to Sustainable Enterprise*. Sheffield: Greenleaf Publishing.

Part V

Sports events and sustainability

14 Formula E's 'green' challenge to motorsport events, spaces and technologies

The London e-prix as a case study

Damion Sturm

National context: introducing Formula E and the London e-prix

Motorsport rarely offers a model of sustainability. Economically it is expensive, socially it is often exclusive and privileges the elite, while politically it is most often used as a symbolic tool for ambitious nations and corporations to self-brand and self-promote. Motorsport's environmental reputation is also problematic: burning fossil fuels, leaving large global carbon footprints and the wanton waste of resources including its impacts on green spaces and locations. While large motorsport series such as Formula One and the World Endurance Championship have shifted towards hybrid technologies, their transformation to, or at least recognition for, sustainable efforts arguably has been negligible. Conversely, for Formula One, there has been a notable decline in audiences primarily due to their slower and quieter hybrid-era cars.

Enter Formula E. Created in 2014, Formula E is a global motor-racing series that promotes sustainable forms of mobility through electronic car-racing. For its fourth season (2017/2018), the series is scheduled to race in 10 different global locations that take in Asia, Africa, Europe and both North and South America. Formula E has been devised as an alternative and futuristic vision of motorsport rather than as a series to directly rival Formula One. The series is premised on 'green' technologies, with the electronic racing cars deploying battery packs and hybrid technologies to underpin the race action on offer. Outside of attempts to reduce the pollution and waste associated with traditional motorsport, Formula E also targets relationships with global 'smart' cities to spread its sustainability message. Where possible, events are staged in major cities, such as Paris, Monaco, Montreal, Berlin, New York and Hong Kong, and raced in central city locations. London hosted the event in the first two seasons of Formula E, staging races in Battersea Park, a Grade II listed Victorian park, in 2015 and 2016. While this was notable for providing racing in a central London location, staging 'green' races within this green space proved controversial as the subsequent discussion shall demonstrate.

Priority issues: Formula E's sustainability challenge

Formula E proclaims to provide 'the unique fusion of entertainment, sustainability, technology and innovation. We are fighting climate change by offering electric vehicles as a solution to air pollution in city centres and breaking down the barriers to the electric vehicle market'.[1] On its website, the sport acknowledges and outlines a range of contemporary environmental issues outside of motorsport. Global air pollution harmfully impacts on 80 per cent of urban residents breathing polluted air, while 6.5 million allegedly die annually from premature air pollution related illnesses. In addition, global transport in 2015 produced one quarter of all fossil fuel carbon emissions; this is expected to rise to 50 per cent by 2050. Formula E strives to initiate change by providing zero emissions, using recycled tyres and reducing its carbon footprint (freighting equipment by sea and road whilst clustering events in global locations). The sport also entered into a global partnership with the UN Environment in 2017 to improve inner city air quality, profile alternative energy solutions and promote the increased uptake of electric vehicles. With France and the UK banning all petrol and diesel cars by 2040 (Asthana and Taylor, 2017; Chrisafis and Vaughan, 2017), a global shift to hybrid technologies is anticipated. In this vein, major car manufacturers Renault, BMW, Citroen, Jaguar, Audi, Mercedes and Porsche have joined, or are joining, the series, aligning electric motor-racing with future 'green' road car developments. Finally, with an emphasis on cities and city racing, the series advocates the construction of temporary rather than permanent race tracks to utilise existing infrastructure, including encouraging public transport by not providing spectator car parks.

Trends: how 'green' are Formula E events?

Despite increasing attempts to provide more 'green', ecology-friendly and environmentally sustainable events, most major sports events have been criticised for non-realistic environmental measures. Indeed, since the 2000s, the sustainability and legacy of most Olympics and World Cup environmental practices have been challenged as forms of 'greenwashing', misrepresenting their actual value or impact (Boykoff and Mascarenhas, 2016; Miller, 2018). Similar criticisms remain across motorsport and the contestable claims for various events and series (Miller, 2016; Trantor and Lowe, 2009).

The rhetoric and realities around Formula E's 'green' credentials remain less certain due to the environmental concerns, issues and controversies raised in some locations. To date, Formula E's uptake, interest and acceptance has been moderate across its first three seasons. The addition of major car manufacturers lends weight to the series' technological initiatives and its growing short-term relevance, but the television viewing figures remain small (dwarfed by Formula One). Live spectatorship is also often problematic, implying that associated tourism impacts are minimal. Finally, collectively, audiences have bemoaned the almost silent cars (derided as 'vacuum cleaner racing') and the present need for drivers to change to a second car mid-race as an inefficient and insufficient form of hybrid-battery power.

From a marketing perspective, Formula E offers the host cities opportunities to self-brand by having technologically 'green' cars racing around iconic city-scapes. In turn, this has potential longer-term benefits for tourism via its global media images evoking notions of destination marketing. Furthermore, there is also a perceived positive association for host cities with environmental sustainability messages, although criticisms have flagged that many of these 'smart cities' have their own dubious sustainability credentials as major contributors to persistent environmental issues.

Government policies: legislating motor-racing in a UK 'green' space

As one of the pre-eminent global cities, London was targeted as a host nation for Formula E in its inaugural 2014/2015 season. However, pre-existing legislation prevented staging motor-racing events on most public roads in the UK. Hence, alternative locations for a city-based London event were sought. A five-year deal was struck to provide the season-ending races (staged as double headers) within Battersea Park. Opened in 1858, Battersea Park is a 200 acre green space in the London Borough of Wandsworth. As noted earlier, it is also a Grade II listed Victorian park complete with green spaces, sports grounds, a zoo, waterways, wildlife and a range of historical monuments. In 2004, it reopened after an £11 million, two-year refurbishment by the Heritage Lottery Fund.

Although a protracted process for temporarily racing in Battersea Park, the organisers of Formula E noted its heightened media significance, public interest and potential for raising awareness by racing near the city centre. To allow the Formula E event to take place within Battersea Park, a Venue Use Agreement replete with planning permission, public consultation and Safety Advisory Group consultations were required. Additionally, given its historic listing, the event needed to satisfy a heritage impact assessment, as well as the Heritage Lottery Fund, who work to ensure that the park's heritage features are protected.

Intriguingly, the heritage impact assessment viewed the normal use of, and access to, large sections of the park for three weeks as unacceptable. Nevertheless, despite stern public opposition, anger at perceived inadequate consultation times and 'green' concerns raised by a range of protest groups, Formula E was granted permission to use Battersea Park.

Case study: issues of staging Formula E in Battersea Park

Running Formula E motor-racing within Battersea Park reveals the contradictions and tensions that can arise when attempting to stage a 'green' event within a 'green' space. Branded as a greener version of Formula One and the sustainable future of motorsport, Formula E organisers place an emphasis on bringing electronic motor-racing to street circuits around major cities rather than specially designed permanent racing tracks. Formula E also targets larger urban audiences, anticipating crowds of 40,000–60,000 for the first London event. By comparison, organisers suggested staging a similar event at a permanent circuit within the UK, such as Donington Park in Leicestershire, would likely only attract 5,000 attendees. Collectively the series seeks to educate on environmental issues, promote alternative technologies and to advocate for reduced noise and air pollution. Of course, via the media, having sustainable cars racing around iconic city landmarks lends itself to branding opportunities for the host locations and for positive public relations as 'smart' cities that are environmentally conscious. In principle, with the creation of the London e-prix, the stage was set for the successful running of a sustainable motor-racing event in a traditional central city park. In reality, the gulf between perceptions of what a 'green' event looks like and the notable impacts on a 'green' space were marked.

Focusing on the 2015 London event in season one, an estimated crowd of 27,000 on Saturday 27 June and 28,500 on Sunday 28 June attended the London e-prix. Despite concerns about inflated figures, the event had been capped at 30,000 per day and reflected audience numbers reported at other Formula E events. Tickets had intentionally also been priced low, with early-bird tickets between £8 and £15. Alternatively, the cheapest adult race day pass of £99 at the British Formula One Grand Prix provides a striking contrast for prices between both events, compounded by additional transportation and likely accommodation costs for the Grand Prix in its rural and isolated Northamptonshire location at the Silverstone circuit (annually staged in July since 1950). Strategically, the low pricing and central London setting allowed Formula E to drum up interest in a new and innovative form of sustainable motor-racing that targeted racing fans, the general public and local families. However, located in a 'green' space and historical parkland, the event was enveloped in issues around accessibility, usage and potential damage that brought Formula E's 'green' values into question.

A post-event review by the Wandsworth Borough Council in 2015 flagged up many of the issues raised around noise complaints, restricted access, environmental damage and growing public opposition to staging Formula E within Battersea Park. As the Formula E website, *current-e.com*, surmised,

> Given the astonishing vehemence and vocal nature of local opposition to the race, however, as well as issues that the venue itself presented (a very narrow track; difficulty in siting grandstands due to trees; obscured visibility for audiences; disruption to park users during set up and break down; disruption to set up due to imposed limitations on working hours; impeded access around the track for event workers), it might be time to default to another location.
>
> ('Battersea hanging in the balance', para. 4)

More pertinent was the collective persistence of five protest groups who opposed the continuation of the event. The Battersea Park Formula E Action Group, the

Warriner Gardens and Alexandra Avenue Residents, the Battersea Society, the Prince of Wales Drive Mansion Blocks and the Friends of Battersea Park, insisted that the event be stopped while citing a range of issues also documented in the Wandsworth Council's review. For the race itself, despite the relative silence of the racing cars, the noisy overhead helicopters broadcasting the event to global television audiences were pinpointed, while also noting the use of public address systems and loud music. More significant, however, was the perceived disruption, closures and destruction that staging the event precipitated.

Despite Formula E paying £1m in compensation, of which the Council suggested £200,000 would go directly back into the park, as well as repaving some of the pathways, concerns were raised at the damage caused. Large machinery was needed within the park to erect barriers, spectator points, and establish the track by widening carriageways. Additionally, thousands of concrete barriers and fences were transported to and from the park. As such, the installation was a noisy and disruptive affair which (un)surprisingly, also transformed previous green areas into tarmac. Opponents suggested that such processes transformed a conservation area into a construction site. Collectively, the set-up and de-rigging left its own environment footprint via closures to public spaces and the zoo (including needing to remove animals during the event), the cancellation of school sport events, while damaging trees and disturbing wildlife. Health and safety elements were also called into question. Closing a popular 'green' space and historically listed Grade II park during the busy summer months for almost three weeks also met with condemnation from residents, park users and other vocal protest groups. Collectively, many challenged representations of Formula E in Battersea Park as a 'green' event and advocated for its removal.

Intriguingly, the council voted to retain the event in 2016, meaning a continuation to closing large sections of the park while also imposing an increased one month timeframe to allow more set-up and de-rigging time. Nevertheless, there were concessions made around noise (reducing public announcements and promoting headphone usage during the event), fewer helicopters flown and tighter restrictions around lorry usage pre- and post-event. Assurances to repair, reinstate and improve the park were also made. Nevertheless, such concessions seemed to only further enrage the persistent opposition groups. Taylor (2015) noted that, 'there was a "sustained and vociferous" opposition to the event, with 400 residents making direct contact with the council and 2,576 signatories on an online petition by Save Battersea Park' (para. 8). Additionally, allegedly 62 per cent disagreed or strongly disagreed to the staging of the event via the council's online consultation. Although the event returned at Battersea Park for Formula E's second season in 2016, this would be its last iteration. Not only were the oppositional groups more vocal and resurgent, but legal proceedings were also prepared against the council. The Battersea Park Action Group filed pre-action proceedings based on Battersea's illegal closure (London public parks cannot be closed for more than six consecutive days), as well as to protect the park on environmental and historical grounds from perceived commercial exploitation. Subsequently, the legal threat and heavy public opposition has forced Formula E out of Battersea Park, out of London and out of the UK since 2016. Nevertheless, rumours persist of a proposed London e-prix being staged around its streets and iconic landmarks in the not-too-distant future.

Case studies: Formula E in Miami and Formula One in Melbourne

The green event versus green space controversy at Battersea Park is not commonplace to Formula E. Admittedly, it should be noted that the series has currently only run for three seasons and that not every location renewed. For example, races were formerly staged in Beijing, Moscow and Putrajaya (Malaysia), while Hong Kong, New York and Montreal were new additions for season three. However, there has been a sense of stability and prolonged longevity to the series, reinforced by the increasing number of manufacturer-teams recently joining Formula E, notably Jaguar, BMW, Audi, Mercedes and Porsche, that are seeking to push the sustainable technological innovations further. Additionally, new locations are continuing to sign up, including Santiago (Chile), Sao Paulo and Rome for season four.

The prime concern noted for Formula E seems to be around the impact of closing city streets for a motor-racing event, with calls to potentially reconsider using existing permanent race tracks (as is done for the Mexican e-prix). In the United States, the Formula E locations have included Miami, Long Beach for two seasons and New York from season three. The Miami event had elements that replicated the controversy at Battersea Park. Originally slated as a five-year deal, the Miami contract was terminated after one season, with little disclosure or explanation. Primarily, however, it would appear 'green' concerns were at the heart of the event's demise. Run at the popular Biscayne Boulevard, the event incurred costs of approximately US$2m to convert the area into a suitable street-racing track. There was also outrage at the need to seal 'green' spaces around the waterfront, covering these over with tarmac. Collectively, negative press coverage and public opposition questioned the 'green' credentials of an event needing to transform and replace a green space. Moreover, rather than promoting green events and sustainable practices, it appeared that Formula E was being used primarily for image-building and as a beautification project within the Miami area.

Elsewhere, a more notable and ongoing issue has been the racing of Formula One cars around Albert Park in Melbourne, Australia. Although the sport has introduced hybrid technologies in recent times, a history of dubious 'green' practices related to its exorbitant expenses and excessive waste has long been associated with Formula One. In 1996, the Australian Grand Prix shifted from a street-race in Adelaide to racing around a public park in Melbourne. Despite a public outcry, including the formation and efforts of the Save Albert Park protest group, the race was ushered in by the local Victorian Government. Opened in 1864, Albert Park is a 560-acre public park, 3 km south of the Melbourne CBD (Central Business District) with numerous green spaces, a lake, sports facilities, a golf course and an abundance of wildlife. Despite being protected by environmental legislation that prohibits a range of activities within the parkland, the Australian Grand Prix Act provided dispensation for the event, superseding the pre-existing legislation.

Staging the Grand Prix raises numerous environmental issues and challenges to notions of sustainable sports events in green spaces. For example, despite being a popular and heavily used public space, Albert Park is closed for nearly three months to accommodate set-up and de-rigging for the four-day Grand Prix race weekend. This also negatively impacts on the sports facilities and other leisure spaces that are both unavailable for public use but often also damaged via the heavy machinery and labour-intensive set up of the temporary race circuit. Although Formula One has dampened the sound of its engines (approximately 130 decibels from 150), the Australian Grand Prix was regularly shrouded in issues around noise pollution and complaints, both from local residents as well as the shrill of the cars still reverberating in parts of the city centre (Lowes, 2004). Much of the Save Albert Park protest group opposition centred on the effects on the ecosystem (disruption to wild life, damage to trees and detracting from public use of a green space), as well as annoyance at the local government's apparent disregard for both the parkland and its associated environmental legalisation. Indeed, ongoing concerns around costs, access and environmental impacts are largely deflected by the local government and race organisers (Tranter and Lowes, 2009), citing its perceived benefits for branding the city, state and for attracting tourists. Thus, despite running at an annual estimated loss of AU$60 million, and despite its disruption and closure of a large public green space for approximately three months, the staging of the Australian Grand Prix in Albert Park shows few signs of abating as it enters its 22nd year.

Finally, other motor-racing events have successfully infused sustainable or perceived 'green' technologies within their series. For example, the Isle of Man TT event consists of two weeks of motor-cycle racing around the Isle. Embedded within this is the 'TT Zero' series, with riders racing on hybrid electric bikes that produce zero toxic emissions, as one of the contested events. From an environmental perspective, even more successful has been the adoption of hybrid technologies in the World Endurance Series. In its flagship race, the Le Mans 24 hours, the LMP1 electronic prototype cars are literally in a class of their own, being a full ten seconds per lap faster than the closest non-hybrid cars. Despite their positive performative results, the immense cost of hybrid technologies saw two successful manufacturers, Audi and Porsche, leave the series in 2016 and 2017 respectively to join Formula E. While indicating a foreseeable future for sustainable electronic motor-racing, their departure is also a likely deathblow to hybrid prototypes in Endurance racing in the short-term. Alternatively, it was announced in August 2017 that the World RallyCross Championship will require all cars to be electronic by 2020.

Further resources

Formula E's sustainability initiatives and linkages provide more details on their alternative technologies, efforts to reduce and recycle, and the broader premise for what they seek to achieve via the various measures and innovations at the centre of the Formula E series.

See http://info.fiaformulae.com/sustainability/

The oppositional and protest groups against staging motor-races in 'green' spaces and public parks can be accessed here in relation to Battersea Park and Albert Park respectively:

http://savebatterseapark.com/issues-at-a-glance/
http://save-albert-park.org.au/

With street racing being legalised on British public roads, London officials have allegedly been in contact with Formula E about staging races within the city centre. One stipulation for any motor-racing event is a reduction in air pollution; Formula E seems preferred to showcase its sustainability initiatives. However, due to the ongoing financial issues with the Silverstone Racing Circuit and the expensive fees for hosting Formula One, London is also being mooted as a future possible site for a London Formula One Grand Prix.

See www.theguardian.com/politics/2017/apr/07/monaco-style-grand-prix-england-public-roads-uk-department-transport
https://joesaward.files.wordpress.com/2017/07/london-gp.pdf

Note

1 http://info.fiaformulae.com/sustainability/

References

Asthana, A. and Taylor, M. (2017). Britain to ban sale of all diesel and petrol cars and vans from 2040. 25 July, *Guardian*. Available at: www.theguardian.com/politics/2017/jul/25/britain-to-ban-sale-of-all-diesel-and-petrol-cars-and-vans-from-2040 (accessed 28 July 2017).
'Battersea hanging in the balance?' (2015). *current-e.com*, 17 November. Available at: http://current-e.com/chatter/battersea-hanging-in-the-balance/ (accessed 25 July 2017).
Boykoff, J. and Mascarenhas, G. (2016). The Olympics, sustainability, and greenwashing: The Rio 2016 Summer Games. *Capitalism Nature Socialism*, 27 (2): 1–11.
Chrisafis, A. and Vaughan, A. (2017). France to ban sales of petrol and diesel cars by 2040. 6 July, *Guardian*. Available at: www.theguardian.com/business/2017/jul/06/france-ban-petrol-diesel-cars-2040-emmanuel-macron-volvo (accessed 25 July 2017).
Lowes, M. (2004). Neoliberal power politics and the controversial siting of the Australian Grand Prix motorsport event in a public park. *Loisir et Société/Society and Leisure*, 27: 69–88.

Miller, T. (2016). Greenwashed sports and environmental activism: Formula 1 and FIFA. *Environmental Communication*, 10 (6): 719–733.

Miller, T. (2018). *Greenwashing Sport.* London and New York: Routledge.

Taylor, R. (2015). Promises of a quieter Formula E 2016 as five groups object to its Battersea Park return. 17 November, *Wandsworth Guardian.* Available at: www. wandsworthguardian.co.uk/news/14037100.Promises_of_a_quieter_Formula_E_2016_ as_five_groups_object_to_its_Battersea_Park_return/ (accessed 28 July 2017).

Tranter, P. and Lowes, M. (2009). Life in the fast lane: environmental, economic, and public health outcomes of motorsport spectacles in Australia. *Journal of Sport and Social Issues*, 33: 150–168.

15 Innovation in sustainable surfing events and mainstreaming sustainability behaviors

Jess Ponting and Sandra Sun-Ah Ponting

Introduction

The World Surf League (WSL) is a professional sporting organization that staged 255 surfing events in 26 countries in 2016. This chapter explores the issues of sustainability at WSL events and attempts to incorporate sustainability not just into the staging of the event but also into event messaging which, given the sport's cultural cache amongst youth and an estimated global audience of 125 million (Beer, 2015), has real potential to influence behaviors beyond those in direct attendance. We focus on a case study of the 2013 Fiji Pro, which leveraged three outside entities in achieving some best practice sustainability outcomes in the staging and execution of the event and in significant sustainability messaging to the global viewing audience. In addition we discuss the very promising, but currently stalled, efforts to incorporate sustainability into the WSL's world championship tour events since 2014.

While a literature on the sustainability of surf tourism has developed (c.f. Martin and Assenov, 2012), sustainability and surfing events is an area that has barely been considered to date. Some research on social impacts of surfing events has been conducted in South Africa, notably Ntloko and Swart (2008) found that the Red Bull Big Wave Africa event had done such a poor job of including local stakeholder groups that it threatened the longevity of the event (which was indeed discontinued shortly thereafter), and Ahmed et al. (2008) concluded that a beach awareness campaign deployed during a surfing event in Durban was largely ineffective. In the first real sustainability assessment of a surfing event undertaken at the Boardmasters Quiksilver Open in the UK, a World Surf League qualifying series event, Whittlesea (2015) found much room for improvement and usefully measured many sustainability metrics to give a ballpark understanding of water and electricity use, and greenhouse-gas emissions from a major beachside surfing event.

Context

Surfing events have an ancient history in pre-colonial Polynesia. Though surfing in various forms was practiced in many parts of the world before the twentieth century including much of Polynesia and Melanesia, Peru, and West Africa it was Hawaii where surfing reach its peak as a central component of cultural expression (Laderman, 2014; Walker, 2011; Westwick and Neushul, 2013). Surfing was woven into the cultural fabric of everyday life in pre-colonial Hawaii where it functioned as an important mode of inter-gender mingling which was made difficult in other areas of life as a result of the *kapu* system of taboos, which kept men and women apart when working or eating. Surfing events attracted large crowds as contestants gambled valuable commodities like livestock, fishing nets, hand hewn canoes, and even their own freedom on the outcome. One contest between Maui and Oahu surfing champions reportedly involved stakes of 16 war canoes and 4000 pigs (Westwick and Neushul, 2013).

The first World Surfing Championships were held at Manly Beach in Australia in 1964 and were won by local surfer Midget Farrelly with a crowd of around 65,000 in attendance. While the event was indeed billed as a world championship contest, an international sporting body did not sanction it and only Australia, the United States and Peru were represented. In 1965, a true world championship sanctioned by the newly formed International Surfing Federation was staged in Peru and won by Peruvian Filipe Pomar. In 1966, Australian Nat Young won the World Championship event in San Diego in front of 80,000 spectators (Heimann, 2016; Warshaw, 2010). From their beginnings, surfing championship events have faced the challenges of large audiences on fragile coastal, beach and intertidal environments.

Professional surfing events began with the formation of the International Professional Surfers (IPS) in 1976. The IPS was taken over by Australian Ian Cairns and changed its name to the Association of Surfing Professionals (ASP) in 1984. The ASP was purchased by Zosea Media, a group led by billionaire Dirk Ziff in 2013 and was ultimately rebranded the World Surf League (WSL) in 2015 (Heimann, 2016). The WSL now oversees 11 international 'tours' comprised of 255 events in 26 countries (WSL, 2016). The most watched events are the World Championship Tours (WCTs) which, in the case of men, consists of 11 events in 8 countries, and in the case of women consists of 10 events in 6 countries.

Priority issues

Surfing is an activity practiced by more than 35 million people from the 101 member countries of the International Surfing Association (O'Brien and Eddie, 2013), 5.3 million in the United States alone (The Outdoor Foundation, 2015), and growing at 30 percent per year (WSL, 2016). Practiced by world leaders including the 44th President of the United States, former Prime Minister of Australia Tony Abbott, and current Canadian Prime Minister Justin Trudeau, the United States Outdoor Foundation (2015) ranked surfing as the fourth favorite outdoor activity in the US (behind running, bicycling, and skateboarding) amongst youth aged between 6 and 24 years in terms of frequency of participation across 4.4 billion outings.

As well as attracting large crowds of spectators to these contests, the WSL has a large and growing following of its contest broadcasts over the Internet and television. New viewership records were set during the 2014 Billabong Pipeline Masters when 6.2 million people tuned in to watch via the WSL's youtube channel alone (Minsberg and Corasaniti, 2015). This record was broken the following year with the Billabong Pro Tahiti that claimed a facebook reach of 58 million people, 1.9 million viewers online, and 12 million television viewers across Australia, Brazil, Hawaii, France, and Portugal (Stapelberg, 2014). As of November 7, 2017, the WSL had 6.5 million Facebook followers (up 1.9 million from mid-2016), 2.6 million Instagram followers, and almost 2 million Twitter followers. The WSL's potential global audience has been estimated to be 125 million (Beer, 2015). Interest in WSL events is likely to grow even further with the inclusion of surfing in the lineup of sports for the 2020 Tokyo Olympic Games.

Given the large reach of the WSL, the international nature of its tours both in terms of event locations and event broadcasting, and the popularity of surfing as an action sport, surfing is well positioned to "punch above its weight" in terms of influencing attitudes and behaviors. The global surfing community has spawned a large number of surfer-driven non-government organizations that aim to improve surfing's sustainability performance across its many facets including manufacturing, retail, travel, media, environment, and events (c.f. Borne and Ponting, 2015). Many also see the potential for surfing – the popular appeal of which has seen its imagery used to sell everything from education, to motor vehicles, computers, watches, cell phones, breakfast cereals, holidays, alcohol, Hollywood films, and perfume – to act as an "on-ramp" for broader society to embrace sustainable behaviors (Whilden and Stewart, 2015).

Trends

Perhaps counter-intuitively, given the spiritual overtones of surfing's public image and the fact that its participants are completely and literally immersed in the natural environment, the surfing industry has been slow to embrace sustainability principles into its products and business practices for fear of it falling flat in the market place (McKnight, 2015; Palladini, 2015; Tomson, 2015). In an attempt to generate some real data on the sustainability attitudes and behaviors of surfers, in 2015 the Center for Surf Research at San Diego State University administered an online survey consisting of 44 questions covering a range of issues, including sustainability as it relates to the surf industry and surf travel. Results of the survey were reported at the Inaugural Conference of the International Association of Surfing Academics at San Diego State University in September of 2015 (Ponting, 2015; O'Brien and Ponting, 2018). In total, 3049 surveys were attempted, yielding 2994 viable responses from 68 countries of origin. The vast majority of responses were from the United States (55 percent) and Australia (18 percent). Respondents came from an additional 66 countries.

The sample was 80 percent male with an average age of 34 and more than 10 years of surfing experience, surfing three times per week, owning four surfboards, and with a mean annual household income of US$75,000. The survey data suggest that the respondents generally hold attitudes that reflect an interest in sustainability. For example, Figure 15.1 shows that only 28 percent agree that the surf industry is doing enough to ensure its products are sustainable, 75 percent are likely to buy a sustainable surf product over a non-sustainable product. Only 40 percent of respondents believed that the surf industry is giving sufficient support to environmental and humanitarian organizations in surfing destinations. If price and performance were comparable, 92 percent of the sample would buy a surfboard made from sustainable materials over one that was not. The survey also sought to determine the sample's willingness to pay various percentages over and above comparable prices for sustainable surf products and surf tourism products (see Figure 15.2). The data suggest that up to

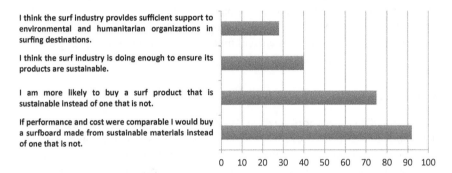

Figure 15.1 Percentage of respondents who agree or strongly agree with statements about sustainability in the surf industry.

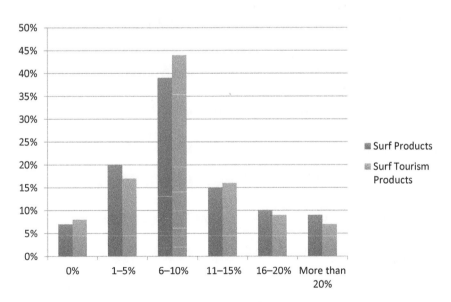

Figure 15.2 Willingness to pay over and above market price for sustainable surf, and surf tourism products.

75 percent of surfers are willing to pay a premium of at least 10 percent for sustainably produced products.

Figure 15.3 summarizes the results of six questions in which respondents were asked to rank their level of agreement with statements relating to sustainability. The results show high levels of concern about sustainability in surf destinations, and demonstrate that past and future purchasing decisions have been and will be based on that concern.

While not directly asking participants about World Surf League events, the survey provides insight into the sustainability attitudes and behaviors of the surfing population, which comprises the WSL's broadcast and on-site event audience. Clearly this population's concern about the sustainability of surfing's presence in surfing destinations is not being adequately reflected by the surfing industry. An indication of the lack of sustainability leadership from "big surfing" (Schumacher, 2015) is the existence of multiple organizations attempting to steer WSL events toward a more sustainable trajectory from the outside in.

Voluntary codes

Before the 2014 takeover of the ASP World Tour by Zosea Media, the sponsoring brands of many WCT events had engaged with outside entities in an effort to incorporate elements of sustainability. In particular: SurfCredits, a non-profit that raised funds from the viewing audience to support destination communities and environments; STOKE Certified, a sustainability certification business specifically targetting the surf and snow industries; and Sustainable Surf, a non-profit with a number of programs designed to catalyze sustainable change in the surf industry and beyond (these organizations are explored in more detail below).

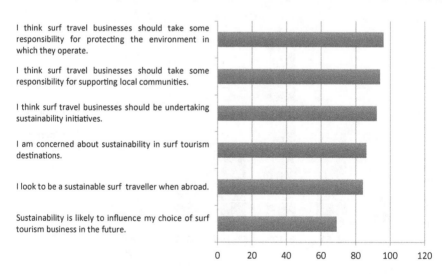

Figure 15.3 Percentage of "agree" and "strongly agree" responses to surf tourism sustainability statements.

Beginning in 2014, the Zosea Media ASP/World Surf League has flirted with the idea of partnering with these organizations for more sustainable event outcomes, but formal arrangements have not yet been established. For example, in 2016 a meeting was held between the WSL, surfboard manufacturers and a range of sustainability consultants, including Sustainable Surf and STOKE Certified, to discuss the notion of using the WSL's event platform to promote the use of more sustainable surfboards by requiring certain sustainability standards from the athletes' equipment (Carroll, 2016; Smith, 2016). Separate talks were also held with Sustainable Surf and STOKE Certified on the topic of rolling out third party sustainability certifications for WCT events but nothing tangible has developed from these meetings.

In 2016, the WSL established a partnership with Columbia University, which took the form of a US$1.5 million gift from billionaire WSL owner Dirk Ziff to his alma mater to establish a program known as "WSL PURE" (Protecting, Understanding, and Respecting the Environment). According to the single landing page developed to date for this effort, PURE is the WSL's "effort to defend our oceans. PURE will celebrate, inspire, and accelerate the efforts of individuals, families, communities, companies, and organizations around the world who act to improve and promote ocean health" (WSL PURE, 2017). All these efforts are highly commendable and are poised to have a very significant positive impact. However, they have all stalled. This is perhaps as a result of a senior executive shake-up in 2016 and 2017 that saw a new CEO installed and a radical redesign of the WCT, set to take effect in 2019. The WSL acknowledged receipt of, but did not respond to, the authors' questions on its future directions with regard to event sustainability. As such, a look back to pre-Zosea Media events can demonstrate the power of collaboration with outside organizations determined to help improve WCT event sustainability for the future.

Case study: the 2013 Fiji Pro

The 2013 Volcom Fiji Pro was the last of the WCT contests in Fiji to be organized and executed by the title sponsor of the event rather than the WSL, which has run the event since 2014. The event was significant in that it was one of only two WCT events that leveraged all three external organizations (SurfCredits, STOKE Certified, and Sustainable Surf's Deep Blue Event Program), providing turnkey sustainability solutions for WCT events at the time. The results were demonstrably positive. In the following paragraphs the origins and roles of these external organizations are explored, as well as their current status in relation to sustainable WCT events.

SurfCredits

SurfCredits launched in 2012 and was designed to function as a mechanism for incorporating corporate social responsibility (CSR) at WCT events. The program utilized the WCT's webcast platform to employ an online donation system that linked surfers, destinations, audiences, athletes, communities, aid projects, and sponsors to benefit host communities in WCT event destinations. Webcast announcers encouraged viewers to donate $25 to pre-vetted non-profit organizations doing important humanitarian, conservation, or research work in event destination communities. In return, donors received five times the cost of their donation in discounts with supporting online surf retailers, a free event t-shirt (also valued at $25), and an entry into a draw to win a week for two at a high end resort at the event location. Prior to this, while some event sponsors undertook CSR initiatives on an ad hoc basis, there was no formal or standard approach across the WCT. In its first 18 months of operation, SurfCredits was deployed in eight ASP events raising tens of thousands of dollars at each location, positively impacting the lives of many hundreds in those locations, and giving away free surf trips to locations including Fiji, Indonesia, Hawaii, and Costa Rica. A survey of 1000 WCT event viewers who had purchased a SurfCredit found that 83 percent of participants felt more positive about the philanthropic efforts of the ASP as a result, 84 percent felt more positive about sponsoring brands, 78 percent felt more positive about WCT athletes and their level of concern for the places they visit on the WCT, and 95 percent felt more tangibly connected to destinations, their communities, the environment, the contest, and the ASP (SurfCredits, 2013). Qualitatively, participants felt that it was: "So awesome to see the commercial arm of surfing finally giving back. I will buy SurfCredits whenever they are offered"; and, that SurfCredits was a "Great way to progress events out of the 'we came, we saw, we conquered' era".

Prior to the 2014 WCT season, events were funded and organized by the sponsoring brands. SurfCredits had spent two years developing relationships with these brands and was gaining significant traction with them. Following the purchase of the ASP by ZoSea media in 2013, the 2014 season was run entirely by the new look ASP (soon to be rebranded as the WSL) with sponsoring brands paying for naming rights only. SurfCredits now had to be accepted by the ASP to be activated at WCT events. SurfCredits pitched their ongoing involvement to senior members of the new ASP team in May 2013. Despite projections of donations to event destinations of between $500,000 and $1.2 million per year within 5 years at no cost to the ASP/WSL, the pitch was unsuccessful. The ASP/WSL chose instead to support a non-profit (Waves for Water) founded by an ex-pro surfer that made ad hoc deliveries of water filters to post disaster locations. These deliveries were self-described as "guerrilla" in nature, meaning they were not generally approved by local authorities, not articulated with locally driven initiatives, and not accompanied by formal training or follow up impact and efficacy assessments. The relationship between ASP/WSL and Waves for Water appears to have petered out by the end of 2014. With no way to continue its business model into the 2014 WCT season, SurfCredits was rendered obsolete overnight and shut down.

STOKE Certified

STOKE Certified is a sustainability certification program based on the Global Sustainable Tourism Council's criteria, specifically targeting the surf and snow industries (O'Brien and Ponting, 2018). The STOKE Surf standard contains 143 criteria across the broad areas of sustainable management, social and economic impacts management, cultural heritage impacts management, and environmental impacts management. Almost 400 compliance indicators guide members towards best practices for each criterion and encourage year over year improvement. By the time of the 2013 Fiji Pro, STOKE Certified had been working with the Tavarua Resort for three years and had developed comprehensive sustainability management and reporting systems.

STOKE Certified, which also has a sustainable events standard (with 93 criteria and 279 compliance indicators), met with the WSL in 2016 and offered to help develop a standard for WSL events based on a blend of their existing surf resort and events standards. Though the meeting ended positively, no subsequent progress has been made. In the meantime STOKE has expanded to include 15 resorts in nine countries and one destination. The destination standard is new in 2017 and works at a regional level. The first region to be benchmarked against the STOKE Destination standard is Peniche, Portugal – the location of the Rip Curl Pro Portugal WCT contest. In addition STOKE has developed, or is developing, standards for surf schools, surf charter boats, and man-made surf parks. The latter is of particular interest, given the 2017 purchase of a surf park technology company (Kelly Slater Wave Company) by the WSL and the inclusion of a WCT event at a surf park facility in the 2018 WCT season. STOKE remains committed to helping the WSL incorporate sustainability into its events moving forward.

Sustainable Surf, Deep Blue Events

A diluted interpretation of the Global Reporting Initiative, the Deep Blue Event standard sets a low and readily achievable bar for sustainable events while still effecting important improvements in sustainability performance. The program was developed by Sustainable Surf, a non-profit with the mission to: "Be the catalyst that transforms surf culture into a powerful force for protecting the ocean playground" (Sustainable Surf, 2017). The Deep Blue Event program launched in 2011 at the Rip Curl Pro WCT event in San Francisco and was promoted as a designation of more "ocean friendly" events with clear pathways for reducing environmental impacts, while also providing social benefits for the local community. In practical terms, Deep Blue Events assesses sustainability across a total of five criteria and five compliance indicators. These are as follows: Waste – 25 percent waste diversion from landfill and a commitment to not use plastic straws; Energy – 25 percent of total event power from renewable sources; Community Support – support at least three NGOs working on local issues; Climate Change – 50 percent of the event's CO_2 footprint to be offset or mitigated; and, Transportation – provide and promote alternative transportation for staff, athletes and spectators where applicable. Compliance with these criteria and indicators is self-reported by event organizers or Sustainable Surf and as such Deep Blue Events cannot be considered for third party sustainability certification. The program has perhaps been most effective in mobilizing community volunteers to perform on-site waste separation to achieve its landfill diversion targets, sourcing biodiesel alternatives for event generators, empowering local environmental organizations and social charity outreach, and offsetting or mitigating excessive CO_2 production by events to approach or achieve carbon neutrality.

While Sustainable Surf continues to activate its Deep Blue Event program at WSL-sanctioned events at the world qualifying series (WQS) level that are not under the direct control of the WSL, its last real engagement with a top level WSL WCT contest was in 2015. In the interim period the program has continued to grow outside of the WCT into other water-based board sport disciplines more open to incorporate sustainability into their events, notably stand up paddleboarding and kiteboarding. Close to 30 events have now been designated Deep Blue Events.

2013 Volcom Fiji Pro

Despite the recent lack of engagement with outside sustainability organizations, in the past, the WSL and its sponsors have had great success producing events which were demonstrably sustainable and which produced positive outcomes for the event destinations and their communities. In addition, the webcast, television and social media around some events have been utilized in ways that had significant reach educating the surfing public and those viewing the events about sustainability concerns, solutions, and everyday behaviors that can be adopted to make positive change. Thus past events have afforded glimpses into what a WCT event that fully leverages its reach and influence to activate sustainability standards and initiatives onsite and to communicate these across their viewing platforms to many many millions of viewers might look and feel like. Perhaps the best example of this was the 2013 Volcom Fiji Pro when all three of the organizations profiled above were involved in helping the ASP to deliver an event that incorporated sustainability into its messaging and on-ground activation.

Through the STOKE Certification of the resort staging the Fiji Pro, the Tavarua Island Resort, assessing much of the events' compliance was a fairly simple process. The full range of Tavarua's sustainability initiatives, many of which would not have been captured by the Deep Blue Event standard's five criteria, were acknowledged and promoted through video vignettes that played throughout the event webcast. SurfCredits raised almost $10,000 for non-profits Loloma Foundation (which provided scholarships and school supplies for 250 school children who would otherwise might not have been able to attend school) and Give Clean Water (a government sanctioned organization that provided permanent clean water solutions for 750 people). A trip for two to the Tavarua Resort was given away to a WSL supporter who had purchased a SurfCredit. The event was declared a Deep Blue Event having diverted at least 40 percent of the waste produced from landfill, mitigated 100 percent of its carbon footprint to be carbon neutral, supported local non-profits through SurfCredits, and with transportation around the event taking place by boats the CO_2 emissions for which were mitigated in total.

Despite being a 'light green' certification, Sustainable Surf's Deep Blue Event standard still represents the pinnacle of sustainability achievement by WSL events to date. The Deep Blue Event standard is a very user friendly, turnkey sustainability solution for the WSL, particularly when complimented by other organizations such as STOKE Certified and SurfCredits. The coalescing of outside organizations at the 2013 Fiji Pro resulted in real engagement with, and benefit to, local communities with demonstrably reduced environmental impacts.

Other work

Many studies have explored various aspects of sustainable events including but certainly not limited to: struggles to incorporate sustainability messaging into events (Laing and Frost, 2009); the growing demand for sustainable events and the need of the events industry to respond (Pelham, 2011); the efficacy of blending existing sustainability approaches in the events context (Musgrave, 2011); and the role of policy (Getz, 2009), legislation (Paterson and Ward, 2011), and professional associations (Dickson and Arcodia, 2009) in encouraging and facilitating sustainable events. In the context of surfing events, the majority of existing work has focused on assessing economic benefits (c.f. Breedveld, 1995; Carlsen, 2003; Downey, 1991; Huff, 2011; Murphy and Bernal, 2008; O'Brien, 2007; O'Neill et al., 1999; Pulford, 2007) with one study also appraising the role of surfing events in influencing spectator attitudes towards sponsoring brands (Randhawa, 2016), and one other assessing sustainability metrics (Whittlesea, 2015).

Further resources

Additional information on sustainability in surfing events can be sourced from the following organizations:

Sustainable Surf Deep Blue Events http://sustainablesurf.org/deep-blue-event/
STOKE Certified www.stokecertified.com/
Center for Surf Research http://csr.sdsu.edu/
Surf Park Solutions http://surfparksolutions.com/
WSL PURE www.wslpure.org/

References

Ahmed, F., Moodley, V. and Sookrajh, R. (2008). The environmental impacts of beach sport tourism events: a case study of the Mr. Price pro surfing event, Durban, South Africa. *Africa Insight*, 38 (3): 73–85.

Beer, J. (2015). Why a shark attack was the perfect ad for the World Surf League. Available at: www.fastcocreate.com/3054673/behind-the-brand/why-a-shark-attack-was-the-perfect-ad-for-world-surf-league (accessed May 26, 2016).

Borne, G. and Ponting, J (eds) (2015). *Sustainable Stoke: Transitions to Sustainability in the Surfing World.* Plymouth: University of Plymouth Press.

Breedveld, J. (1995). Rip curl pro/qui women's classic surfing contest: economic impact assessment. *Australian Leisure*, 6 (4): 15–16.

Carlsen, J. (2003). Riding the wave of event sponsorship: sponsorship objectives and awareness at the Margaret River masters surfing event. In R. L. Braithwaite and R. W. Braithwaite (eds), Riding the Wave of Tourism and Hospitality Research: Proceedings of the Council of Australian University Tourism and Hospitality Education Conference, Coffs Harbour, 2003. Lismore, Australia: Southern Cross University.

Carroll, N. (2016). *Nick Carroll on: A Quietly Radical Notion.* Available at: www.coastalwatch.com/surfing/20618/nick-carroll-on-a-quietly-radical-notion (accessed August 24, 2017).

Dickson, C. and Arcodia, C. (2009). Promoting sustainable event practice: the role of professional associations. *International Journal of Hospitality Management*, 29: 236–244.

Downey, B. (1991). The tourism impact on Victoria of its special sporting events: Including case studies of the 1989 Bells Beach Easter Surf Carnival and the 1989 Ford Australian Open. Unpublished Master's thesis. Victoria University of Technology, Melbourne.

Getz, D. (2009). Policy for sustainable and responsible festivals and events: institutionalization of a new paradigm. *Journal of Policy Research in Tourism, Leisure and Events*, 1 (1): 61–78.

Heimann, J. (2016). *Surfing 1778–2015.* Koln: Taschen.

Huff, L. (2011). *The Contribution of the Vans Triple Crown of Surfing to Hawaii's Economy and Brand Image.* Brigham Young University – Hawaii Alliance for Marketing Professionals and Students (AMPS).

Laderman, S. (2014). *Empire in Waves: A Political History of Surfing.* Berkeley, CA: University of California Press.

Laing, J. and Frost, W. (2009). How green was my festival: exploring challenges and opportunities with staging green events. *International Journal of Hospitality Management*, 29: 261–267.

Martin, S. A., and Assenov, I. (2012). The genesis of a new body of sport tourism literature: a systematic review of surf tourism research (1997–2011). *Journal of Sport & Tourism*, 17 (4): 257–287. doi:10.1080/14775085.2013.766528.

McKnight, R. (2015). Quiksilver and sustainability: the view from the top. In G. Borne and J. Ponting (eds), *Sustainable Stoke: Transitions to Sustainability in the Surfing World.* Plymouth: University of Plymouth Press.

Minsberg, T. and Corasaniti, N. (2015). Pro surfing looks beyond the TV screen to draw viewers. *New York Times* (New York Edition), February 23, page B1.

Murphy, M. and Bernal, M. (2008). *The Impact of Surfing on the Local Economy of Mundaka Spain.* Davenport, CA: Save The Waves Coalition.

Musgrave, J. (2011). Moving towards responsible events management. *Worldwide Hospitality and Tourism Themes*, 3 (3): 258–274.

Ntloko, N. J. and Swart, K. (2008). Sport tourism event impacts on the host community-a case study of Red Bull Big Wave Africa. *South African Journal for Research in Sport, Physical Education and Recreation*, 30 (2): 79–93.

O'Brien, D. (2007). Points of leverage: maximizing host community benefit from a regional surfing festival. *European Sport Management Quarterly*, 7 (2): 141–165.

O'Brien, D. and Eddie, I. (2013). Benchmarking global best practice: Innovation and leadership in surf city tourism and industry development. Paper presented at the Global Surf Cities Conference, Kirra Community and Cultural Centre.

O'Brien, D. and Ponting, J. (2018). Sustainable Stoke: initiating sustainability certification in surf tourism. In B. McCullough and T. Ellison (eds), *Handbook on Sport, Sustainability and the Environment*. London: Routledge.

O'Neill, M., Getz, D. and Carlsen, J. (1999). Evaluation of service quality at events: the 1998 Coca-Cola Masters surfing event at Margaret River, Western Australia, *Managing Service Quality*, 9 (3): 158–166.

Palladini, D. (2015). Smart business: linking environmental health to corporate wellbeing. In G. Borne and J. Ponting (eds), *Sustainable Stoke: Transitions to Sustainability in the Surfing World.* University of Plymouth Press, Plymouth.

Paterson, M. and Ward, S. (2011). Roundtable discussion: applying sustainability legislation to events. *Worldwide Hospitality and Tourism Themes*, 3 (3): 203–209.

Pelham, F. (2011). Will sustainability change the business model of the event industry? *Worldwide Hospitality and Tourism Themes*, 3 (3): 187–192.

Ponting, J. (2015). *Constructing Nirvana: Implications for the Surf Park Industry*, Sustainable Stoke: Inaugural Conference of the International Association of Surfing Academics, San Diego State University, September 19 and 20.

Pulford, M. (2007). *2007 Rip Curl Pro Economic Impact Report*. Surfing Victoria Inc, Torquay.

Randhawa, K. (2016). The role of sport events in spectator sponsor/brand attitudes – A case study of the Quiksilver Pro. Unpublished PhD Thesis, Department of Tourism, Sport and Hotel Management, Griffith University.

Schumacher, C. (2015). Shifting surfing towards environmental justice. In G. Borne and J. Ponting (eds), *Sustainable Stoke: Transitions to Sustainability in the Surfing World.* Plymouth: University of Plymouth Press.

Smith, C. (2016). *Fascist WSL to Regulate Surfboards: A secret and nefarious plot to save the environment*. Available at: http://beachgrit.com/2016/10/fascist-wsl-to-regulate-surfboards/ (accessed August 24, 2017).

Stapelberg, G. (2014). Billabong Pro Tahiti generates largest audience in pro-surfing history. Available at: www.worldsurfleague.com/posts/66691/billabong-pro-tahiti-generates-largest-audience-in-pro-surfing-history (accessed May 26, 2016).

Surf Credits (2013). *Surf Credits: Presentation to the ASP May 29th 2013*. Unpublished Report.

Sustainable Surf (2017). *About Us*. Available at: http://sustainablesurf.org/about-us/ (accessed November 7, 2017).

The Outdoor Foundation (2015). *Outdoor Participation Report 2014*. Washington, DC: The Outdoor Foundation.

Tomson, S. (2015). Pro surfing and the art of inspiration. In G. Borne and J. Ponting (eds), *Sustainable Stoke: Transitions to Sustainability in the Surfing World.* Plymouth: University of Plymouth Press.

Walker, I. H. (2011). *Waves of Resistance: Surfing and History in Twentieth-century Hawaii*. Honolulu: University of Hawaii Press.

Warshaw, M. (2010). *The History of Surfing*. San Francisco, CA: Chronicle Books.

Westwick, P. and Neushul, P. (2013). *The World in the Curl: An Unconventional History of Surfing*. New York: Crown/Archetype.

Whilden, K. and Stewart, M. (2015). Transforming surf culture towards sustainability. In G. Borne and J. Ponting (eds), *Sustainable Stoke: Transitions to Sustainability in the Surfing World*. Plymouth: University of Plymouth Press.

Whittlesea, E. (2015). Greening Events: the case of Boardmasters surf and music festival, UK. In G. Borne and J. Ponting (eds), *Sustainable Stoke: Transitions to Sustainability in the Surfing World*. Plymouth: University of Plymouth Press.

World Surf League (WSL) (2016). *Sponsorship*. Available at: www.worldsurfleague.com/pages/sponsorship (accessed January 20, 2016).

WSL PURE (2017). *WSL PURE: A Commitment to Ocean Health*. Available at: www.wslpure.org/ (accessed November 7, 2017).

Afterword

Hugues Séraphin and Emma Nolan

Sustainability can no longer be referred to as simply a trend, as it is clear that it has become imperative that sustainability objectives and practices are a feature of every aspect of our social and professional lives. Given the size and importance of the tourism and events industries, understanding the role of sustainability within them has become a significant area of research and sharing examples of best practice has become extremely valuable to both practitioners and scholars.

This book has provided a number of international examples of best practice in the management of destinations, venues, spaces and events. It has, however, also shone a light on some of the ongoing challenges of implementing sustainability procedures and achieving objectives. For example, across several chapters we have seen how many countries have few recognisable or government endorsed certification schemes or benchmarking systems. Although there are a growing number of best practice guides and resources available to the tourism or event manager, there is much scope for more detailed advice and support. Furthermore, some of the key barriers to achieving sustainability goals have been highlighted as a lack of time and resources, insufficient knowledge as well as a lack of support from stakeholders.

One of the most prevalent themes of this book is the importance of the involvement and commitment of all stakeholders. In order to maximise the positive impact of sustainability practices, the coordination and support of stakeholders is essential. Yet a number of case studies in this book have shown how this is a particular challenge. Many case studies have commented on how it is important and fruitful to involve the local community in the planning and management of events and sites, but this remains an ongoing challenge for all those working towards delivering sustainable tourism and event activities. Another key theme that appears throughout the book is the ongoing friction between governments, communities and businesses. A number of case studies highlight the need for better collaborations between governments and society and the challenge of overcoming power struggles in the pursuit of a common goal.

Nonetheless, this book has demonstrated how it is possible to triumph in some of the most challenging of situations. Positive achievements have been cited in the management of resource-intensive, large-scale music festivals as well as within the MICE sector which generates much international and domestic travel thereby contributing to greenhouse-gas emissions. This book has even managed to highlight some of the positive work that is being done within the motorsport industry, which has often been branded as an extremely damaging event as it involves the burning of fossil fuels, the creation of large global carbon footprints and the destruction of green spaces. Additionally, a number of chapters have demonstrated how responsible environmental practices have now become embedded in management practices and how these are used to motivate staff and encourage responsible behaviour in both consumers and suppliers. Given the television audience of a number of large-scale events, this positive influence can also extend beyond those in direct attendance. Furthermore, sustainability credentials, certification and awards are valuable marketing tools and can greatly enhance the image of an event or destination. Several case studies in this book have shown how consumer demand is having a significant impact on the implementation of green initiatives and how green credentials can attract their attention and give a destination, an event or a location a competitive advantage.

All the sustainability credentials, certification and awards, all the environmental practices embedded in management practices that we have presented in that book are to some extent illustrating the framework developed by Visser (2015), who argued that sustainability can be achieved by unlocking change through: transformational leadership; enterprise reform; technology innovation; corporate transparency; stakeholder engagement; social responsibility; and integrated value. Equally important, Visser argues that 'if we are to reach sustainable frontiers … it must begin with changing our collective minds – and only then will we change our collective behaviour' (2015: 1–4). The variety of case studies presented in the book is evidence that we are collectively changing our behaviour, even if the extent varies between organisations and individuals.

We are now at a point in time when there are more sustainability initiatives, guidelines, frameworks and certification schemes in place. There has been a rise in the number of specialised working groups to support the implementation of responsible management practices. There has also been an increase in support from both government and non-governmental organisations in terms of advice, resources, grants and funding. The recognition of the importance of having a green conscience has become more widespread among consumers as well as professionals and the quest to develop more innovative and effective sustainability methods and processes continues to advance. As such, this book has provided timely insight into some of the best examples of good practice from around the world. It has included tips and advice, shared the results of research and investigations, and provided an honest commentary on some of the challenges involved in setting, working towards and achieving sustainability goals.

References

Visser, W. (2015). *Sustainable Frontiers. Unlocking Change through Business, Leadership and Innovation*. Sheffield: Greenleaf Publishing.

Index

Page numbers in **bold** denote tables, those in *italics* denote figures.

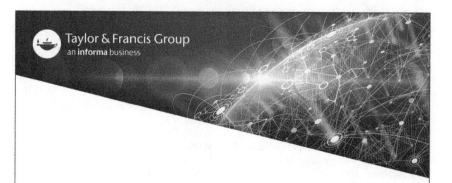